SECURITY FOR UBIQUITOUS COMPUTING

WILEY SERIES IN COMMUNICATIONS NETWORKING & DISTRIBUTED SYSTEMS.

Series Editor: David Hutchison, *Lancaster University*
Series Advisers: Harmen van As, *TU Vienna*
                      Serge Fdida, *University of Paris*
                      Joe Sventek, *Agilent Laboratories, Edinburgh.*

The 'Wiley Series in Communications Networking & Distributed Systems' is a series of expert-level, technically detailed books covering cutting-edge research and brand new developments in networking, middleware and software technologies for communications and distributed systems. The books will provide timely, accurate and reliable information about the state-of-the-art to researchers and development engineers in the Telecommunications and Computing sectors.

Other titles in the series:

Wright: *Voice over Packet Networks*
Jepsen: *Java for Telecommunications*
Mishra: *Quality of Service*
Sutton: *Secure Communications*

SECURITY
FOR UBIQUITOUS COMPUTING

Frank Stajano
University of Cambridge, UK

JOHN WILEY & SONS, LTD

Published by   John Wiley & Sons, Ltd
                  Baffins Lane, Chichester,
                  West Sussex, PO19 1UD, England

                  National 01243 779777
                  International (+44) 1243 779777

e-mail (for orders and customer service enquiries): **cs-books@wiley.co.uk**
Visit our Home Page on http://www.wiley.co.uk or **http://www.wiley.com**

Other Wiley Editorial Offices

John Wiley & Sons, Inc., 605 Third Avenue,
New York, NY 10158-0012, USA

WILEY-VCH Verlag GmbH
Pappelallee 3, D-69469 Weinheim, Germany

John Wiley & Sons Australia Ltd, 33 Park Road, Milton,
Queensland 4064, Australia

John Wiley & Sons (Canada) Ltd, 22 Worcester Road
Rexdale, Ontario, M9W 1L1, Canada

John Wiley & Sons (Asia) Pte Ltd, 2 Clementi Loop #02-01,
Jin Xing Distripark, Singapore 129809

British Library Cataloguing in Publication Data

A catalogue record for this book is available from the British Library

ISBN 0470 84493 0

Produced from PostScript files supplied by the author.
Printed and bound in Great Britain by T J International Ltd, Padstow, Cornwall.
This book is printed on acid-free paper responsibly manufactured from sustainable forestry, in which at least two trees are planted for each one used for paper production.

To Carl Barks
"The Duck Man"
1901-03-27 – 2000-08-25
Master storyteller and meta-inventor
Creator of Gyro Gearloose

Contents

About the author

Frank Stajano is a faculty member in the Department of Engineering of the University of Cambridge (United Kingdom), where he holds the ARM Lectureship in Ubiquitous Computing Systems at the Laboratory for Communications Engineering.

Having been elected a Toshiba Fellow, he spent one year as a visiting scientist at the Toshiba Corporate R&D Center in Kawasaki (Japan), conducting research on ubicomp security and writing this book. While in Japan he also collaborated in research activities with the Universities of Keiō and Waseda.

Prior to these appointments he spent 8 years as a research scientist at AT&T Laboratories Cambridge (formerly ORL), where he took part in several research projects and gained extensive experience of innovative ubicomp systems both as a user and as a developer. He worked on a variety of topics from distributed multimedia to object oriented scripting and web programming, as well as on the security of the PEN (formerly Piconet) embedded networking system.

He holds a Ph.D. in computer security from the University of Cambridge and a Dr. Ing. in electronic engineering from Università "La Sapienza" of Rome (Italy).

Outside computers his main area of expertise is comics, a subject on which he coauthored two books. He is fluent in three languages and is currently learning a fourth. He is also a keen practitioner of Japanese martial arts, in particular jūdō and kendō.

Foreword

Twenty or even ten years ago, computer security was a marginal speciality for geeks who liked to obsess about things like enciphering email. Nowadays, it is centre stage. Cyberterrorism and electronic fraud are the subject of hand-wringing press articles; but that's only the beginning.

Financial and political power are now largely exercised through networked systems. Cash machine and credit card networks decide whether you can get money; burglar alarm networks decide whether the police will come to your house; identify-friend-or-foe systems tell the military which aircraft might be worth intercepting. Most of the investment in cryptography and computer security goes to ensure that these sinews of civilisation will continue to perform dependably in the way that their builders envisaged.

Within another ten years, all sorts of devices that are stand-alone or not even computerized will be connected to the net; your fridge, your heart monitor, your bathroom scales and your shoes might all work together to monitor (and nag you about) your cardiovascular health. There will be more sinister aspects: the military is already funding research on "smart dust" to provide universal surveillance, and tiny robot insects to sting enemies to death.

How will power and control be exercised in this brave new world?

Already, powerful interests are staking out huge territories. Hollywood has bullied the consumer electronics industry into building copyright control mechanisms into a wide range of gadgets; now DVD players, games consoles and even some PCs enforce security rules that are often against their owners' interests and wishes. You may record your lectures on a minidisc recorder, and then find that you can't back up the recordings anywhere. And it's not just "information" goods that end up being controlled in annoying ways by others. Insurance firms in Norway insist that the owners of expensive cars fit an alarm that monitors the car's location using GPS and reports it using a GSM mobile phone. But what's the point of buying a Jaguar if you have to fit an alarm whose log will invalidate your insurance if the car is ever driven at half its rated top speed? For whom is the system providing "security"?

Security in ubiquitous computing is going to be a huge issue, for both engineers and policy people alike. That's why this book is important.

As Frank Stajano worked for years at AT&T Labs, which spawned much of the technology, he can give many good examples—active badges, smart floors, intelligent coffee machines, even CD covers that cause your home music system to play the album when you open them. Many of these have raised surprising new security issues, involving complex trade-offs between usability, privacy, reliability and control.

Protecting large networks of simple devices also raises a lot of difficult technical problems. Conventional solutions, such as public key infrastructures, tend to be unworkable or just simply irrelevant; conventional security policies, such as protecting those transactions deemed "confidential", don't block the attacks we are most concerned about. Here we come to Frank's original work—protection mechanisms with such delightful names as the "Resurrecting Duckling Security Policy", the "Grenade Timer" and the "Cocaine Auction Protocol".

Security in the twenty-first century is going to be a much more complex business. It will include a lot more technical issues and will touch the everyday world at many more points. Developers and policy people are going to have to learn to think in new ways. Frank's book can help make that fun.

Ross Anderson
Cambridge, UK

Preface

The brief and frantically evolving history of computing and digital communications is entering another major paradigm shift.

It took computers barely half a century to evolve from grandiose isolated room-sized machines, affordable only by a handful of major organizations, to inexpensive multimedia-capable PCs, now commonplace in every home and office, connected to form a worldwide internet. The next major evolutionary step, in part already underway, brought about by a synergy of hardware miniaturization, wireless communications and distributed software systems, is going to be *ubiquitous computing* (*ubicomp* for short). No longer just one or two, but hundreds or thousands of computers per human being, now in the form of networked processors invisibly embedded in everyday objects rather than in conventional keyboard-and-monitor boxes.

Many of us have already lost track of the number of objects we own that contain a microprocessor (try listing them). In the future many more objects, from appliances to furniture to clothes, not to mention nanotechnology-based robots, will contain embedded processors, and will also be endowed with short-range wireless networking capabilities. Today, some manufacturers embed audio input hardware in their digital camera so that you can annotate your pictures by voice. This is an inelegant kitchen-sink-style design: why should a still picture camera be encumbered with audio hardware? Tomorrow, though, manufacturers will be able to embed ad hoc networking capabilities into everything, and you will be able to annotate the photographs in your camera by speaking into your cellphone, which already incorporates digital audio hardware as part of its primary function. Devices will be able to share hardware peripherals and offer their services to each other. Industry shares this vision: in 2001, membership in the Bluetooth SIG was almost unanimous among companies in consumer electronics, computing or communications.

However, when everything is capable of spontaneously and autonomously exchanging data with anything else in range, new concerns come about. You like to be able to "beam" your electronic business card from your PDA to that of a new acquaintance, but who exactly is in a position to consult the entries in your address list or diary? As these devices become more and more pervasively integrated in our daily routine, and as they get to know more and more about our preferences and habits, the privacy issues of the secrets held by our digital butlers acquire a new relevance. Besides, if your wirelessly networkable PDA now even carries electronic money, how do you guard against invisible electronic pickpockets who don't even have to touch you to burgle you?

There are many fine books on computer security, and new ones are now coming out on ubiquitous computing, ad hoc networking and specific implementation technologies such as Bluetooth and 802.11. What's missing is a book focusing on the intersection of the two topics: sufficiently specialized on ubiquitous computing that it does not spend most of its page budget on unrelated issues, like most security books do, and at the same time much more detailed than the obligatory-but-not-particularly-insightful security chapter typically found in the current crop of books on wireless networking.

This is it. This is the book written for people interested in "the big picture" on the security issues of ubiquitous computing. It is aimed at a technical audience but does not require prior knowledge of either security or ubicomp. It will also be valuable to readers versed in only one of these two fields, who will find it a gentle introduction to the other.

The style is simple and equations-free. The book opens with a panoramic view of the many facets of the ubicomp phenomenon and continues with a readable jargon-busting primer on security and the important concepts of cryptology. After a survey of these fundamentals, the book focuses on the aspects that make ubiquitous computing security different from that of traditional distributed systems. It provides pointers to first-hand sources and to current research in an extensively annotated bibliography; where appropriate, it also presents new inventions to solve new problems in authentication, availability and anonymity. There is also an appendix reviewing, for comparison, the security solutions adopted in a number of well known distributed systems.

I know from direct personal experience that the engineers, researchers and managers who are interested in a sound technical introduction to ubicomp security are busy professionals whose reading time is limited. With this in mind, my aim has been to produce a readable, technically accurate, up to date and *short* book. This is not a cookbook full of implementation recipes, or an encyclopædia that tells the clueless practitioner what to do in every possible case. It is instead a technical overview of the field, including a broad framework to make sense of it all, a taxonomy of the major problems and a few in-depth discussions of specific problems.

Even though the first commercial implementations of some aspects of the ubicomp vision are now starting to appear, the grand scenario is still definitely a thing of the future; and ubicomp security, which would be a global property of the whole system, certainly hasn't happened yet. I wish it does before the deployment is complete.

For this wish to be granted it is necessary for everyone involved to approach ubicomp with the right mindset, and with a knowledge of what could go wrong. All too often, during the first iteration of building a new system and under pressure from time-to-market requirements, security (one of the least visible properties of a system, whether present or absent) is dismissed as inessential compared to the hard challenge of getting the system to work at all.

However, attempts at retrofitting security to existing designs tend to result in inadequate and vulnerable systems. My aim here is to provide awareness, primarily for system builders but also for the technically aware early adopters. Both the system architects planning entire ranges of ubicomp products and the programmers writing the actual firmware will do a much better job if they understand the security implications of what they do, even if the current focus is just on "getting it to work". The intelligent users, meanwhile, will want to be informed about the risks of the new technology so as to be able to make informed choices on what to accept, reject or demand when they vote with their wallets.

By reading this book you will gain a thorough understanding of the system-level security issues relevant to ubiquitous computing. You will acquire a sound background knowledge with which to assess and evaluate any practical implementation scenarios you might face. I will not try to teach you a series of unrelated cute tricks, but rather to give you a mental key with which to interpret and make sense of any new development in this field. Since the evolutionary speed of ubiquitous computing surprises even computer people, it is my firm belief that this "teaching how to fish" approach is the only one worth following.

Frank Stajano
Kawasaki, Japan

Acknowledgements

I have always been fascinated by gadgets. I am an engineer, both by academic training and by genetic heritage (my grandfather was one too), so this preference should not come as a great surprise to readers familiar with Adams's mercilessly accurate essay on "Engineers, Scientists, Programmers, and Other Odd People" [4, chapter 14]. I have been known to walk around wearing more electronic gadgets than garments and it is with anticipation that I look forward to the ubiquitous computing scenario becoming reality in the average household and workplace.

This book distils several years of research on ubicomp security I conducted at the University of Cambridge Computer Laboratory and at AT&T Laboratories Cambridge in the context of the Piconet project, a short-range wireless networking technology designed to be embedded in devices to allow them to communicate spontaneously with each other (see section 2.5.5).

I am extremely grateful to Andy Hopper, head of AT&T Laboratories Cambridge, for his generosity, co-operation and trust; without his support I would never have been able to carry out this research with such freedom and independence. Over the years I learnt many important lessons from him on entrepreneurship, delegation, money, intellectual property and leadership. A fantastic boss—plus, he loves gadgets as much as I do.

I am equally grateful to Ross Anderson of the Computer Laboratory for years of very fruitful collaboration, for his stimulating comments and suggestions, for his appreciative and encouraging words, and for inspiration in general. Some of the more important topics developed in this book started as papers that we wrote together.

In terms of managing the research process, I am very grateful to Alan Jones of AT&T, who followed my work closely but discreetly, helped with various intellectual property issues and carefully reviewed many of my publications. In addition I had the good fortune to be able to discuss my progress with Maurice Wilkes on several occasions: he gave me strategic high-level advice at key points, dispensing his great wisdom and experience with characteristic modesty and wit. Both of them were very helpful in setting goals and staying on track.

Warm thanks also go to Roger Needham, who voiced encouraging comments on this research on several occasions and helped me get the most out of it.

I am grateful to my parents Attilio and Alessandra and to my dear sister Cecilia for enthusiastically sharing my happiness and excitement about this new book. We meet less than yearly these days, but I can feel how intensely you rejoice at what I do. Thank you for your support and love.

I am greatly appreciative of the dedication and care with which friends and colleagues read drafts of this work at various stages in its evolution: many thanks to Ross Anderson, Richard Clayton, Jon Crowcroft, George Danezis, Hesky Fisher, Mark Lomas, Roger Needham, Eric Raymond, Susanne Wetzel and Stuart Wray[1] for reading the whole thing, and to Jiny Bradshaw, David Clarke, Corrado Giustozzi, Alan Jones, Pekka Nikander, Yutaka Sata and Quentin Stafford-Fraser for reading parts of it. They all offered useful ideas, suggestions and encouragement and gave me a chance to correct unclear passages, inconsistencies and mistakes. Other useful comments, based on the book proposal, came from David Hutchison and Tatsuo Nakajima. But let it be clear, of course, that the responsibility for any remaining errors, misconceptions and omissions is still entirely mine.

The support staff of the Computer Lab of the University of Cambridge have been invaluable. Many wonderful people, too numerous to mention individually, make the lab run smoothly with their professionalism and helpfulness. I am especially grateful to Robin Fairbairns for competent and friendly LATEX help and to Lewis Tiffany for maintaining a well-stocked and very well organized library—I missed this invaluable resource when I moved out of Cambridge, as I knew I would.

Speaking of LATEX, my thanks also go to the members of the comp.text.tex newsgroup community—particularly Anthony Goreham, Heiko Oberdiek and Anthony Williams—for promptly offering their valuable expertise.

While most of the underlying research was conducted in Cambridge, the actual book was produced during my fellowship at Toshiba at the company's Corporate R&D Center in Kawasaki. Thanks to Roberto Cipolla, firstly for introducing me to the Toshiba Fellowship programme and for precious advice about Japan, and secondly for encouraging me to turn my research into a book. Above all, I am very grateful to Toshiba for offering me this fantastic opportunity and in particular to Yukio Kamatani, head of the Communication Platform Laboratory which hosted me, for the absolute trust and freedom with which he allowed me to conduct my research, set my own goals and spend as much time as needed on this book.

I am also grateful to the brilliant editorial team at Wiley that supported me with efficiency, professionalism and enthusiasm during the production of the book: Pat Bonham, Birgit Gruber, Sally Mortimore and Zoë Pinnock.

As for sources, I thank Springer-Verlag GmbH & Co. KG, Academic Press and the Institute of Electronics, Information and Communication Engineering (IEICE) for kindly granting me permission to reprint or adapt some of my previous writings

---

[1] Stuart gets extra credit for carefully reading a full draft in only two days, yet providing six typewritten pages of insightful comments.

[17]   ANDERSON, STAJANO, LEE. "Security Policies". *Advances in Computers* 55, © Academic Press 2001. (Ref.: sections 3.5, 4.2, B.3.)

[236]   STAJANO. "The Resurrecting Duckling—What Next?". Proc. Security Protocols 2000, *LNCS* 2133, © Springer-Verlag 2001. (Ref.: section 4.3.)

[237]   STAJANO, ANDERSON. "The Cocaine Auction Protocol: On The Power Of Anonymous Broadcast". Proc. Information Hiding 1999, *LNCS* 1768, © Springer-Verlag 2000. (Ref.: chapter 8.)

[239]   STAJANO, ANDERSON. "The Grenade Timer: Fortifying the Watchdog Timer Against Malicious Mobile Code". Proc. MoMuC 2000, © IEICE 2000. (Ref.: section 7.3.)

[240]   STAJANO, ANDERSON. "The Resurrecting Duckling: Security Issues in Ad-Hoc Wireless Networks". Proc. Security Protocols 1999, *LNCS* 1796, © Springer-Verlag 2000. (Ref.: sections 4.1, 4.2.)

Table 1. Copyrighted texts I coauthored in the past that I have reused and adapted for this book (see the bibliography for full details of the original publications).

for which they now hold the copyright. (Thanks also go, of course, to my coauthors Ross Anderson and Jong-Hyeon Lee.) As detailed in table 1, for Academic Press the material is from a book chapter, while for Springer-Verlag and IEICE it is from papers published in conference proceedings.

I also thank the following institutions and individuals for supplying me with, and granting me permission to use, pictures of their research work: AT&T Laboratories Cambridge Ltd. (section 2.5), Diego López de Ipiña (section 2.5.4), Steve Mann (section 2.3.2, "photos reproduced by permission of Steve Mann of *CYBORG: Digital Destiny and Human Possibility in the Age of the Wearable Computer*, http://wearcam.org/cyborg.htm"), Xerox PARC (section 2.1) and Roy Want (section 2.1.2). All images in the book are credited to their respective owners in the caption unless they are my own.

Finally, while I reiterate my gratitude towards AT&T Labs Cambridge, the University of Cambridge and Toshiba, I emphasize that the opinions I express in this book are solely mine and should not be attributed to any of these institutions.

Contact information

I use and encourage the use of PGP for secure communication (see the discussion in the second half of section 3.4.3, from page 79 onwards). The fingerprints of my public keys are listed below. The public keys themselves are available from the keyservers and from my web page. I will certainly create and use new keys in the future, especially since `fms-default` will expire soon, but don't trust them as mine unless they have been signed by both of the keys below.

> Key `fms-home`, id 0x399A3121 (RSA) 1024.
> Created 1993-12-04; never expires; cipher: IDEA.
> Fingerprint: E118 38AF FAF6 37AC - 4874 9D1F 3FC3 2FB0.
> Now used primarily to sign other keys.
>
> Key `fms-default`, id 0x1C6D7240 (DH/DSS) 2048/1024.
> Created 1998-07-29; expires 2002-12-31; cipher: IDEA.
> Fingerprint: 58B9 DAB7 4B20 2BF4 C1BE - BCBD B425 898F 1C6D 7240.
> Please use this for normal correspondence.

My web page, with up-to-date email and snail mail contact details, is currently at `http://www-lce.eng.cam.ac.uk/~fms27/`. It might one day move, but it is very unlikely to disappear completely. If it's no longer at the address above, try feeding my name to a search engine.

The web page contains a section dedicated to this book, including an *errata corrige*. It also has details of my other publications and activities.

Chapter 1

Introduction

Ubiquitous computing is the vision of a world in which computing power and digital communications are extremely inexpensive commodities, so cheap that they are embedded in all the everyday objects that surround us. This book examines the security issues of such a scenario.

In this chapter we briefly introduce ubiquitous computing (more on this in the next chapter), we define some basic terminology and we point out the principal security concerns that we shall be facing.

1.1 Scenario

The established trend in consumer electronics is to embed a microprocessor in everything—cellphones, car stereos, televisions, VCRs, watches, GPS (Global Positioning System) receivers, digital cameras. In some specific environments such as avionics, electronic devices are already becoming networked; in others, work is underway. Medical device manufacturers want instruments such as thermometers, heart monitors and blood oxygen meters to report to a nursing station; consumer electronics makers are promoting the Firewire standard for PCs, stereos, TVs and DVD players to talk to each other; and kitchen appliance vendors envisage a future in which the oven will talk to the fridge, which will reorder food over the net.

It is to be expected that, in the near future, this networking will become much more general. The next step is to embed a short range wireless transceiver into everything; then many gadgets can become more useful and effective by communicating and cooperating with each other. A camera, for example, might obtain the geographical position and exact time from a nearby GPS unit every time a picture is taken, and record that information with the image. At present, if the photographer wants to record a voice note with the picture, the camera must incorporate digital audio hardware; in the future, the camera might instead let the photographer

1

speak into her digital audio recorder or cellphone. Even better, the audio data might optionally take a detour through the user's powerful laptop, where a speech recognition engine could transcribe the utterance, so as to annotate the photograph with searchable text rather than just with audio samples—and of course this could be done at any time that the camera detects the proximity and availability of the laptop with the speech recognition service. In this scenario each device, by becoming a network node, may take advantage of the services offered by other nearby devices instead of having to duplicate their functionality.

This vision, as we shall see in chapter 2, was first put forward by Mark Weiser of Xerox PARC [259], who coined the locution "ubiquitous computing" in 1988. Between then and now, many research organizations have started projects to explore various facets of this vision, and some of this research is now materializing into consumer products. In 2001, the most visible commercial incarnations of this idea were two open standards for wireless radio networking: Bluetooth [40, 126], originally thought of as a "serial cable replacement" for small computer peripherals, and 802.11, originally developed as a wireless LAN system for laptops. Estrin, Govindan and Heidemann [102] present a future scenario of ubiquitous embedded networking that encompasses this and much more.

1.2   Essential terminology

Computer people generate neologisms at an alarming rate. The inflation of trendy buzzwords and acronyms is all too often a dubious marketing gimmick to cover the lack of contents, but there are cases in which a new term genuinely is the best way to describe a new technology or a new way of doing things. I leave it to the reader to decide whether my use of new terms in this book falls in the first or the second category, but it seems in any case a good idea to define the most relevant ones in advance.

The focus of this work shall be the examination of **security issues for ubiquitous computing and ad hoc networking**. The *Oxford English Dictionary* [203] (henceforth "the *OED*") defines "ubiquitous" as

> Present or appearing everywhere; omnipresent.

With **ubiquitous computing** we refer to a scenario in which computing is omnipresent, and particularly in which devices that do not look like computers are endowed with computing capabilities. "A computer on every desk" does not qualify as ubiquitous computing; having data processing power inside light switches, door locks, fridges and shoes, instead, does.

As we saw in section 1.1, we envisage a situation in which all those devices are not only capable of computing but also of communicating, because their synergy then makes the whole worth more than the sum of the parts. We do not however expect a fixed networking infrastructure to be in place—certainly not one based on cables. It would be less than practical to run data cables between switches, locks and fridges—not to mention shoes. A wireless network infrastructure looks more plausible: as happens with mobile telephones, a base station could cover a cell, and a network of suitably positioned base stations could cover a larger area. But we are interested in a broader picture, in which even this arrangement may not always be possible or practical: think of a photographer taking pictures in the desert and whose camera wants to ask the GPS unit what coordinates and timestamp to associate with the picture. The computing and the communications may be ubiquitous, but the network infrastructure might not be. In such cases the devices will have to communicate as peers and form a local network as needed when they recognize each other's presence. This is what we mean by **ad hoc networking**. The *OED* defines "ad hoc" as

> Devoted, appointed, etc., to or for some particular purpose.

The wireless network formed by the camera and the GPS receiver is ad hoc in the sense that it was established just for that specific situation instead of being a permanent infrastructural fixture.

Finally, it would perhaps be desirable to define **security**, not because the term is new or unfamiliar, but because it is overloaded, and may be interpreted differently by different readers.

A common mistake is to identify security with cryptology, the art of building and breaking ciphers (*cryptography* and *cryptanalysis* respectively). While it's true that cryptology gives computer security many of its technical weapons, to identify the two is to miss the big picture and to expose oneself to less glamorous but probably more effective attacks. As demonstrated by Anderson [11, 8] with a wealth of case studies, what fails in real life is rarely the crypto.

In a nutshell, security is really risk management. Security is assessing **threats** (bad things that may happen, e.g. your money getting stolen), **vulnerabilities** (weaknesses in your defences, e.g. your front door being made of thin wood and glass) and **attacks** (ways in which the threats may be actualized, e.g. a thief breaking through your weak front door while you and the neighbours are on holiday), estimating costs for the threats, estimating probabilities for the attacks given the vulnerabilities, developing appropriate **safeguards** (*a priori* vaccines) and **countermeasures** (*a posteriori* remedies), and implementing the ones for which the certain price of the defence is worth spending compared to the uncertain loss that a potential threat implies.

In this context it is apparent that cryptology is only one of many tools, not the discipline itself. Amoroso [7], whose clear terminology we adopted in the

previous paragraph, offers a rigorous overview of this process. Schneier, author of
an extremely popular cryptography textbook [227], candidly admits in a later book
[228] to having previously missed the forest for the trees.

Having clarified this, I shall give an overview of computer security mechanisms
for the uninitiated reader in chapter 3.

1.3 Problems

Ubiquitous computing imposes peculiar constraints, for example in terms of connectivity, computational power and energy budget, which make this case significantly different from those contemplated by the canonical doctrine of security in
distributed systems.

A well-established taxonomy subdivides computer security threats into three
categories, according to whether they threaten confidentiality, integrity or availability. Let us review these three fundamental security properties given the preconditions of ubiquitous computing.

Confidentiality is the property that is violated whenever information is disclosed to unauthorized principals[1]. Everyone realizes that wireless networking is
more vulnerable to passive eavesdropping attacks than a solution based on cables:
by construction, information is radiated to anyone within range. It is natural to
expect that the security requirements of a wireless system will include addressing
this concern.

Integrity is violated whenever information is altered in an unauthorized way.
This applies both to information within a host and to information in transit between
hosts. Imagine a wireless temperature sensor on your roof that relays its measurements to a display inside your house (at ORL we built a prototype of such a device for Piconet in 1998, as part of a playground of simple communicating devices
which also included fans, displays, logging nodes and so on (see section 2.5.5);
but a much nicer, if less versatile, commercial version could probably be bought at
Radio Shack even then). If an attacker modifies either the sensor's firmware or the
transmitted messages so that the displayed temperature is off by 10 degrees then,
if you are sufficiently gullible, you may be cheated into wearing the wrong type of
clothes for that day's weather. If this does not look like a terribly dramatic security
violation, imagine instead that the sensor is monitoring a patient's temperature in
a clinic or, even better, that it is part of an alarm system for a nuclear power plant.
As happens with confidentiality, the wireless nature of communications increases
the vulnerability of the system to integrity violations: if the receiver listens to the

---

[1]We call *principals* the entities that can perform actions; this general and somewhat ambiguous
term encompasses without distinction humans, machines that act as representatives for humans, and
machines that don't.

strongest signal that "looks right", an attacker wishing to substitute forged messages for the original ones only needs to shout loudly enough, without having to splice any cables. As for the integrity of hosts, as opposed to that of messages in transit, the ubiquitous computing vision of *unattended* devices ready to communicate with whoever comes in range clearly makes it likely that an attacker will sooner or later tamper with such unattended devices if this can bring her any benefits.

Availability is the property of a system which always honours any legitimate requests by authorized principals. It is violated when an attacker succeeds in *denying service* to legitimate users, typically by using up all the available resources. As we remarked about integrity, the fact that ubiquitous computing implies unattended devices opens the door to many abuses. If we envisage that these ubiquitous hosts might accept mobile code that roams from one of them to another, then denial of service might also be caused by malicious programs that lock up the host device.

While illustrating the three fundamental security properties of confidentiality, integrity and availability we have repeatedly referred to "authorized principals". It follows that a fundamental prerequisite of a secure system is the ability to establish whether any given principal is or is not authorized to perform the action it is requesting. To define "who is authorized to do what" is the duty of the *security policy*, a concise specification of the security goals of the system. In order to ascertain whether the policy authorizes a principal to perform an action, there is also a need for *identification* (finding out who the principal claims to be) and particularly *authentication*[2] (establishing the validity of this claim). **Authentication** is one of the foundations of security: it is easy to come up with examples that demonstrate that, in its absence, the three fundamental properties can be trivially violated. (Looking for example at confidentiality, even if your communications are protected with military-grade encryption, you are still liable to suffer from a disclosure threat if you have unknowingly established your encrypted channel with a recipient other than the one you intended.) Since authentication is such a central issue, we shall examine how various existing systems deal with it and then turn to the peculiar problems encountered in performing authentication in ad hoc networking, where the absence of infrastructure makes the traditional approaches impracticable.

We shall also look more closely at a peculiar aspect of confidentiality that is not quite mainstream: **anonymity**. Most of the attention devoted to confidentiality concentrates on how to prevent disclosure of the *contents* of messages, which leads naturally to cryptology. Sometimes, however, the really sensitive information is not in the body but in the header. Given the same number of pages, a detective or a spy will generally find an itemized phone bill for his target much more revealing than the transcript of any individual phone call. This sort of attack is called *traffic*

---

[2]Here we refer in particular to *identity* authentication, but it is reasonable to discuss the authenticity of other kinds of information. The term has therefore wider applicability in the general case.

analysis. The danger is not limited to the world of secret agents: credit cards and loyalty cards record your spending patterns, cash machine transactions and cellular telephone calls timestamp your whereabouts, and the fusion of all these logs can be used to build disturbingly detailed and intrusive dossiers on private individuals. As we design the technology that will enable ubiquitous computing, we have a duty to protect future users (ourselves included) from what could otherwise turn by default into an Orwellian ubiquitous surveillance.

We shall examine each of these problems in turn: I have dedicated one chapter to each of the boldface terms in this section. Finally, an appendix offers a brief survey of deployed network security solutions.

1.4   Notation

Existing notations for encryption are many and varied. To some extent, each author seems to come up with his or her own preferred flavour. I shall not break with this tradition: in the interest of explicitness, I shall adopt my own personal variation that will allow us to mention the cipher explicitly where this is useful, and to identify the function being performed without relying on implicit inferences from the key in use. We shall use the function names E, D, S, V, h and MAC respectively for encryption, decryption, signature, verification, hash and message authentication code (see chapter 3 for definitions of these terms), with optional subscript and superscript to indicate key and algorithm. So

$$\mathrm{E}(m),\ \mathrm{E}_K(m),\ \mathrm{E}_K^{\mathrm{AES}}(m)$$

respectively indicate the encryption of message m, the encryption of message m under key K and the encryption of message m with AES under key K.

There is much less disagreement over the rest of the notation. I shall, like most authors, indicate a symmetric key shared between A and B as K_{AB}, whereas for public key cryptography I shall use keys that mention only one principal in the subscript: K_A will be A's public key and its inverse K_A^{-1} will be A's private key.

I shall place a delta (for "definition") over the equal sign (like this: $\triangleq$) when I mean "is hereby defined to be equal to" as opposed to simply "is equal to".

As you probably guessed, numbers enclosed in square brackets (like this: [92]) are references to the annotated bibliography at the end of the book.

For protocols, I shall adopt the classical notation whereby

$$A \rightarrow B : m$$

indicates that principal A sends message m to principal B—with a notable exception in section 8.2. This should not be confused with the superficially similar notation used in appendix A to define the domain A and range B of a relation R, as in

$$R : A \rightarrow B.$$

For dates, I shall use the ISO standard notation of year-month-day; among its many advantages, its monotonic big-endianness[3] means that a simple string sort also works as a chronological sort. (This rule does not apply to the publication dates in the bibliography, though: there, the inscrutable BIBTEX does whatever it likes.)

For money, as an engineer I refuse to write "ten thousand dollars" as "$10k", which is just as nonsensical as writing "s10μ" for "ten microseconds". The scaling prefix "k", being indeed a scaling *pre*fix and not a cute abbreviation for the string ",000", is placed *before* its fundamental unit to form a new derived unit; and the correct SI order is "value, space, unit", not "unit, value". I shall therefore write "10 k$".

Some authors draw fine distinctions between the related terms of "confidentiality", "secrecy" and "privacy". The definitions vary subtly from author to author, often in contradictory ways; the only common ground seems to be that "privacy" describes personal secrets as opposed to organizational ones (for which some authors use "secrecy" and others "confidentiality"). I feel that there is little clarity to gain in officially assigning arbitrary nuances to these almost synonymical terms. In this book I shall normally use "confidentiality" (whose meaning I define in section 3.1), and my occasional use of "secrecy" and "privacy" shall not imply a purposeful technical distinction.

---

[3] Any given digit weighs more than any digit on its right.

Chapter 2

Ubiquitous computing

As we saw in the introduction, "ubiquitous computing" (or "ubicomp" for short) literally denotes a situation in which computing is everywhere. This, however, may mean many things, and indeed different authors have used the term in significantly different ways. In this chapter we shall meet several different views on the ubicomp phenomenon by reviewing some of the works that have contributed to defining this field.

Ubiquitous computing is not yet a reality for the general public, but it is now mature and even *fashionable* as a research topic: it is hard to find a research institution without at least one ubicomp-related project. Therefore I am not aiming for an exhaustive survey (it would be hard to know where to stop) but for a representative sampler that will give you a flavour of what ubicomp may mean, in the widest sense.

The projects presented in this chapter are not all on the same level of maturity or concreteness. Some of them are fully developed systems that are of interest for the engineering aspects: they show practical implementations of the technologies that might make ubicomp work. Others, instead, are little more than thought experiments, future promises, or perhaps proof-of-concept demonstrations that do not yet scale beyond the single-instance prototype: still, to dismiss them sceptically would be narrow-minded—their interest is in the new ideas and visions they suggest. All of them contribute to our understanding of what ubicomp might become once it reaches its intended audience of non-technical users.

The relative size of the sections of this chapter will of course show my bias, and I offer no apology for this. This should definitely not be interpreted as me asserting that the only significant ubicomp research is that conducted in Cambridge at ORL/AT&T, but rather as an acknowledgement of the fact that I have been working in that lab for over 8 years. While for the projects developed at other institutions I can offer you an informed summary based on reading their publications and occasionally visiting their facilities, for the ORL/AT&T laboratory I am in a position to give you a first person account of my daily experience of interacting with the ubicomp systems we developed and deployed. Giving substantial space to that section is therefore an explicit choice.

For a panoramic view of current ubicomp projects, with a particular focus on context-aware applications, I recommend Rehman's extensive online directory [215]. The best stand-alone survey on ubicomp to date is perhaps the article by Abowd and Mynatt [2]. First hand accounts of relevant research are to be found in the proceedings of conferences such as the well-established *Mobicom* [3], dealing with issues of mobile computing in general, and the newer and more focused *Ubicomp* [247] (formerly "Handheld and Ubiquitous Computing"), both held under the auspices of the Association for Computing Machinery.

2.1 Xerox PARC

The Palo Alto Research Center of Xerox in California is the birthplace of, among other things, the window-based GUI and the Ethernet. It is here that ubiquitous computing was first envisioned by the late Mark Weiser (1952–1999), principal scientist and later CTO of PARC.

Weiser coined the locution "ubiquitous computing" in 1988 as the name for the new research programme he started at PARC's Computer Science Laboratory. His early writings [259, 260], particularly the 1991 *Scientific American* article (referenced in practically all the scientific ubicomp publications you are likely to come across), helped define the field. His concise high-level retrospective [258], which appeared posthumously in the IBM Systems Journal, neatly chronicles the main landmarks and the underlying philosophy in the evolution of this research theme at PARC.

2.1.1 Disappearing computing

The invention of automatic computing is widely recognized as one of the great technological breakthroughs for humanity. But Weiser points out that, despite the fabulous high-tech advances of the past few decades, this technology is still extremely immature. To put things in perspective, he compares the invention of computing to that of writing.

Writing, he argues, was perhaps the first instance of "information technology": it was the invention that allowed us to store concepts and ideas for later retrieval as opposed to relying exclusively on human memory. Writing is pervasive in the modern society: books are only a small aspect of the global phenomenon, since there is writing everywhere—on magazines, on leaflets, on signs, on labels, on walls, on buttons and dials, on packaging (from container crates down to chewing-gum wrappers) and, to a first approximation, on any imaginable man-made artefact. Most importantly, we do not think of reading and writing while we make use of signs, labels and so on: we just take the act for granted as something completely spontaneous and we instead concentrate on the activity that the written word supports [259]:

> The most profound technologies are those that disappear. They weave themselves into the fabric of everyday life until they are indistinguishable from it.

Obviously, writing is indeed ubiquitous and has "disappeared" in the above sense, but computing hasn't yet. When we use a computer, the focus is still squarely on the tool rather than on the task. For Weiser, ubiquitous computing is not so much about having traditional computers everywhere, but rather about having computing *capabilities* everywhere, embedded in the environment in such a way that they can be used witout noticing them. Computing will become ubiquitous when it supports the user's activity unobtrusively, instead of being the focus of attention.

Another example chosen by Weiser to emphasize the same point is that of electric motors: there was a time, about a century ago, when the electric motor, being the big technological innovation, was the central item in the factory workshop. A single motor, through appropriate mechanical transmissions, powered dozens of tools and machines. Nowadays, instead, electric motors are inexpensive commodities and each tool (drill, saw, fan, vacuum cleaner...) can get its own—or several. In a typical car, he observes, there may be over twenty electric motors, several of which get activated by any single action, with the driver largely unaware of the details. Here is, therefore, another technology that has successfully "disappeared" into the background.

2.1.2 Tabs, pads and boards

The ubiquitous computing project at PARC aimed to explore this vision of disappearing computing and, to this end, built a variety of computing devices no longer bound to the PC model of CPU box, monitor and keyboard. These experimental devices included the inch-size Tab, the foot-size Pad and the yard-size Board. The original inspiration for exploring this range of sizes came from observing the many sizes of writing that surround us, from small labels on pushbuttons and book spines, to longer pieces of text on books, notebooks and loose sheets of paper, to large lettering on signs, walls and whiteboards. As a first attempt to make the computer technology blend in the environment in the same way as writing, the PARC researchers aimed to replace the monolithic, self-centric desktop-bound computer with many dedicated devices [260]:

I [...] adopted the slogan that, for each person in an office, there should be hundreds of tabs, tens of pads, and one or two boards.

The **ParcTab**, created and described in detail by Want *et al.* [255], was a handheld device the size of a deck of playing cards with a 128×64 pixel touch-sensitive monochrome display and three physical buttons on one side for optional one-handed operation. It suited left- and right-handed users equally well, since one could flip it (and rotate the display picture by a half-turn) to place the buttons on the other side (see figure 2.1).

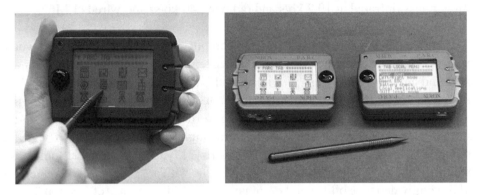

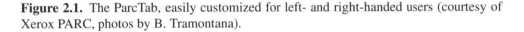

Figure 2.1. The ParcTab, easily customized for left- and right-handed users (courtesy of Xerox PARC, photos by B. Tramontana).

From many points of view, including the Unistroke [120] pen-based text input system that was implemented on it, it was a precursor of the similarly-sized pen-based PDAs that gained commercial popularity in the late 1990s with the unexpected success of the Palm Pilot organizer.

Unlike the PDAs it predated, though, it was not conceived as a stand-alone device: its designer Want, who had previously created the Active Badge while at Olivetti (*q.v.*, section 2.5.1), equipped it with a (badge-compatible) infrared interface which enabled the device to communicate with transponders in the building. This made the ParcTab a component of a building-wide ubiquitous computing infrastructure rather than a self-contained unit. The ParcTab relied on the availability of servers in the network, to which it delegated data storage and most of the computational activity. Thanks to this thin client architecture, the ParcTab had little local memory and a processor of limited computing power, which allowed for a relatively long battery life (if compared to, say, the mobile phones of the day) of a couple of weeks between recharges.

Xerox researchers Lamming and Flynn [166], of the sister lab in Cambridge then known as RXRC, used the ParcTab as a memory prosthesis in an application called Forget-me-not. ParcTabs worked as self-writing diaries by timestamping and logging the locations visited by the user, the encounters with other people, the phone calls placed and received (from PBX data—phone number and duration, not a transcript), the programs used at the workstation, the emails sent and received (!) and so on. A cute icon-based custom GUI equipped with a basic filtering facility made the diary available on the screen of the ParcTab in a compact and easily reviewed form.

The **ParcPad** was a precursor to the tablet computers that were briefly popular in the mid-1990s. It had a 640×480 pixel display with pen input and it featured both wireless (infrared at 19.2 kb/s and radio at 240 kb/s) and wired (1 Mb/s) communication channels.

The ParcPad was intended as a "scrap computer": like scrap paper, you would not carry one with you; instead, you would just temporarily pick up one of the many you'd find anywhere you went. For this paradigm to be practical, there had to be a way to carry the user's state from one device to the other. To this end, Kantarjiev *et al.* [151] describe their struggles in trying to run the X Window System on the ParcPad over a wireless channel. It is interesting to compare this effort with the similar one later undertaken by Richardson *et al.* [217] at ORL, which at some point also involved a tablet-shaped computer (albeit one with a 25 Mb/s ATM connection and moving video capability) and eventually evolved into VNC (cf. section 2.5.1).

The whiteboard-sized **LiveBoard** featured a CSCW drawing system supporting remote collaboration between several boards. As Goldberg and Richardson point out [120],

> keyboards do not work well for large wall-sized displays [...], because a keyboard is fixed and can't be reached from all parts of the display.

To address this issue, the ParcTab's Unistroke pen input method was adopted for the LiveBoard as well. Moreover, in a neat application of the ubicomp paradigm, the ParcTab could be used as an input device for the LiveBoard—users sitting around the conference desk could scribble on their personal ParcTabs and have the output displayed on the LiveBoard.

2.1.3   Calm technology

Weiser and Seely Brown [261] use the locution "calm technology" to describe an important aspect of their vision of ubiquitous computing: the fact that computing should no longer monopolize the attention of the user. In many cases, computing activity should quietly take place in the background and make its outcome accessible to the peripheral perception of the user in an unobtrusive way.

The visually striking example chosen by the authors to illustrate this concept is a piece of techno-art called the Dangling String (figure 2.2). A red plastic cable

Figure 2.2. The Dangling String, a moving sculpture by artist Natalie Jeremijenko, that animates when there is traffic on the Ethernet (courtesy of Xerox PARC, photos by B. Tramontana).

hangs from a small motor connected to the Ethernet and hidden in a corner of the ceiling. Every packet travelling on the network causes the motor to emit a pulse, which makes the string twitch. When the network is busy, the string jumps about constantly; when it is uncongested, the string only vibrates every few seconds. The Dangling String is more fun than a window-based packet monitor, it is always on, and—unlike the arrogant Microsoft Office paper clip—does not demand your attention: you are free to take notice of it (perhaps subliminally) if you're interested, or to ignore it if you're not.

2.2 Norman's Invisible Computer

In his influential and fascinating 1998 book *The Invisible Computer* [200] Don Norman, cognitive psychologist [171], usability pioneer [199] and former Apple Fellow, develops the Weiser theme of the disappearing computer and takes it further, exploring its viability in the commercial world.

As one of his first examples he comes back to the case of the electric motor already mentioned by Weiser and further points out how a similar situation existed even in the home: he exhibits a 1918 advertisement from the Sears Roebuck catalogue which proudly offers a "home motor". This versatile device can be combined with an endless list of attachments in order to help out its lucky owner with a variety of household chores. It can then act as a mixer, a fan, an egg beater, a vibrator [*sic*], a sewing machine and so on.

Nowadays it would feel ridiculous to disconnect the motor from the sewing machine in order to attach it to the egg beater. Instead, it feels natural for each appliance to have as many motors as it needs, of exactly the right size and power,

permanently embedded into it. And it seems queer that, only a century ago, ordinary people could be persuaded to buy a "home motor": who cares about motors
anyway? What people really want, rightly argues Norman, is the mixer, the fan and
the sewing machine, not the motor.

Yet, on the computer front, we are nowadays in the same situation. Ordinary
households are persuaded to buy a "personal computer" which is then used for such
diverse activities as browsing the web, writing letters, managing home finances,
editing photographs and videos and so forth. All of these activities are shoehorned
into the same keyboard-and-mouse interaction paradigm: the PC is likened by Norman to a Swiss-army knife that can be used to perform the job of many tools, but
never as well as any of the individual specialized tools[1]. Because it is so extremely
multipurpose, it is not very good at anything and it is too complex to use and maintain in good working order.

So the author argues that each one of the activities previously mentioned would
be better served by its own dedicated information appliance—a simple device that
would not look or (mis)behave like a computer, despite having rather similar internals. In order not to lose the current benefit of being able to share data between
those activities (e.g. so as to be able to include a photograph in a letter), those
appliances should also be capable of sending information to each other.

Norman's case is appealing and compelling, but it has its critics. Among them
is Odlyzko [201], whose main objection is that the mature market described by
Norman (for whom, while the feature-rich PC is geared towards the propellerhead[2],
now that the market is mature the new product should target the masses and become
simpler) will be destabilized and made new and immature by the tide of innovation
triggered by the very introduction of information appliances. Like many others,
Odlyzko is also sceptical about the claim that data exchange between independent
devices made by different manufacturers at different times is going to work out as
smoothly as promised. Another objection is that the tradeoff between flexibility
and ease of use may need to be resolved differently for different users—possibly
even for different members of the same household, some of whom will therefore
find a "simple information appliance" too simple and inflexible for the tasks they
would like to perform.

Personally I would also add—especially after my experience in Japan[3]—that
the envisaged information appliances, although they may be smaller than the computer they replace, are still physical objects, whose minimum size is determined by

---

[1] Anyone needing proof of this should try viewing a DVD on a computer and attempt to single out
a specific frame using mouse-operated rewind, slow motion and pause buttons; then do the same on
a regular DVD player using the jog-shuttle dial.

[2] Norman politely says "technology enthusiast" and "early adopter".

[3] Having to spend one year in an 18 m^2 one-room flat has given me quite a different perspective
on the value of *space* from that of the typical American homeowner.

the requirements of their user interface. If I had to have one such physical appliance for every application I use, I just wouldn't know where to put them! Maybe things wouldn't be so bad if appliances came in the extremely regular shape of magazines or books, and could be quickly and efficiently stored on a bookshelf when not in use[4]: I do have many thousands of books and magazines (and comics!) at home and they cause me no problems. But if one of the important reasons for building separate appliances is that each needs a differently shaped interface—incorporating the appropriate combination of keyboards, pens, dials, knobs, microphones, displays, printers and whatnot—then how could we hope to have all those appliances fit neatly on a shelf like books when we wanted them out of the way?

At any rate, and apart from all this, the real merit of Norman's book is not so much in the technical details but in its holistic analysis of the business case for the post-PC information appliance. Having the best technology does not necessarily guarantee success in the marketplace, and neither does being the first. Norman's instructive analysis presents examples that range from Edison's phonograph to the Apple Macintosh and distils from them a strategy to make the information appliance a commercial success. He explains that a successful product stands on three equally important legs, of which raw technological performance is only one; the other two are marketing and user experience. His observations are important lessons if we are to build a ubicomp future that will stand a chance of actually being *adopted* by the general public.

2.3 MIT

Over the years, the Massachusetts Institute of Technology has hosted many research initiatives related to ubiquitous computing. Here is a sampler.

2.3.1 Tangible bits

During a visit to the Media Lab in 1996, the highlight of which was a display of wireless Lego-based mini-robots[5], I was shown several demos in the spirit of "calm technology": mapping computer information onto everyday low-tech and non-threatening objects. There was also an emphasis on supplying information using non-intrusive "background" channels, as opposed to attention-grabbing "foreground" methods—the strategy demonstrated by the Dangling String mentioned in section 2.1.3.

---

[4]Unlike today's computers which, owing to their Laocoöntean wiring even more than to their bulk and non-stackable shapes, are very difficult to move from their semi-permanent place on one's desk.

[5]The delightful "Lego Mindstorms" product line was a result of research cooperation between MIT and the Danish toy maker.

In the ambientROOM by Ishii *et al.* [141] (a free-standing cubicle outfitted with physical interfaces to the computing world), the wallpaper was an abstract light pattern that changed dynamically based on some remote activity, such as the number of people in a nearby meeting area or the activity of a hamster elsewhere (metaphorically representative of, say, the activity of one's baby child at home). The light pattern itself, generated optomechanically by reflecting light off water ripples triggered by the activity being monitored, was permanently "live" without being an annoying distraction; it was instead pleasant and soothing.

Similar use was made of audible cues, with hits on the web server represented by the sound of raindrops. An average level of traffic mapped to a soft rain in the background, while a sudden silence or a thunderstorm would be noticed, perhaps prompting the user into looking for information about the cause.

Network activity, too, was translated into sound (appropriately rendered as car traffic) and then metaphorically hidden inside a little spice jar: uncorking the glass jar released the sound, and you could also monitor other entities by uncorking different bottles.

An analogue clock on the wall was used as an *input* device: if the user wound back the clock's hands to a previous time, the sound and light patterns of the room would then no longer indicate real-time activity, but that which had happened at the time displayed on the clock face.

Outside the ambientROOM, the metaDESK [248] also translated a computer interface into tangible bits, but this time for active and direct manipulation as opposed to background awareness. A toy building placed on the desk would cause a map of the surrounding area to be projected on the desk; and the map faithfully followed the building if this was moved around or rotated. Placing a second building on the desk imposed a second constraint on the map, which rescaled and reoriented itself accordingly (now perforce ignoring the individual orientations of the two buildings, which might be inconsistent). A flat-panel display could be brought over the desk area and would show a 3D rendering of the map from that viewpoint. These were all ways to interact with computer models by intuitively manipulating tangible objects, without having to go anywhere near a computer.

2.3.2   The WearComp

In this chapter we are exploring many different ways in which computing may become ubiquitous: for example by migrating from desktop machines onto tabs, pads and boards; by becoming invisibly embedded into appliances; by affecting non-computing aspects of our environment at the periphery of our perception. Not least, computers may become ubiquitous by becoming something you *wear*—and few people have been wearing computers for longer than Steve Mann, now associate professor at the University of Toronto, who built his first prototypes in high school in the late 1970s and early 1980s [179], before the first portable computers were available commercially.

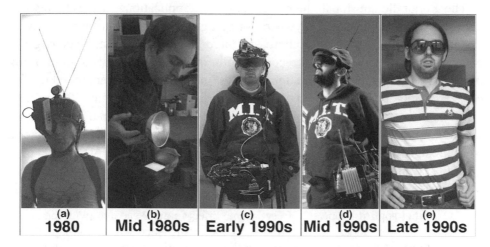

Figure 2.3. The evolution of Mann's WearComp and WearCam, sampled approximately every five years. In the most recent photograph (e), the computer is hidden under clothing and the display looks like an ordinary pair of sunglasses (courtesy and Subjectright (S) Steve Mann).

The invention for which Mann is best known, which he perfected while a graduate student at MIT in the 1990s, is the WearComp/WearCam [183], a body-worn combination including a camera, a display, a chord keyboard, a radio transceiver, a computer, a battery and, to put it all together, a substantial amount of wiring.

This is a markedly different take on the ubiquitous computing theme: in this case "the computer is everywhere" not because it's embedded in everything that surrounds the subject, but because it's embedded in the subject himself. From the early prototypes (figure 2.3) that made him appear as a cyborg—particularly owing to the attention-grabbing head-mounted gear including miner's helmet with spotlight, over-the-eye display, camera and antennas—Mann has continuously refined his hardware taking advantage of the latest evolutions in miniaturization of the relevant electronics. One of his recent display devices (not pictured) looks like a normal pair of bifocals, giving no clues to onlookers that the wearer may be carrying and using a computer[6].

One of the distinctive features of the wearable computer is that it is always on and ready for use, its display being permanently available in the wearer's field of vision. This, too, is a way for computing to disappear into the perceptual

---

[6]Ironically, now that he no longer looks like a science-fiction-movie cyborg, Mann introduces himself as one and is indeed the star of a movie called *Cyberman*.

background of the user, although the approach is radically different from (oppo-site to?) that of the Dangling String of section 2.1.3.

The author did not stop at the more predictable applications such as being able to receive email anytime and anywhere, or being able to take notes unobtrusively by single-handedly typing on a chord keyboard in the pocket while keeping eye contact with the interlocutor. The combination of a camera feed and a radio link allowed remote users to "see through the eyes" of the WearCam-equipped cyborg and, where appropriate, send him comments or reminders in real time (figure 2.4).

Mann's more innovative uses of the wearable computer centred around auto-matic manipulations of the video stream from the camera, making the computer a visual prosthesis that augmented the perceptual capabilities of the wearer. Digital visual filters, for example, could mediate the experience of seeing, implementing a fish-eye lens or a stroboscope [180]:

> One filter applied a repeating freeze-frame effect to the WearCam (with the cameras' own shutters set to 1/10,000 second). This video sample-and-hold technique let me see the unseeable: writing on moving automobile tires and the blades on a spinning airplane propeller. [...] Beyond just enabling me to see things I would otherwise have missed, the effect would sometimes cause me to remember certain things better. There is something very visceral about having an image frozen in space in front of your eyes. I found, for example, that I would often remember faces better, because a frozen image tended to remain in my memory much longer than a moving one. Perhaps intelligent eyeglasses of the future will anticipate what is important to us and select the sampling rate accordingly to reveal salient details.

Image processing allowed the frames from a panning movement of the camera to be stitched into a larger picture, available offline as a panoramic view (figure 2.4). Image recognition allowed superimposition of relevant textual information on the scene being viewed—a previously entered shopping list would appear as a floating tag over the cashier as a reminder to the wearer during a refund transaction; or a virtual self-adhesive note could be stuck on a building (!) to remind the wearer of something that needed to be done once there. Face recognition by the machine could float a name tag over known faces found in the current view to avoid the embarrassment of not remembering a person's name. Other "memory prosthetic" uses for the system included finding a lost garment by reviewing previous footage in which it appeared.

Biometric sensors monitoring quantities such as heartbeat and footsteps were used as additional inputs. This way, if the wearer were hypothetically attacked by a gun-toting villain, heuristics could infer a situation of perceived danger from such measurements and dispatch a distress call via radio, annotating the current camera scene with some text explaining that the wearer might be in danger and unable to call for help himself [178].

Figure 2.4. Views from a WearCam are stitched together into a "pencigraphic image composite". In the lower left corner Mann receives a text comment from his spouse, to whom the scene is being transmitted in real time via radio link (courtesy and Subjectright (S) Steve Mann).

An interesting aspect of Mann's work from the point of view of this book is his active focus on personal privacy issues [177], often enlivened by a healthy streak of provocative sensationalism. Here are a few highlights.

- Pointing out the growing spread of surveillance cameras not only in high risk environments such as banks and airports but also in lower risk areas such as shops and even city streets, he notes that we are being watched everywhere we go. He offers the WearCam as a distributed alternative, arguing that a "neighbourhood watch" arrangement in which people watch out for each other's safety would be less intrusive and less subject to totalitarian abuse than the current centralized arrangement in which the feeds from street cameras—soon equipped with automatic face recognition—all converge into the hands of governments or big businesses.

- Since Mann has been watching the world through a recording camera for years, he has developed some interesting personal insights into the privacy issues surrounding the act of taking pictures of people. Some of these are reflected in his proposal of "subjectright" (as opposed to copyright), according to which the rights to a picture belong to the subject that appears in it. (This is explained in further detail at http://www.wearcam.org/subjectrights. htm.)

- At a more basic level, Mann notes that the eye-mounted display of the Wear-
  Comp gives its user a degree of privacy not available with a laptop or PDA:
  the passenger in the next seat on the aeroplane won't be able to read your
  screen, and in fact won't even know that you are using a computer.

- The latest and least obtrusive version of the WearCam is described by its creator as an equalizer that gives individuals the same power (of recording their
  images whether they like it or not) that "the system" uses towards (against?)
  them: even in places where photography is not allowed, such as some stores
  or banks, the wearer may covertly relay his see-through-my-eyes viewpoint
  to his spouse back home and get real-time advice about the ongoing transaction (see figure 2.4 on page 19), as well as keeping evidence of what happened in case of subsequent dispute [178]:

  > If we are going to be under video surveillance, we may as well keep
  > our own "memory" of the events around us, analogous to a contract in
  > which both parties keep a signed copy.

  In a more dramatic scenario, if covert WearCam were widespread, they might
  capture police brutality and human rights violations more effectively and
  safely than today's handheld camcorders, which are likely to be spotted by
  the perpetrators and thereafter confiscated or destroyed.

- Other small projects from Mann explore the relationship between man and
  technology without resorting to the complex system engineering efforts of
  the WearCam. An example is a satire on the "seat licences" that are commonly used by commercial software: a chair (see figure 2.5) allows you
  to rest on it for a few minutes once you swipe your card in its reader, but
  sharp spikes pop up from the seat as soon as your licence expires [175]. The
  deeper meaning of this is to get you thinking about software licences, intellectual property and their consequences, as computing evolves from "porta-
  bles" through "wearables" to "implantables". Another example is a garment
  that gives its voluntary wearer an electric shock whenever network connectivity is lost, the point being that the wearer can now claim that disconnection
  is physically painful [176]:

  > 'Painful Disconnect' makes real the notion that denial of the right to
  > self-surveillance by friends and family is equivalent to possible torture
  > or other mistreatment.

  Some researchers find these projects irritating "because they are not real science". Of course they're not: they're opinion pieces. Some of them have
  even appeared in art exhibitions. The author is deliberately provocative and

Figure 2.5. SeatSale. You get a seating licence by swiping a photo ID card in the reader, but when the licence expires you have to get off the chair—unless you are a fakir (courtesy of Steve Mann).

has a gift for stimulating interesting discussions whether one agrees with him or not.

Mann has just written two books, one full of mathematics [182] and one for the general public [181], about his inventions and his experience of life as a cyborg. Since they were only published after my manuscript was closed, you will not find a review of their contents here; however, given the track record of originality of the author, my guess is that the second one in particular is likely to be an interesting, controversial and thought-provoking read.

2.3.3 Auto-ID

Perhaps the most ubiquitous technological mark of our society is the humble bar code: there is hardly any consumer product nowadays that does not display the familiar pattern of thin and thick lines somewhere on its packaging.

The Auto-ID project at MIT, blessed by the sponsorship and cooperation of several major retailers and manufacturers, aims to develop a successor to the bar code [192]. There will be two simple but critical innovations: one, the new system will be based on radio rather than on optical scanning, so it will be possible to read the tag without requiring that an operator align the printed code with the reading device. Two, it will have a much larger identifier space, so that it will be possible to embed a serial number in the code (making all tags different) as opposed to just a model number.

The first point, doing away with line-of-sight laser scanning, opens up many more opportunities to acquire tags. The bar code requires a manual alignment operation for each item that is scanned—which is costly (human intervention) and slow (items to be scanned need to be processed one by one). This means that bar codes are not acquired very frequently—as a matter of fact, they are rarely ever acquired anywhere other than at the point of sale. The cost of the hardware is even now sufficiently low that it would be perfectly feasible to incorporate a laser scanner in a fridge; however, very few users would actually go to the trouble of scanning every item every time they put it in or take it out of the fridge, and this is why even high-end fridges don't come with bar code readers. With the "ePC" (electronic Product Code) chip envisaged by the Auto-ID project, instead, the fridge could automatically list its contents—and so could the bookshelf and the medicine closet. Reading an RFID (radio frequency identification) tag such as the ePC does not require line of sight; besides, it is possible for several tags to be in the field of the reader and still be read correctly and efficiently using appropriate algorithms for anti-collision.

Some of the proposed scenarios include the medicine closet warning you about drugs that you should not take together, the washing machine warning you about the presence of a red sock in a load of whites, and the microwave oven directly following instructions from the packaged food on the time and power necessary for perfect cooking.

There is a trade-off between the cost of the tag itself and that of the acquisition operation: for the bar code, manufacture of the tag is practically free (some sort of label would have to be printed on the packaging even if there were no bar code) whereas acquisition is comparatively expensive because it requires manual intervention. For the ePC, on the contrary, the tag (a passive RFID transponder) is expensive[7], but the cost of reading it is negligible. Clearly, at current prices, for many cheap items it is not economically practicable to adopt ePCs, whereas bar codes pose no problems. There will be cases, though, in which the active functionality gained by the object through the Auto-ID will be sufficiently valuable that it will compensate for this extra cost.

The goal stated in the first Auto-ID tech report [192] is to bring the price of tags down to 0.1 $. The FAQ section of the consortium's web site [193] goes further, or at least it did in mid-2001, citing 0.01 $ as a requirement before the tags can be cost effective on everyday products and ambitiously forecasting that 0.05 $ ePC chips would be feasible by the end of the year.

> More technically, we do not believe conventional silicon chip based technology can go much below this price point at any volume. To get below the 5 cent barrier, we expect to need breakthrough new memory technologies, perhaps using magnetic materials, printed integrated circuits, or organic techniques.

---

[7]In 2001, RFID transponders could be bought for about 0.9 $ a piece in quantities of 100.

Figure 2.6. Two ring binders with identical bar codes on their spine.

The second point we listed, global uniqueness of codes even for identical products, makes it possible to build a system in which individual objects are tagged with their properties.

The inventory control system of your company can record that this is the VGA projector that was sent in for repair in October, whereas that is the one that was lent to the branch office for two months. The ring binders lying here on my desk as I am writing this sentence (figure 2.6) carry identical bar codes on their spine labels, which would be useless to me even if I had a bar code reader. These codes were only of use to the merchant who scanned them at the till when they were sold. However, if the manufacturer had marked these binders not just with bar codes but with Auto-ID codes, I could tell them apart and tag each of them with a list of the papers it contains; with Auto-ID readers continuously sensing the contents of my bookshelves and desk, I could later ask my computer system to give me the location of any specific paper ("It's in the binder labelled 'MISC 07', currently on your desk"). Even better, if the tags were sufficiently small and cheap, I could label the individual papers themselves, and then even the table of contents of each ring binder could be compiled automatically.

While we are at it, this is an appropriate place to mention the issue of **address space cardinality**, which affects all tagging systems and is therefore relevant to several other projects presented in this chapter.

There exist two main variations of the printed bar code: the 12-digit UPC[8], whose decimal representation looks like X-XXXXX-XXXXX-X, and the 13-digit EAN[9], which looks like X-XXXXXX-XXXXXX. The first digit describes the type of code; the last is a checksum; the two blocks in the middle give the manufacturer code (100,000 possibilities for UPC; 1,000,000 for EAN) and the product code (100,000 possibilities for each manufacturer). Naturally enough, manufacturer codes are assigned by the respective consortium, while product codes are assigned by each manufacturer.

Nobody should be overly surprised that these numbering schemes are running out of space. Most numbering schemes do, sooner or later—from postal codes to car number plates, and from telephone numbers to IP addresses. The obvious remedy is to allocate more bits. Where the code is bound by physical constraints, as in the case of car number plates, the increase is somewhat cautious—perhaps a digit or two at a time; but where the code's length only matters in cyberspace, the tendency is for outrageously licentious jumps—witness IP, going from 32 to 128 bits. After all, bits are cheap; what's *really* expensive is having to overhaul the deployed infrastructure to accommodate the revised format. This is an incentive to move to address spaces of astronomic cardinality, in the hope that this will be the last of the necessary expansions. Of course this hope may still be vain, in so far as the availability of so many more codes may soon encourage new "wasteful" uses that had not even been imagined at the time of the expansion.

It would be grossly superficial to consider the issue only in terms of the number of bits and say for example that, since the mass of the Earth is 6×10^{24} kg ($\approx 2^{92}$ g), 92 bits of addressing suffice to assign a different code to each gram-sized fragment of the Earth (including mantle and core), and therefore must definitely be adequate to tag the whole conceivable range of present and future man-made artefacts. This flawed reasoning fails to take into account the problem of *partitioning*. Assigning all numbers centrally is a solution that does not scale, so a hierarchical alternative is often adopted: as described above for the bar codes, the central agency only assigns blocks of numbers for the entities at the top level (the manufacturers), and then each one of those assigns the numbers for the next level down (the products). More levels can be introduced if necessary. This dramatically reduces the effective number of addressable entities owing to the wastage within code ranges that have been allocated at the top levels (with some margin, necessarily) but not actually used at the "leaf" level of the tree. To alleviate the problem of wastage the partitioning may be made mobile (like IPv4, and unlike bar codes), but at the expense of extra

---

[8]UPC = Universal Product Code, a standard issued by the Uniform Code Council [249] and used primarily in the USA.

[9]Since the scheme is adopted globally in 45 countries, EAN now confusingly means International Article Numbering Association rather than European Article Numbering as it used to.

complication in decoding.

Brock [51] offers a particularly clear analysis of these issues in his report on the design of the Auto-ID's code. All things considered, a code space of 96 bits was chosen, partitioned to give 2^{28} ($\approx$ 256 million) manufacturers, 2^{24} ($\approx$ 16 million) product types per manufacturer and 2^{36} ($\approx$ 64 billion) serial numbers per product. Even so, Brock wisely acknowledges that these boundaries may eventually be exceeded—for example if every person on Earth were allowed to be a virtual "manufacturer" who assigned her own codes to objects of choice. To cater for this, the remaining 8 bits are assigned to a "header" that specifies one of 256 possible partitioning schemes, with the one described above being the only scheme currently defined.

In closing this section it is worth noting that the UCC and EAN are themselves investigating the use of RFID tags [250].

2.3.4 Oxygen

The Oxygen project is a very large container for a complete ubicomp solution, spanning all levels from hardware to system software to user interface and knowledge management, and all fields from speech and image recognition to microprocessor design and software radios. Given the extremely wide range of topics involved, and the fact that the project is still in its early stages, what we shall do here is simply to sketch the envisaged outcome; the interested reader is referred to the programmatic article by Dertouzos in *Scientific American* [88] and to the project's web site [191] where results will be posted in due course.

From the point of view of the user experience, Oxygen promises to be a world in which computation is available anywhere at negligible cost (like oxygen—or, more technologically, electricity). The abundance of computing power will be spent to make computing systems adapt to the way humans work, instead of the reverse paradigm to which we have been subjected so far. Users will be able to ask for results in a way that is natural to them ("print that picture on the nearest uncongested printer"), using natural language instead of computer syntax and speech and gestures instead of typing and clicking.

The hardware to be deployed to support this vision includes the following three kinds of entities.

H21s: handheld devices acting as PDAs, personal communicators (integrating the functions of cellphone, radio, pager, email and so on) and universal remote control units.

E21s: more powerful computing servers, typically mains-powered, embedded in the environment (home, office, car...) and capable of affecting it with functions such as controlling the air conditioning, the lighting and so on.

N21s: dynamic networks allowing the previous classes of devices to discover each other's services and make use of them.

2.4   HP's Cooltown

The Cooltown project at Hewlett-Packard Laboratories, as described by Kindberg and Barton [156], implements a vision of ubiquitous computing based on web technology and tagging. Places and objects can, on request, emit a globally unique URL that represents them. The request will typically come from a user's PDA which will then act as the user interface for the entity that identified itself.

For example, a user entering a conference room will pick up on her PDA an infrared beacon emitted by the room and containing the URL of the web page for the room. The PDA will then surf to that page and show the user all the services that the room offers.

Although the intended purpose is somewhat different, there are obvious similarities between this approach and that of the Auto-ID seen above in section 2.3.3. Functionally, Cooltown is meant as a way for nomadic users to control the devices around them, whereas Auto-ID is meant as a way for objects to convey information about themselves. But this distinction can easily be blurred, and at an abstract level there are no fundamental constraints that would prevent either of these systems from providing the functionality of the other.

Technologically, the two main differences are that Cooltown is not worried about the line-of-sight limitations of bar code readers (in fact it explicitly envisages their use alongside infrared transceivers—which themselves lack the penetration properties of radio) and that Cooltown is explicitly based on WWW standards and protocols.

The first point is linked to the fact that Cooltown usage is explicitly based on the paradigm of a human interacting with objects and the environment, so it's no problem for that human to scan a bar code when she points her universal web browser at the things with which she chooses to interact.

The second point is a practical issue that gives Cooltown simplicity and robustness: by adopting the web model, Cooltown takes advantage of a mature, well-understood and demonstrably scalable architecture that delivers contents and services in a vendor- and service-independent way.

By using her PDA as a repository of bookmarks, the speaker walks up to the projector in the conference room and uploads ("beams") into it the URL of her presentation. (In Cooltown, she no longer has to carry her own laptop around.) Then, reversing roles, she acquires the tag of the projector and surfs to the page that implements the projector's user interface. From there she can advance slides as required, controlling the shared projector with her personal PDA.

The versatility of the web model of interaction, including CGI and client upload via forms, can be exploited for less obvious applications. A Cooltown camera recognizes the user by acquiring her URL (which contains a special subsection dedicated to web clients that are cameras), perhaps through a user badge (see section 2.5.1). Then, by surfing to that section, the camera finds a form through which photos can be uploaded to the user's page via HTTP POST.

Huang *et al.* [135] interestingly describe the practical challenges faced by a non-technical user wishing to publish digital photographs on his web page: even when there is wireless connectivity between the camera and the computer, the operation is far from trivial and typically involves tedious repetitive operations such as the renaming of dozens of files. Ubicomp environments will live up to their promise only after solving all these practical issues. Cooltown's choice of web protocols is a stable and well-understood base for experimentation in this domain.

2.5 ORL/AT&T Labs Cambridge

The Olivetti Research laboratory in Cambridge, UK (later Olivetti-Oracle Research Laboratory, now AT&T Laboratories Cambridge), where the Active Badge was invented in 1989, was an early player in the ubicomp game. This systems-oriented research centre developed several new technologies revolving around the global vision of **sentient computing** put forward by the lab's director Andy Hopper.

The core idea of sentient computing is to make computing systems reactive to the physical world: as the user's context changes, the applications should adapt to the new environment and serve the user in the manner that is most appropriate to the new circumstances. The enabling technology that makes this possible is that of inexpensive digital sensors (including cameras, microphones and compasses) that could be deployed in large numbers. Sentient computing leads to "do-nothing technology" (the user's presence is sufficient to make things happen, as opposed to having to request things explicitly with button presses) and to "global smart personalization" (systems automatically reconfigure themselves with the preferences of the current user). Says Hopper [134]:

> Central to any good working relationship is a degree of mutual understanding between the two parties. The problem with conventional human-computer interaction is that responsibility for understanding, or the lack of it, lies wholly with the user. [...] Instead of bringing the user to the computer, let us take into account that people live and work in a real physical world, and make this notion—the concept of space—integral to the operation of our computer systems. We need to make computer systems aware of the physical

environment—shifting part of the onus of understanding from user to machine. Awareness comes through sensing, and that implies the need for appropriate sensor technologies to collect status and location data.

Many research groups around the world are currently working on the related
topic of "context-aware computing"—systems that reconfigure themselves
depending on the "context" (whatever this may mean) of their user. It is interesting
to note the significant number of cases in which the context information consists
primarily of the user's *location*.

Outdoors, the Global Positioning System provides absolute geographical coordinates with an accuracy of around 10 m. Originally developed for military uses,
the technology was found to be extremely useful for civilian air and sea navigation and is now being widely deployed in commercial car navigation systems[10].
Handheld receivers are also available for bikers and trekkers.

The ORL/AT&T laboratory has been investigating location technologies for
over a decade and has been responsible for pioneering contributions in the field of
indoors location systems—from the Active Badge, whose spatial resolution is at the
room scale, to the Active Bat, accurate to a few centimetres; and from the vision-
based TRIP system, which locates objects via special 2D bar codes, to the weight-
sensitive Active Floor, which can recognize people from their walking patterns.

The ubicomp-related research conducted at AT&T Labs Cambridge has not
been limited to location technologies, though: further relevant projects have included Virtual Network Computing (VNC), which lets you access your personal
computing environment from anywhere, and the Prototype Embedded Network
(PEN), a short-range wireless communication system with an emphasis on low
power.

2.5.1   The Active Badge

The Active Badge [254], in a pattern common to many other inventions, was born
out of frustration. Our workplace was spread out on three floors of a narrow building and the researchers would frequently be in places other than their own offices,
discussing ideas with colleagues; finding a specific person often involved phoning their office and then, in sequence, the hardware lab, the meeting room, and
the offices of other colleagues who might know the whereabouts of the intended
callee. One of the researchers, Roy Want, took up Hopper's half-serious challenge
to create a system that addressed this problem, and came up with the Active Badge
(figure 2.7 shows a later version of the device, *circa* 1992).

---

[10]At the time of writing (2001) these are mostly seen in high-end rental cars in Europe and America, but they are commonplace consumer electronic items for motorists in Japan.

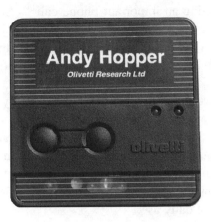

Figure 2.7. The Active Badge (courtesy of AT&T Laboratories Cambridge).

The principle on which the Active Badge is based is very simple. The device is worn by users like a conventional name badge—which it also is. Its infrared transmitter periodically sends out the badge's identifier, which is picked up by fixed sensors deployed throughout the building. Because the infrared signal bounces off walls without penetrating them, the detection of a signal by any given sensor indicates that the corresponding badge is located in the same room as the sensor. By collating sightings from all the sensors in the building, the system knows where individual badges are and can offer services such as the automatic redirection of phone calls. The hardware is cheap and easy to build because the underlying technology of infrared signalling is widespread in consumer equipment such as remote control units and is therefore commercially mature, with its components widely available as commodity items.

This system was first deployed across the lab as an experimental prototype in early 1990 and was subsequently adopted by other academic and industrial research institutions in Europe and America including the University of Cambridge, Imperial College London, the University of Twente, Digital Equipment Corporation, Xerox, Bellcore and MIT. The Badge was at one point even sold as a product by our parent company Olivetti, though it never reached commercial acceptance in the marketplace. We used the system continuously for about ten years until we replaced it with the higher resolution Active Bat system (described in section 2.5.3 next); this means that we can now speak about it from extensive practical experience and not just as an intellectual experiment.

In our lab, the Active Badge soon became an essential part of the infrastructure: researchers really liked the fact that they could freely wander away from their office even if they were expecting an important phone call[11]. Sometimes, when a new start-up company was formed from one of our research projects, their move to new premises was followed by the deployment of an Active Badge network, because the researchers from our lab hated to forgo the convenience of the badge after having experienced it at ORL.

Wearing the badge was always voluntary, but few if any people ever decided to opt out. I did, for a certain time, in part also as a kind of social service to ensure that new employees would not be forced to wear one because of unanimous peer pressure; but this did not change the overall picture, and most staff members have been consistently viewing the system as a sci-fi asset of the lab rather than as a privacy threat. The following statement by Want *et al.* [254] (emphasis mine) has been validated by years of daily use:

> There is a danger that in the future this technology will be abused by un-scrupulous employers. If it is, then legislation must be used to protect us from this kind of technology abuse. However, it is our conclusion that *amongst professional people responsible for their own work time*, it is a very useful and welcome office system.

This acceptance was fostered by some explicit policy decisions: firstly, badge sightings were never logged—they were used instantaneously and then thrown away. Secondly, we committed to **reciprocity**. Everybody wore a badge, and everybody had the xab application (figure 2.8) running on their workstation all the time; this displayed a list of all the staff members with their current location, nearest phone number and number of people in the same room. So, yes, your boss could watch you, but in return you could watch him yourself if you were so inclined. As a matter of fact the boss even installed badge sensors in his *home*, which relayed his position via ISDN to the badge server at the lab[12]. This "ethical foundation" of reciprocity helped make it clear that the purpose of the system was not to monitor staff but to help lab members find each other.

At some point a new facility was added to the system: you could now set a "watch" on someone and you would get a beeping alert when their location changed. This was meant for the situation in which A wanted to contact B, but the badge system told A that B was in a meeting, which A did not want to disturb. By putting a watch on B, A could catch him just as he walked out of his meeting. One of the researchers complained that this would facilitate abuse of the system by curious snoops or petty thieves who could sneak into someone's office during the lunch hour, safe in the knowledge that they would get advance warning of their

---

[11]This was before everyone in the civilized world (except yours truly who still stubbornly refuses to carry one) had a cellular phone.

[12]He did this primarily to support automatic *teleporting* of his desktop session between work and home, described next on page 33.

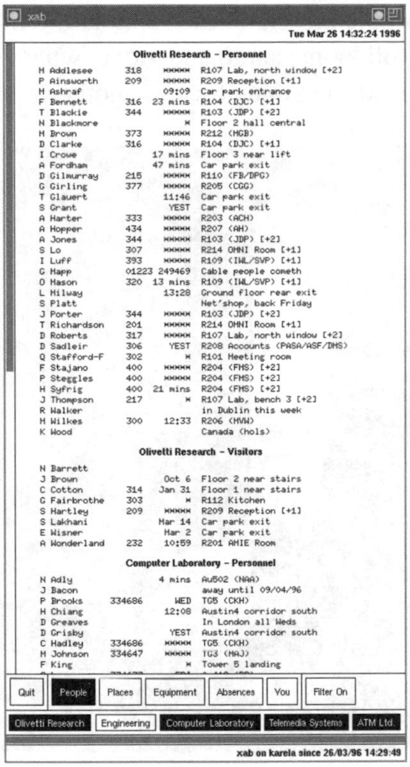

```
xab                                                    
                                        Tue Mar 26 14:32:24 1996

                        Olivetti Research - Personnel

    M Addlesee      318    xxxxx    R107 Lab, north window [+2]
    P Ainsworth     209    xxxxx    R209 Reception [+1]
    M Ashraf               09:09    Car park entrance
    F Bennett       316    23 mins  R104 (DJC) [+1]
    T Blackie       344    xxxxx    R103 (JDP) [+2]
    N Blackmore            x        Floor 2 hall central
    M Brown         373    xxxxx    R212 (HGB)
    D Clarke        316    xxxxx    R104 (DJC) [+1]
    I Crowe                17 mins  Floor 3 near lift
    A Fordham              47 mins  Car park exit
    D Gilmurray     215    xxxxx    R110 (FB/DPG)
    G Girling       377    xxxxx    R205 (CGG)
    T Glauert              11:46    Car park exit
    S Grant                YEST     Car park exit
    A Harter        333    xxxxx    R203 (ACH)
    A Hopper        434    xxxxx    R207 (AH)
    A Jones         344    xxxxx    R103 (JDP) [+2]
    S Lo            307    xxxxx    R214 OMNI Room [+1]
    I Luff          393    xxxxx    R109 (IWL/SVP) [+1]
    G Mapp          01223 249469    Cable people cometh
    O Mason         320    13 mins  R109 (IWL/SVP) [+1]
    L Milway               13:28    Ground floor rear exit
    S Platt                         Net'shop, back Friday
    J Porter        344    xxxxx    R103 (JDP) [+2]
    T Richardson    201    xxxxx    R214 OMNI Room [+1]
    D Roberts       317    xxxxx    R107 Lab, north window [+2]
    D Sadleir       306    YEST     R208 Accounts (PASA/WSF/IMS)
    Q Stafford-F    302    x        R101 Meeting room
    F Stajano       400    xxxxx    R204 (FMS) [+2]
    P Steggles      400    xxxxx    R204 (FMS) [+2]
    H Syfrig        400    21 mins  R204 (FMS) [+2]
    J Thompson      217    x        R107 Lab, bench 3 [+2]
    R Walker                        in Dublin this week
    M Wilkes        300    12:33    R206 (MMW)
    K Wood                          Canada (hols)

                        Olivetti Research - Visitors

    N Barrett
    J Brown                Oct 6    Floor 2 near stairs
    C Cotton        314    Jan 31   Floor 1 near stairs
    G Fairbrothe    303    x        R112 Kitchen
    S Hartley       209    xxxxx    R209 Reception [+1]
    S Lakhani              Mar 14   Car park exit
    E Wisner              Mar 2     Car park exit
    A Wonderland    232    10:59    R201 AMIE Room

                       Computer Laboratory - Personnel

    N Adly                 4 mins   Au502 (NAA)
    J Bacon                         away until 09/04/96
    P Brooks        334686 WED      TG5 (CKH)
    H Chiang              12:08     Austin4 corridor south
    D Greaves                       In London all Weds
    D Grisby               YEST     Austin4 corridor south
    C Hadley        334686 xxxxx    TG5 (CKH)
    M Johnson       334647 xxxxx    TG3 (MHJ)
    F King                 x        Tower 5 landing

  [Quit] [People] [Places] [Equipment] [Absences] [You] [Filter On]

  [Olivetti Research] [Engineering] [Computer Laboratory] [Telemedia Systems] [ATM Ltd.]

                               xab on karela since 26/03/96 14:29:49
```

Figure 2.8. The `xab` application, displaying badge sightings on an X Windows workstation (courtesy of AT&T Laboratories Cambridge).

victim's return. The issue was addressed by resorting to the reciprocity principle: whenever user *A* set a watch on user *B*, *B* would receive a notification. This made the feature acceptable and a new social protocol naturally developed around it: on receiving the notification, *B* would phone *A* to say "I'm back now, were you looking for me?".

Many other projects in our lab made use of the location information provided by the Active Badge to enhance some other service. In our distributed multimedia systems Pandora [133] and Medusa [265] you could videophone someone by name as well as by phone number[13], and videomail would be automatically annotated

---

[13]Observe that "by phone number" effectively means "by location" unless we are dealing with mobile telephony: when you dial 321123 you are not actually calling "George", but "George's office". Cellular phones reverse this situation—and therefore are wide-area person-tracking devices in their own right—in part also owing to the interesting social convention that the mobile terminal is a strictly personal item that is never shared. When the fixed phone on your desk rings and you're not in the immediate vicinity, it is acceptable for a member of your family (at home) or a colleague (at work)

with the names of the people present in the room at the time of the recording. We also experimented with follow-me audio and video, where media streams would be redirected while you moved from one office to another.

Figure 2.9. The Smart Beverage Dispenser (courtesy of AT&T Laboratories Cambridge).

Ward, Naylon *et al.* interfaced the coffee machine[14] to the badge system so that clicking the badge button when walking up to the machine selected the user's preferred beverage from a list featuring, among others, coffee, chocolate "and the revolting *mokaccino*, a subtle blend of coffee and chocolate" [24]. This can be seen as a light-hearted example of "global smart personalization": the appliance (see figure 2.9) automatically adapts its behaviour to that preferred by its current user.

Another example of global smart personalization comes from the teleporting

---

to answer it for you; but it is considered bad manners for anyone to do this with your *mobile* phone, even when you temporarily leave it on your desk.

[14]It is interesting to note the frequency with which hackers take caffeine not just as a substance that keeps them awake during late-night programming sessions but also as an inspiration for whacky computer recreations. See for example the CMU coke machine that users could query via finger(1) to ensure that they would be issued a can that had had time to cool down [58]; the Trojan Room coffee pot at the University of Cambridge [235], later to become the first webcam; the ParcTab-augmented coffee pot of Xerox PARC, which allowed a public-spirited researcher to alert colleagues electronically whenever a fresh pot had been brewed [258]; and the Hyper Text Coffee Pot Control Protocol (HTCPCP/1.0), which made its way to an appropriately dated Internet RFC [184].

system [217] and from its better known open-source successor VNC [218, 25] (Virtual Network Computer), both developed by Richardson *et al.*

These systems allow a user to maintain a GUI session (a "desktop") that can be accessed from any other computer used as a thin client, with the state of all open applications being preserved as the user moves from one thin client to the next. They implement personalization in the sense that any computer can become "your" computer just by connecting to the networked server that runs your desktop. You can use any currently "physically free" computer (meaning one with nobody sitting in front of it) to access your remote resources, even one whose screen is locked or taken by someone else's session. You don't have to log in—the thin client that will display your remote desktop is overlaid on top of whatever is already there, without disturbing the existing session.

This Virtual Network Computer paradigm can be very useful on its own but becomes even better if augmented by location information: you can then simply walk up to a computer anywhere and have "your" desktop appear on it, with the cursor still in the middle of the sentence you were typing, and without having manually to launch the VNC client and feed it your password. Note that in actual practice the "teleporting" action (i.e. making the remote desktop appear on the local workstation) is not triggered automatically by the movement of the user: we also require an explicit click of the badge button. It would otherwise be embarrassing to have one's desktop randomly appearing on nearby screens—particularly ones being used by others—as one moved around the building. The click action also allows the user to select a specific destination screen in rooms where several are present. Having said that, the action of teleporting *away* (to nowhere) is indeed automatic, and triggered simply by the user moving to another location. This do-nothing operation is also an advantage for security: since your desktop disappears from the screen once you leave the room, there is no danger of accidentally leaving your session open for a passer-by to abuse.

In the above we may observe the badge being used as an authentication device. Because the badge is considered to be a personal device that is always with its owner, it is treated like a physical key. Whoever holds my key can open my filing cabinet, and whoever holds my badge can recall and access my VNC desktop. When the badge started being used in this way (which happened when we allowed it to unlock doors, way before teleporting) we introduced a challenge-response protocol to thwart replay attacks (see section 3.4.3).

It is interesting to note that by far the most commonly used function of the Active Badge system turned out to be not the automation of some manual task but simply the ability to view, in a very basic textual form (see figure 2.8 above), the location of all the lab members. Most people at the lab always keep a badge window running for the whole duration of their login session. Apart from the obvious use of figuring out where to go or phone to actually meet a specific colleague, a more subtle social benefit is the ability to check in advance whether the colleague is free or already busy with someone else.

Figure 2.10. A tob ("transmit-only badge") is used to track the location of this trolley-mounted oscilloscope (courtesy of AT&T Laboratories Cambridge).

We soon realized that the facility to locate colleagues could be fruitfully extended to that of locating frequently borrowed objects. Prime candidates for this were the "good" oscilloscope (this was mounted on a trolley so that it could be wheeled from the main hardware lab to wherever it was needed; but engineers would frequently hoard it in their offices for days, to the dismay of their colleagues who had to broadcast distressed-sounding email requests; see figure 2.10) and the label maker whose successor is shown in figure 5.1 on page 115. Originally this was done by sticking ordinary badges on the objects; in 1993 we developed a smaller, simpler and more energy-efficient "transmit-only[15] badge", or tob, which we ended up deploying on all our computer equipment—printers, computers, switches, cameras, microphones, displays and other networked peripherals.

While the usefulness of tracking the location of our peripatetic oscilloscope is immediately obvious, it may seem odd to want to label items such as printers or desktop computers which, after all, don't move very often. The benefit of this practice is that it enables an application running on a given machine to ask the system what equipment is available in the same room. Relying on static configuration files for the same purpose would be a maintenance nightmare, especially in the experimental environment of a research lab where researchers continually augment their

---

[15]While a transmission facility was obviously necessary for any badge to communicate its location, the full version of the badge could also *receive* messages from the network. This allowed additional functionality such as paging (the arrival of the sandwich man prompted the receptionist to issue a broadcast that made all badges play a tune recognized by users as "food, glorious food!") and challenge-response.

workstations with new gadgets and *do* move equipment around more often than you might think. In fact the badge-driven teleporting described earlier in this section relies heavily on tob information to find out which machines in the current room can work as a VNC viewer.

2.5.2 The Active Floor

The Active Badge requires you to tag every object or person you wish to track. We also decided to investigate systems that did not impose this requirement. A pressure-sensitive floor, for example (a staple of sci-fi action movies), can detect users walking on it. In the transition from science fiction to engineering, though, one has to address a variety of practical concerns.

Firstly, what should be the spatial resolution of the sensing floor? If too low, it will be sufficient to activate a *Mission Impossible*-style alarm but not to detect where an individual is in the room. If too high, cost will become an issue, and it will be difficult even to route wires from the individual sensors to the electronic circuits that process and aggregate their readings.

Secondly, the requirements for mechanical robustness of the sensors are not trivial to fulfil. A floor must be able to withstand fairly rough treatment above and beyond being walked upon—including having heavy objects dropped upon, being subjected to shearing stress when someone runs and stops, being subjected to high pressure from canes, high heels or chair legs, having liquids spilled on and so on. Furthermore, the fact that the floor is two-dimensional obviously means that the number of (suitably rugged) sensing elements to be deployed grows with the square of the chosen spatial resolution. One proposal of adopting boolean microswitches arranged in a sub-centimetre grid (in the hope of getting a simple bitmapped output that would show the shape and orientation of the shoes of the people treading on it) attracted the comment that it would be cheaper to pave the floor with banknotes of the highest denomination.

The final design, described by Addlesee *et al.* in [5], consists of 0.5 m × 0.5 m carpeted floor tiles made of plywood and steel, supported at the corners by load cells in the shape of cylindrical metal pads (see figure 2.11). Each cell supports four tiles and acts like a precision scale[16]. Compared to alternatives such as the microswitch array, this arrangement offers several practical advantages: the surface is sufficiently robust and stable to be used as an ordinary floor, installation is relatively easy and the tiles can be carpeted without affecting the floor's sensing ability.

---

[16]The resolution is about 50 g with a range of 0–500 kg and a precision of 0.5%. In the prototype Active Floor, the output of each cell is sampled at 500 Hz.

Figure 2.11. A detail of the construction of the Active Floor, showing a bare tile, a carpeted tile and a load cell (courtesy of AT&T Laboratories Cambridge).

As a sensing system, the Active Floor offers some interesting properties. First and foremost, it does not require prior marking of the items to be tracked—it will always accurately report the total weight of the objects in a given area. A peculiar feature that few other sensing systems possess is that, with the Active Floor, an object can never "obscure" another: to evade detection, items would have to be suspended from the ceiling. If any sizable object is moved from one desk to another (or brought in or taken out of that office), or if a person enters or exits the room, the floor will notice.

At the same time, though, it is difficult to extract higher level meaning from the raw sensor data. One can track the position of the centre of gravity of a moving object but it is difficult to establish the identity of the particular object that is moving. A comparison with a database of objects of known weights somehow brings us back to a priori tagging—and in any case the method is incapable of distinguishing multiple instances of the same artefact, e.g. three laptops of the same model. Besides, when several objects move at the same time, the problem of locating their centre of gravity no longer has a unique solution. Various heuristics may be applied, but a really robust solution is needed before the floor can reliably be used as a location system.

It is nonetheless possible to extract some pretty remarkable results out of the data produced by the floor: even though the experimental setup was somewhat constrained[17], the cited authors reported reasonable success in identifying people based

---

[17] A single subject was examined at a time, and the subject would cooperatively step in the middle

on their gait [5] thanks to HMM-based analysis techniques originally developed for speech and face recognition.

2.5.3   The Active Bat

The badge system could not resolve position at higher granularity than the room; as such it could not support some more advanced location-aware applications. For example the cited location-based VNC teleporting (section 2.5.1) works well with individual offices where each room only contains a few workstations, but it would be useless in an open-plan environment with tens or hundreds of desks all labelled as being in the same "location".

Starting in 1995, Ward *et al.* [257, 256] developed a new active tag that signalled its position using ultrasound as opposed to infrared. The name "Active Bat" for this successor of the badge is of course a reference to the flying mammal that uses a location system based on similar sensing technology.

Given the much lower speed of the ultrasonic signal compared to that of the infrared (think speed of sound vs. speed of light), it is possible to measure the time of flight of the pulse from transmitter to receiver with sufficient accuracy to yield a precise distance measurement between the two.

In the Active Bat system (figure 2.12), the ultrasound transmitter ("bat") is attached to the mobile object as the tag, while the receivers are placed at known locations on the ceiling. Bats are individually addressable and, at regular intervals, a base station sends a radio command (whose delivery is instantaneous compared to that of the ultrasound message) to a specific bat, ordering it to transmit an ultrasonic pulse. At the same time the base station notifies the ceiling receivers that that particular bat is now going to transmit. The receivers, laid out on the ceiling at regular intervals, measure different flight times depending on their relative location to the transmitting tag. Then, using trilateration[18], the system works out the position of the tag in three dimensions with respect to the known positions of the ceiling receivers. The controller then addresses another bat and starts a new cycle.

Substantial engineering has brought the initial prototype to a mature system that scales well both in the size of the area to be covered and in the number of bats that can be tracked simultaneously. The current version is deployed on all three floors of our laboratory and can locate bats with an accuracy of about 3 cm. The bats themselves are about the size of a thick lighter and have now completely replaced badges and tobs in our lab.

The software back-end that supports the Active Bat is considerably more elaborate than the one for the badge. Application programs would have little use for

---

of the designated target tile.

[18]This is the dual technique to the better known "triangulation". It uses the sides of a triangle, rather than its angles, to determine the position of the third vertex.

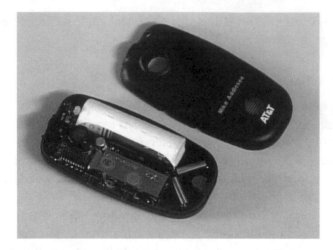

Figure 2.12. The Active Bat (courtesy of AT&T Laboratories Cambridge).

the actual centimetre-resolution 3D coordinates of the individual bats. A layer of spatial indexing middleware, developed by Steggles *et al.* [243], raises the level of abstraction by processing the bat sightings and generating events when something of interest occurs, such as when the containment zone of a tagged entity (say, a person) overlaps that of another (say, a wall-mounted screen, meaning that that person is now in a position to interact with the screen, point at parts of it and so on). Applications can register interest in specific spatial events and will be notified by the system when these occur.

High resolution location information enables users to interact in new ways with the ubiquitous computing system: you can activate individual objects in your surroundings, or signal your intention to use them, merely by going near them. But to what does this translate in practice? Perhaps one of the most interesting new uses for this enhanced information is the ability to define "virtual buttons". As a developer of ubiquitous computing applications you may print a label saying "email me an image of this whiteboard", paste it on the edge of the whiteboard, define a 3D region around the label, register it in the system and associate it with the appropriate sequence of actions. Your users can now click their Active Bat on top of that label and receive a dump of the whiteboard in their email inbox. (And note how the interpretation of "email *me*" follows the identity of the owner of the bat.)

As a programmer, you can define virtual buttons wherever you like in 3D space, which users can click using their bat as if it were a mouse. In our laboratory we now have distinctive "smart posters" on the walls (figure 2.13) that not only describe an application but also let you control it by clicking your bat over the appropriate self-describing areas of the poster [26, 23].

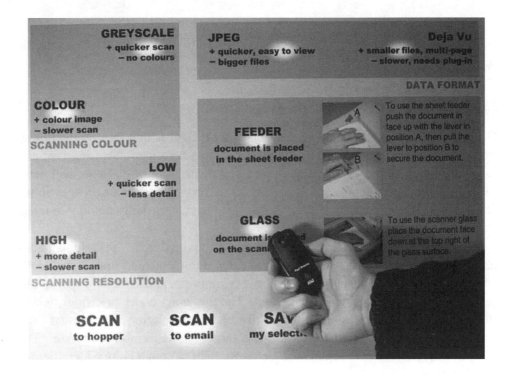

Figure 2.13. A smart poster acting as the computerless user interface for a public document scanner nearby. The user is about to scan the document currently on the glass (courtesy of AT&T Laboratories Cambridge).

Of course, having such buttons near walls makes it easier to label them with printed notices, but this is just a notational convenience. You can also define "activation regions" whose associated action is triggered simply by spatial overlap, without requiring a button click. For example you can equip your office with many cameras and have a follow-me videophone by associating an active region with the coverage area of each camera. As you walk around, from your desk to the whiteboard and from the window to the office of your colleague, the system automatically keeps you in shot by switching to the camera and microphone that best cover your current position.

Badge emulation (room-level location), desk-resolution teleporting, smart posters and follow-me video do not exhaust the uses of the Active Bat. Another interesting ubicomp development is to tag mobile objects such as digital cameras and audio recorders. The camera can then mark each photograph not only with a time stamp but also with the name of the photographer, since location information from the bats of the photographer and the camera tells the system who was holding that camera when the picture was taken.

All these applications give us a glimpse of how the availability of high resolution location information might redefine the ways in which we interact with the ubiquitous computing systems of the future.

2.5.4   TRIP

The problem with active tags like the badge and the bat is that they contain powered electronics. As a consequence they have a non-zero manufacturing cost and they need a battery replacement every now and then. Both of these are bad news when you want to tag gazillions of objects (e.g. every book in your home). So we devised an alternative system where the tags would cost virtually nothing to make and require no external power.

The TRIP project, or Target Recognition via Image Processing, originally developed by Henty and Jones at ORL and later reimplemented and extended by López de Ipiña [173, 172] at the University of Cambridge, makes use of special targets designed for easy optical recognition. The two inner concentric rings, which are solid, appear as ellipses regardless of the relative orientation of target and camera, and this invariant helps in locating the target and determining its size. The outer two rings, which are segmented, define by their pattern a unique identifier for each target.

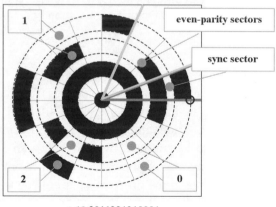

* 10 **2011221210001**

Figure 2.14. A TRIP target, showing (anticlockwise from East) the sync sector, the two redundancy sectors and the remaining 13 data sectors, for a total of 3^{13} valid codes (courtesy of AT&T Laboratories Cambridge and Diego López de Ipiña).

TRIP targets can be generated at essentially no cost on a conventional laser or inkjet printer and pasted on the objects to be tagged. Their physical size is not fixed: depending on the application they usually range in diameter from one to ten centimetres, but there is no reason why one could not draw targets over a metre wide (and I'll soon describe an application that would benefit from this). The only system constraints are on the minimum size *in pixels* of the acquired image (about 40×40), so it is acceptable to make the targets smaller if one is prepared to move the camera closer to the target or to acquire images at a higher resolution.

The encoding method used, in which black-black is reserved for the sync sector, allows for 3^{15} (≈ 14 million) different codes. If desired, some of the bits of the identifier space may be used as redundancy—i.e. as an error detection code. In the current implementation, a sample of which appears in figure 2.14, two sectors are used in this way, leaving 3^{13} (≈ 1.6 million) valid codes. This is a useful trade-off between the number of available codes and the robustness of the recognition: with careful tuning, the rate of false positives can be reduced to arbitrarily low values. If needed, a larger code space could be obtained by adding further segmented rings— even just a third one would yield 7^{15} (≈ 4.7 trillion) codes—at the cost of requiring a larger image of the target (in pixels) for the recognition.

There are at least two ways in which such a system may be used. In one, TRIP is used as a location system. With suitable inverse geometrical transformations, the position and size of any recognized tags in the scene are transformed into geometrical coordinates with respect to the position of the camera. Depth information (i.e. distance between target and camera) can be extracted from the size of the target in the acquired image if the size of the original is known. This can be done by using some bits of the code (4 ternary sectors in the current implementation) to encode the physical radius of the printed tag, at the expense of a further reduction in the cardinality of the code space ($3^9 \approx 20,000$ codes). For absolute positioning, the camera is static[19] and its position and orientation have been accurately surveyed. Depth information could also be extracted through stereoscopic operation, by correlating the views from different cameras pointing at the same scene. Multiple cameras are desirable anyway, in order to guarantee coverage of the designated area regardless of the orientation of the tag. Such a system may be used for similar applications to the ones made possible by the Active Bat we described in section 2.5.3, such as the follow-me videophone.

In the second and simpler mode of operation, TRIP is used to detect not the precise 3D location of an object but merely the presence or absence of specific tags in the current scene. A virtual jukebox, for example, allows you to select songs by showing the appropriately tagged CDs to the camera.

An application that better illustrates the power of the system and the usefulness

---

[19]One could imagine relaxing this condition if the position and orientation of the moving camera were dynamically assessed using some other high precision location system, but the errors would compose and it would be difficult to produce a robust and accurate system.

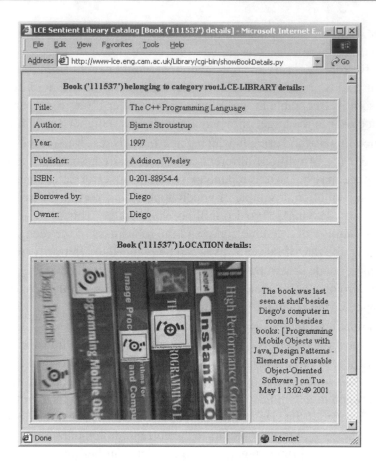

Figure 2.15. The web interface to the TRIP Sentient Library. The query shows the result of a search for Stroustrup's *The C++ Programming Language*. The bookshelf where the book was last seen is identified, and the titles of nearby books that were recognized are also mentioned. Note, in the captured video frame, a small cross in the centre of the TRIP target for the relevant book (courtesy of Diego López de Ipiña).

of being able to tag a large number of objects at no cost is the TRIP Sentient Library (figure 2.15): having tagged all the books in the lab with a TRIP target on the spine, you can walk around with a camcorder every week and film all the bookshelves. Then the videotape is postprocessed and, for each book, the system stores in a database the most recent frame containing that book. This way, when you query the database for a book, you are shown a picture of where it was last seen.

We have also thought of an application that would make use of very large targets: the Active Car Park [241]. As a matter of fact we *already* have a pretty "active" car park, even without any ubicomp additions, in so far as demand exceeds supply; it is common for staff members driving into work to try the front of the building, then the back, only to be forced to look for alternatives elsewhere—a process that the heavy morning traffic makes slow and frustrating. If we painted a TRIP target in each car bay, making them large enough so that cameras pointing at the car park from the top floor of our building could recognize them, then the system could tell which spaces were still free (because their targets would not be obstructed by a car) and this information could be consulted by users via cellular phone as they drove towards the office.

2.5.5 PEN

While the systems we have so far described have all been, one way or another, sensor systems (with an associated software back-end, sometimes of remarkable complexity), another essential component of ubiquitous computing is a facility for short range wireless communication.

Around 1994–95 we realized that the then-current infrared communication facility, included in most new laptops[20] in the form of an IrDA port [140], was inadequate for do-nothing ubicomp because of its propagation characteristics. The infrared signal follows the laws of optics and therefore it is often necessary to point the transmitter at the receiver in order to ensure a good connection. Even if reflections on walls and furniture may sometimes help propagate the signal and therefore relax the line of sight requirement, it is certainly not possible for a device on your desk to communicate with one inside your closed handbag or briefcase. We decided that radio was a much better medium to use and set out to build a system to meet the requirements of ubicomp communication.

Our aim was to build a system that could be embedded in everything as a universal communication facility. We would probably not have started this project had Bluetooth been there at the time—we would have just *used* Bluetooth ourselves, concentrating instead on ubicomp applications. But since we had to build the infrastructure ourselves, we ended up with something slightly different. While Bluetooth supports continuous media (e.g. voice) and relatively high bit rates (of the order of Mb/s), we placed a deliberate emphasis on low power consumption (for a battery lifetime of at least a few months) and consequently on short range (a few metres) and low bit rate (in the tens of kb/s).

Short range and low bit rate follow naturally from the quest for power saving, but they also have intrinsic merits. In ubicomp communications, many devices need to talk to each other simultaneously. A given frequency can only be reused when the transmitting device is out of range of whatever other device is currently using that frequency, and in this context a short range is an asset. Short range also means

---

[20]But seldom used by applications.

Figure 2.16. A PEN node, revealing its insides, and a lowercase pen for size comparison (courtesy of AT&T Laboratories Cambridge).

that, except for routing[21], "connectivity suggests proximity"—a useful location hint for ubicomp applications: devices that I can contact by radio are devices that my owner can see and reach. The low bit rate helps stake out an application space in which devices exchange brief nuggets of information as opposed to large lumps of data or continuous media streams. This, in turn, encourages a "mostly off" duty cycle[22] that is advantageous not only to battery lifetime but also to temporal reuse of the radio frequency, again helping towards the goal of allowing many pairs of devices to use the channel concurrently.

Our system, originally called Piconet and later renamed PEN (Prototype Embedded Network) to avoid confusion with the Bluetooth usage of the term, was first built and described by Bennett *et al.* [31]. A more recent and higher level overview of the system and its applications is offered by Jones and Hopper [146], while some more technical papers by Girling *et al.* [114, 115] describe in further detail the special low power communication protocols of the system (how do you contact a device that spends over 99.9% of its time asleep?).

---

[21]Not implemented in our system, although Stefanova [242] experimented with it.

[22]This may look like a paradox—it would be logical to argue that a lower bit rate forces one to occupy the channel for a longer time in order to transmit the same amount of data. However, this fails to take into account that resource availability contributes to the definition of the application space: an environment in which the channel has a capacity of megabits per second attracts different usage patterns from a 10 kb/s one. Witness the change in attitude between users of dial-up modems, ISDN, ADSL and always-on LAN-based connections.

PEN is built around a self-contained unit, the "node" (figure 2.16). In its current prototype form the node is about the size of a deck of playing cards; but in due course it ought to fit in the corner of a chip. It contains a CPU, some RAM, a generous amount of flash memory for OS and application, a radio transceiver module and some I/O ports to which one can attach peripherals such as sensors and actuators. But of course this is only the engineer's view, which needs to be turned on its head in order to describe the real goal of this research. Nobody is interested in PEN nodes with peripherals attached to them: as per Weiser's "disappearing computing" paradigm, what we want is ordinary objects endowed with PEN communication facilities so that they can talk to each other. The new name of our system, with its accent on *embedding* the network, is appropriate and revealing.

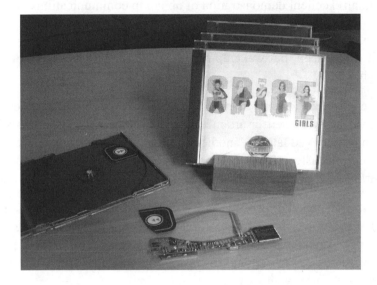

Figure 2.17. Cyberspice. The music starts playing as soon as you open the CD case (courtesy of AT&T Laboratories Cambridge).

Endowing everyday objects with communication capabilities can be another way to move the user interface from computers to the real world. In a popular application of PEN, called Cyberspice after the spice jar of section 2.3.1 "and a pop group that were popular at the time" [146], opening a compact disc case causes the room to be filled with hi-fi music from the corresponding album (figure 2.17). We filled the unused space under the disc holder of the standard CD case with a miniature circuit board implementing a transmit-only subset of the standard Piconet functionality. We also added a magnetic switch to detect whether the case is open or closed. When the case is opened, a message is sent from the CD case to the jukebox server, which starts playing the appropriate disc based on the identifier of that particular CD case. A flat button inside the case can be used to skip to the following track. This application demonstrates that even a very low band-width communication facility may be sufficient to enable useful synergies between different components of the ubicomp system.

Embedded wireless connectivity is extremely convenient for deploying an ad hoc array of sensors. As an illustration we have conducted a few practical ex-periments with PEN-enabled thermometers, using them to diagnose temperature problems in the home or office. The sensors can be distributed in the environment in the exact spots where one wishes to monitor the temperature—a process that would be substantially more cumbersome with wired devices. Various types of nodes from a general purpose modular toolkit cooperate to collect the temperature readings, in an excellent demonstration of ubicomp communications [146].

- The **sensor** nodes are battery-powered. Once deployed they spend most of their time asleep, but wake up regularly to sample the temperature and talk to other nodes.

- The **cache** nodes are mains-powered, so they can afford to be listening all the time. Whenever a sensor produces a reading, the cache node stores it, so that it can be retrieved later by another node querying the temperature even while the sensor is asleep. A cache node may serve several sensor nodes, and it is desirable that each sensor node be covered by at least one cache node.

- The **logger** node collects all the new readings it finds from sensor or cache nodes and stores them in its long-term memory. It keeps a log of all past readings as opposed to just the most recent ones. It is battery-powered so that it can be carried around to collect data automatically from many static nodes as the user walks past them.

- The **download** node is interfaced to a PC. It sucks data from other nodes and transfers it to the PC for processing (statistical analysis, graph plotting etc.).

We have used this type of setup to monitor the efficiency of the air conditioning system in our machine room when it appeared that some of the computers were not being adequately cooled. Compared to the paper chart recorder depicted in figure 2.18 the PEN sensors are smaller, so they interfere much less with the chilled air flow they are supposed to measure; they are cheaper, so more of them can be de-ployed; and they produce a digital output that is much more convenient to postpro-cess. They can for example be used to produce a single table or graph correlating the readings of several sensors at different points in the room.

The convenience of tetherless deployment is not limited to input devices such as sensors: it is equally advantageous for output devices such as displays. We have

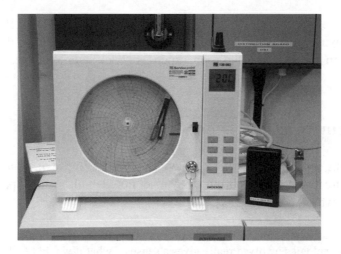

Figure 2.18. A paper chart temperature recorder and a PEN temperature sensor (courtesy of AT&T Laboratories Cambridge).

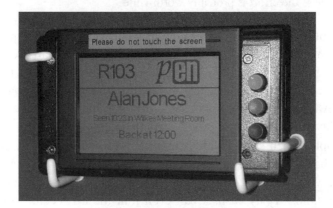

Figure 2.19. A dynamic room tag combining PEN, a cholesteric display and a data feed from the Active Badge system. Because they are wireless, such tags can be very easily deployed throughout a building (courtesy of AT&T Laboratories Cambridge).

built a low power wireless display by coupling a PEN node to a special cholesteric LCD that requires energy only to *flip* the state of its pixels, not to maintain it—in other words, once you have written a bitmap to the display, it will stay on indefinitely even if you remove the battery. This allows us to treat the device somewhat like a printed tag, and indeed we have used this type of PEN node as a door tag (figure 2.19). Compared to a traditional display there is still no noticeable energy penalty in changing the information on the display a few times per day, so we update the door tag dynamically with information from the Active Badge (or Bat) system, showing who is inside the room at the time. We can also display a short message from the owner of the room, such as "back later" or "please do not disturb".

2.6 Security issues

The preceding sections of this chapter have given us a glimpse of what the ubicomp-enabled future might perhaps bring. As Weiser noted in his seminal paper, we don't really know what's coming [259]:

> Neither an explication of the principles of ubiquitous computing nor a list of the technologies involved really gives a sense of what it would be like to live in a world full of invisible widgets. To extrapolate from today's rudimentary fragments of embodied virtuality resembles an attempt to predict the publication of Finnegan's Wake after just having invented writing on clay tablets. Nevertheless the effort is probably worthwhile.

What about security? We don't know in what ways the ubicomp scenario can be abused by ingenious attackers, and we don't know who the attackers are going to be. You'll find that they probably won't be limited to the computer villains to whom the press incorrectly refers as "hackers". Here too, therefore, the imagination effort will be worthwhile, and an important step will be to identify what exactly we want to protect. Maybe something we take for granted right now...

For example, when store loyalty cards were introduced, many people did not see any drawbacks in a system that gave them a discount in exchange for telling the merchant what they had bought. "After all, the merchant already knows what I bought and, unless I pay cash, it can even link the till receipt to my cheque or credit card account." This is true in theory; but, in practice, it requires a little too much work to be worth doing. The store card takes away the guesswork and makes it possible for the merchant to build an accurate profile of your purchasing pattern at very little cost. A crucial consequence is that such profiles can be traded among merchants *and merged* to build disturbingly exhaustive dossiers. Imagine the dossier obtained by combining the log of all your transactions with supermarkets, airlines, bookstores, car hire outfits, banks, highways, phone companies and so on. Even a very partial subset of it will reveal where you were on any given day, whether and when your household had any guests, whether your overall diet is healthy, whether you are addicted to tobacco or alcohol[23], what kind of books, newspapers and videos interest you, what dangerous sports you practise and so

---

[23]Perfectly legal in many jurisdictions, but you might consider your vices to be your own business.

forth. Clearly some of this information might be of interest not only to direct marketers but also to insurers and employers, for whom being able to steer clear from risky parties carries a direct financial advantage. In the different but related context of web scraping, Garfinkel [110, chapter 4, page 88] appropriately notes:

> Ultimately, the wide availability of this information might create powerful new social filters through which only the boring and reserved will be able to pass.

The sceptic who believes that customer profiling has no serious drawbacks other than perhaps junk mail would do well to read Garfinkel's book for plausible scenarios and for some well-documented real world anecdotes. Among them is the case of an Arizona supermarket, sued by a customer who fell in the store and injured his leg, whose defence included exhibiting logs showing that that customer was a frequent buyer of liquor [110, chapter 7, page 159].

It is thus worth examining the envisaged ubicomp futures with an eye to their potential security implications. The point of this section is not to expose alleged flaws, but to ask questions—the kind of questions that are best asked *before* the envisaged systems are actually built and deployed.

2.6.1 The disappearing computer

The disappearing computer, for example, may disappear so well that users lose not just control but even *awareness* of what is actually going on. While this is a welcome strategy to hide irrelevant complexity, it can easily become a liability. The "reactive room" built at the University of Toronto in the early 1990s [75] was a ubicomp-equipped conference room in which lights, cameras and other equipment went on and off automatically based on user behaviour; but there have been informal reports of it providing so little feedback to its users as to be nicknamed the "possessed room". This is a serious usability problem and an even more serious security problem: if you can't tell what your computer is doing when you are online, how can you be sure it's not transmitting your documents to a malicious destination[24]? And if you already can't tell with your visible computer, how can you hope to tell with the invisible ones inside your appliances? Weiser himself [258], in summarizing the ubicomp research carried out by his group, acknowledged this as one of the major unresolved questions:

> If the computational system is invisible as well as extensive, it becomes hard to know what is controlling what, what is connected to what, where information is flowing, how it is being used, what is broken (vs what is working

---

[24]With a slow external modem it would at least be obvious that an uncalled-for data transfer is taking place; but with a modern high speed network connection this is no longer the case.

correctly, but not helpfully), and what are the consequences of any given action (including simply walking into a room). Maintaining simplicity and control simultaneously is still one of the major open questions facing ubiquitous computing research.

The tension between security and usability (see section 2.6.7 below) is always going to be a difficult problem. If users can't easily tell the difference between the secure and the insecure state of a device, they risk using it in the insecure state without meaning to do so. The user interface of the security functions of any ubiquitous computing gadgets is therefore particularly important.

2.6.2   The voting button

The ParcTab is an example of a wireless multipurpose handheld controller. Among the many uses for such a device, Weiser envisages that of "voting button" [259]:

> In presentations, the size of text on overhead slides, the volume of the amplified voice, even the amount of ambient light, can be determined not by accident or guess but by the desires of the listeners in the room at that moment. Software tools for instant votes and consensus checking are already in specialized use in electronic meeting rooms of large corporations; tabs can make them widespread.

What if the voting mechanism, once in place, is adopted for less trivial items? (Say, who gets to represent our group at the conference in Hawaii.) Can other people see how I vote, perhaps by setting up a silent listening ParcTab? Can anyone vote multiple times by pretending to be different people? Do we have to (and will it be reasonable to) trust an all-powerful arbitrator who sees everyone's votes and then only reveals the anonymized results? In chapter 8 we shall explore many of these points in an exaggerated context meant to make the underlying trust issues unambiguous.

2.6.3   The input recognition server

Pen-based input on handheld devices such as the Palm Pilot and other commercial successors of the ParcTab is often much slower than what a skilled typist can achieve on a keyboard, even when using Unistroke-style alphabets. Suggestions for alternatives have included self-correcting approximate string matching against a large dictionary, and speech recognition. Given the limited memory and processing power available on the handhelds, such tasks will typically be offloaded to a wirelessly connected computing server. The server—presumably a shared resource—receives the raw input (ink or voice) from the palmtop, processes it and returns the recognized result. For best recognition performance, the server will retain some kind of state about each user's input (at minimum, statistical profiles and an adaptively evolving custom dictionary; potentially, full transcripts). In such an arrangement, anything the user writes on this personal device is transmitted, processed and maybe stored on the server. Can we still consider the notes taken on such a device as being private? Can notes be intercepted on their way to or from the server? Can they be reconstructed *a posteriori* by someone who attacks the server[25]? But you should not make the mistake of considering secrecy as the only security concern. Can someone pretend to be you to the server and spoil your server state so that recognition is no longer accurate—or, more amusingly, so that it is biased towards intentionally embarrassing misspellings? What if someone just disables the server and thereby prevents you and anyone else in that meeting room from taking notes efficiently?

2.6.4 The Home Medical Advisor

The appendix of Norman's book [200] presents many imaginative examples of information appliances. One of them is the *Home Medical Advisor*:

> The age of medical sensors that are sufficiently inexpensive, rugged and reliable for the home is just emerging. [...] A physician may ask that critical sensor readings be automatically transmitted to the primary health care center. That way when patients called or visited, their physicians would already have their measurements and recent medical history. [...] They would also make such consultation more productive by providing an information record that will help both the patient and the physician know the facts, instead of relying upon the patient's faulty memory.

Do you think you should be able to review and decide what information your appliance will make available to your doctor? Is there a chance that your medical data will also automatically end up in the database of your health insurer? (Observe that legal protection such as "nobody is allowed to share your data without your explicit consent" is usually defeated by procedural countermeasures such as "please authorize us to manipulate your data in any way we see fit, or we won't be able to provide our services to you".)

Can someone modify the recorded measurements so that your doctor will diagnose a terrible illness? The worry would prevent you from working with full efficiency during that crucial week in which the contract is due. It might even cause you to become ill for real (ulcer or whatever). This would be an attack on you and your company. Alternatively, *you* could use the incorrect diagnosis for a fraudulent claim. This would be an attack on your insurer. Looking at who stands

---

[25]This may include taking it apart physically after the users and their palmtops are no longer in the building.

to gain and lose from each attack scenario is important, since it provides us with insights on who has an incentive to make the device or system secure, and on what "secure" actually means in each context.

2.6.5   The Weather and Traffic Display

Another example from Norman is the *Weather and Traffic Display*:

> Want to know the weather forecast or traffic conditions for your daily commute? Just look up on the wall at the weather and traffic display. It's somewhat like a clock, meant to be hung on the wall, perhaps in the kitchen. The clock is an appliance that continually shows the correct time. If you aren't interested in the time, you don't look at the clock. If you want the time, there it is, effortlessly available. So, too, with the traffic display.

The main difference between the traffic display and the clock is that the clock has no external dependencies. People can't stop your clock by attacking something else. But they might stop your traffic display without even coming near it, by attacking the server or the communication channel. Can someone make your display go blank? More subtly, can someone make it display plausible but wrong information, causing you to waste two hours in a traffic jam?

2.6.6   The Home Financial Center

Another neat one is the *Home Financial Center*:

> Imagine a simple information appliance that specializes in home finances; bill paying, family financial reviews, and at the end of each year, income taxes. The financial appliance is networked to the bank and perhaps a stockbroker and financial advisor.

Do you have any idea how many network probes you get on your home computer every time you go online? (Try installing a personal firewall some time, just for fun.) And how many do you think you will get per day once you install that "always on" connection? OK, now add the monetary incentive.

2.6.7   Security versus usability

As a usability expert, Norman correctly points out the following dilemma:

> In the ideal world, it would be possible to go to an information appliance, turn it on and instantly use it for its intended purpose, with no delay required for the electronics to warm up, no delay for the underlying computer systems to turn on and establish the context. All information appliances would work like our calculators: when you needed them, you would simply push

the "on" button and start calculating. Because of the privacy issues, this simplicity is denied us whenever confidential or otherwise restricted information
is involved.

Both usability and security are usually neglected at the start of a project: technology
dominates. But neither is easy to retrofit. Can we design them in—both of them—
from the start? Are they compatible at all? This is an open research problem.

In practice, if the user must *choose* between the two, security usually loses.
If paranoid security measures make the system too awkward to use, they will be
switched off entirely so that the user can finally get some work done. The challenge
is to make the two properties coexist in harmony.

The tension between the conflicting requirements of security and usability is
well illustrated by the problem of password-protecting one's personal computer.
These machines are notorious for taking an irritatingly long time (of the order of
minutes) to bootstrap, and this has been an invariant over the past twenty years
despite an increase in processor speeds of almost three orders of magnitude. While
this is bad in itself, having to wait for a piece of machinery to warm up is not
totally unreasonable. What is more frustrating is not to be able to devote one's
attention to much else while this is happening. It would be nice to switch the
machine on, turn around to swap a few jokes with a colleague, and then come
back to a working computer. Instead, the login prompt appears after a few minutes
of disk whirring, but when you feed it your password it takes another couple of
frustrating minutes before your desktop becomes fully populated and responsive.
If you have a more secure setup in which several levels of the system independently
ask you for a password[26], the problem is compounded: on some of my computers
I get a password request from the BIOS, another one a few minutes later from the
operating system, and another one a little later from PGPdisk (an encrypting file
system—and one that I highly recommend, by the way). After that, more passwords
are needed for the higher layers: one to connect to the ISP, one for SSH to secure
the connection, one for the mail server and so on and so forth. No wonder that
people leave themselves logged in at the end of the day (hopefully after locking
their machine), once they've built up all this state.

From the point of view of usability, having accepted passwords as a necessary evil[27], I would at least prefer the system to ask me for all these passwords all
together, just when I switch the system on, and then use them one by one as appropriate, so that I could concentrate on something else during the boot process and
then come back to a working machine. From the point of view of security, though,
it will be hard to implement this satisfactorily: how can the machine ensure that

---

[26]And they had better be all different, of course, or there would be little point in the exercise.

[27]This may be a limiting assumption: perhaps a better solution to this problem might come from
the adoption of other methods of authentication.

these passwords are distributed to their legitimate software recipients and that no malicious program can trick the system into giving it one or more passwords that were not meant for it? How can the machine prompt me about each of the passwords I must enter, if the relevant pieces of software have not been launched yet? And won't we be back to square one (forced interaction followed by a long wait) whenever I make a mistake while entering one of the passwords?

2.6.8   The WearCam

The WearCam raises interesting privacy issues, many of which are discussed by the author himself. While Mann presents the device as something that gives individuals the same evidence-gathering power as the organizations that deploy and control surveillance cameras, he acknowledges that it could be turned against its user [177]:

> There is of course the chilling prospect that people could be *required* to wear a NetCam, and this should be guarded against, for it provides a road (or maybe a superhighway) toward an Orwellian dystopia. That raises the important question: who owns the data? Well, as with traditional photography, the photographer owns the data. NetCam is an augmented memory system, and if we choose to extend our brain with augmented memory, this memory should attain the same level of protection as our own thoughts. In order to prevent NetCam from being used as a thought-control device, it is necessary to enforce this ownership through encryption. If law enforcement had the power to seize NetCam data, we'd basically be living in a Clipper-like world. We'd be giving law enforcement the power to reach into our brains and read out our memory. In a sense, we'd have thought police.

The tight integration between man and machine, to the point of "mediated reality" (the wearer only sees the world through the machine's camera and filters), creates a new privacy vulnerability. Nobody can, against your consent, force you to reveal what you did or what you saw, short perhaps of torturing you; but it takes only moderate force to steal your wearable computer from you and look inside it to review past footage.

It may be possible and desirable to restrict access to the wearable for anyone other than the owner; the usual trade-off between security and usability will resurface, but it is probably feasible to ensure that extracting secrets from the machine be almost as difficult as extracting them from the mind of its wearer. (This is not simply a problem of access control but primarily one of tamper resistance; useful insights on the matter come from Anderson and Kuhn [14] and, at a different level, from Sammes and Jenkinson [224].)

An elegant way to address the problem is to transmit the filmed material wirelessly to a remote server, which is what Mann actually does, instead of storing it in the wearable. The data may even be distributed among many servers whose physical and cyberspace locations are hidden.

Having secured the data, however, the video evidence held on the remote server(s) is still going to be a desirable target. In fact, for the kind of attackers ready to torture a victim or throw her in jail to make her reveal what she saw, there will be an even greater incentive to apply such pressure to the WearCam cyborg so as to gain access to the stored footage. In such unfortunate circumstances, merely using the WearCam exposes the wearer to increased risks—of privacy loss, of bodily damage or more.

This comment should not be read as saying that the WearCam is *bad*: to a large extent, similar comments could be made about the use of encryption in general. What we are doing here is *raising awareness of relevant security issues*.

A note on motives: if the WearCam is meant, among other things, as a response to the proliferation of intrusive surveillance cameras, it is not entirely clear how the retaliatory action of wearing yet another camera does much to impede this intrusion. While it may be true that reciprocity makes the surveillance camera people more accountable for their actions, it does not do anything to restore any lost privacy. It is not entirely unreasonable to view the WearCam itself as a privacy intrusion (on others), and the reciprocity argument as an *excusatio non petita* to justify its otherwise dubious ethical legitimacy.

From another point of view, however, if personal WearCams became widespread, the justification for large-scale (UK-style) deployment of government-run surveillance cameras would be greatly reduced. Since this technological reincarnation of a peer-to-peer neigbourhood watch would be more than sufficient to protect the law-abiding citizens, it might initiate a process through which the intrusive centralized surveillance is repudiated by the general public, because there is no further benefit to be gained in running its obvious societal risks. This goes to show how some fundamental security issues at the system design level may sometimes have wide repercussions on society and policy.

2.6.9 Networked cameras and microphones

Talking of wearable cameras we should not ignore the less futuristic static cameras that are already commonplace for doorbells, computer-based videophones and perhaps other home uses. From the ubicomp perspective, they will all produce digital streams, routable to the most appropriate viewing client, as in this scenario from Brumitt and Cadiz [54]:

> While current devices tend to perform only standalone functions [...], the increasing connectivity of devices should allow more complex interactions. [...] A camera used for infant monitoring might be able to direct its output to whatever display is most conveniently located for the parent.

Can your neighbour eavesdrop on the radio link (passive attack)? Can she redirect/splice the stream to her TV (active attack)? Can she turn on your camera remotely? And, if you're thinking "I'm safe because I'm not going to have any networked cameras in my home anyway", what about the microphone that came with your sound card? Is it not permanently connected to your computer? The question is not academic—accessing someone else's `/dev/audio` across the Internet as an eavesdropping device was an exploit that caused some consternation in the early 1990s [55, 74].

Even better, what about that truly ubiquitous network microphone that you certainly *do* have at home, probably in several instances? How can you be sure it's not being turned on remotely when you least expect it? It's called a telephone, by the way, and yes, some modern ones support such a "remotely-controlled eavesdropping" facility [170]. On hook does not necessarily mean disconnected. Are you sure yours isn't one of them? And what about your cellular phone?

2.6.10   Auto-ID

Does the Auto-ID scenario have any security implications? Well, yes, when you think that items can be scanned unobtrusively and from a distance. There will be people who set up concealed detectors and list the contents of your suitcase as you walk past them. It will be a bit like X-ray vision, as far as the tagged objects are concerned. Talking of which, busty females should expect the exact make, model and cup size of their underwear to become rather widely known among their lecherous male colleagues. They might fight back in kind, of course: globally unique serial numbers will allow them to find out and publicize which ones of their colleagues have not changed *their* underwear since the previous day.

The reader should observe this case as one in which the problem is privacy, but encryption is not the answer. A simple-minded solution might be to affix the code only to the packaging, instead of to the product itself; but this would defeat many of the additional benefits of the scheme, such as the ability of the washing machine to warn you that you've mistakenly dropped that precious white lace garment in a load of blue jeans.

2.6.11   The Active Badge and other location systems

Many of the visitors witnessing the Active Badge system express privacy concerns about it. Many other widespread technologies—from door-opening entry cards to cellular telephones to the login facility of distributed computer systems—can be used to infer the location of individuals, but they do not attract the same level of attention. Perhaps this is simply because, unlike the badge, they do not make location tracking their primary and official purpose: with those technologies, your location *could* be tracked; with the badge, it definitely is. From this viewpoint, the badge as a research project should at least be credited for its *explicitness*—for having brought up the issue in a clear and unambiguous way. The correct attitude, from a security point of view, is to use this explicit and exemplary case study to understand more about our requirements on the security of location information; and then apply this new knowledge not only to the badge but also to all these other systems from which location can be inferred, regardless of whether this is their primary purpose or not.

The first question to ask is perhaps one of control: can I turn it off? The answer for the badge is, in the first instance, yes: just put it in your pocket and the infrared signal will no longer reach the sensors. However, the real answer is more elaborate. Firstly, there are the organizational aspects—the actual question being: am I *allowed* to turn it off? This is what Want *et al.* refer to when, in the quote on page 30, they say "among professional people responsible for their own work time". In our lab wearing the badge was completely voluntary; but it would be easy to imagine different policies elsewhere, particularly in workplaces where employees are required to clock in and out. In this case the question becomes: if I turn it off, will I be spotted? If I do not like the system to notice the fact that I am leaving my room to go and talk to a colleague in another division, I can leave the badge face-up on my desk and, to the system, it will look as if I never left my room. This is a feature, not a bug—at least from some viewpoints[28]. The system tracks the location of badges, not of people, and I can break the association between my position and that of my badge whenever I find it desirable to do so.

Those who value the above "plausible deniability" as a feature should check whether other location systems offer the same privacy protection or not. While the Active Bat was being developed, my colleague David Clarke observed that its higher spatial and temporal resolution meant that the system could tell whether a bat was lying on a desk or being worn. With the bat system, you can take off your tag, but the system will know you did. One of the security lessons here is that system features may change: unless you are protected by an official policy that guarantees, for example, your plausible deniability with respect to not wearing the badge, it is up to you to check whether any new technical developments change the *status quo*. Of course, at a higher level, even *policies* might change, so continuous vigilance is required to stay on top of what's happening.

Another question is: who gets to know? In the badge system, the location of each badge was acquired through the room sensors by the central system and

---

[28]As usual, security means different things to different parties. It's a security hole to those who believe the badge should provide unforgeable location information, and a security feature to those who believe it should provide a useful location service while respecting the privacy of its users. The first step in security, as in most other activities, is to gain awareness of one's objectives.

was then distributed to all the local clients that requested it (figure 2.8). It was also distributed globally through a web page of similar design to the xab screen, though people had access to a boolean switch that removed their entry from the page. Jackson [143] proposed an elaborate system in which users would have finer grain control over the recipients of the location information: each query would be filtered through a user-defined script that could return the truth, a half-truth or a lie depending on the identity of the requester, the time of day, the current location of the badge owner and so on. Another important part of his work was an analysis of the system looking for the minimum subset of components that the user needed to trust with confidential location information.

Mann [178] proposed to *reverse* the Active Badge architecture: instead of having transmitting tags that send their ID to room receivers, one could have receiving tags picking up the ID of room transmitters. (This is the same arrangement, *mutatis mutandis*, as that of the GPS system.) Then the location would only be known to the badge wearer, who could decide whether to divulge it and to whom. The main advantage of this scheme is that it keeps the Trusted Computing Base (section 3.5.2) very small.

However, it is rarely useful for the badge wearer to be notified of her own location, especially indoors—most practical applications involve communicating that location to other principals, as in the case of teleporting ("hey, I'm here, so move my session to this computer"). This can still be implemented in the reversed architecture: the user simply tells the system her location when she wants to teleport. The implications are firstly that a transmit path from the badge is still required[29] in order to issue the command implied by the button press; and secondly that, by issuing the command, the user also reveals her position at that time, even if this is not required by the application—just as in the case of a door-opening magnetic card or a money withdrawal at an ATM. The Smart Beverage Dispenser is another example of this.

Other applications, such as xab or the automatic rerouting of phone calls, require users to reveal their position on an ongoing basis, in which case the privacy gain from the reversed architecture is much smaller. It may at first seem that this arrangement gives the user greater control, but the same could be obtained in the standard Active Badge system by allowing the user to customize whether and when the badge should beacon[30]. The disclosure issue here is not a function of the system architecture but of the application, which *requires* that data in order to function. If the user does not trust the application, or its users, or the system on which it runs, this problem has to be addressed on its own merits.

---

[29]Bidirectional communication is a necessity anyway if we are to support challenge-response; see section 2.5.1 on page 33.

[30]Which was not done because it was felt to go against the "do-nothing technology" spirit.

Note that, for physical reasons, the reversal of the architecture is not directly possible with the Active Bat: if all the ceiling receivers were to emit ultrasound simultaneously, the "reverse bat" would have a very hard time figuring out who said what.

2.6.12 Recording gadgets and other devices that Hollywood dislikes

In closing this chapter it is worth mentioning another significant point of view, namely the controversial one from which the *owner* of the device is regarded as the potential enemy against whom to guard.

The fundamental, inherent and defining characteristic of digital technology is the possibility of reproducing and duplicating source material without loss of quality. To most people this is an obvious benefit over analogue technology. To commercial content producers[31], though, this is a serious preoccupation, in so far as it opens the door to unlimited unpaid copying.

There is consequently significant economic pressure on the equipment manufacturers to limit the inherent possibilities of digital gadgets so as to impede illegal copying by technical means. These precautions, however, are all but foolproof: Anderson [11, chapter 20] gives copious technical details. One of the side effects of these elaborate attempts at making digital bits uncopiable (likened by Schneier [229] to attempts at making water not wet) is that other perfectly legitimate uses of the devices are also made impossible. For example I recently bought a Sony Minidisc recorder in order to record my own university lectures for review and improvement. To my extreme disappointment I found out that these discs cannot be backed up. Gilmore [113] is a sharp-witted advocate of the consumer side on this issue.

This problem is going to be directly relevant to ubiquitous computing. Before going too far in any direction on the technical front, it would be wise to get acquainted with both sides of the argument and form an independent and responsible idea of what should be the *right* behaviour of the systems we are going to build.

---

[31]Commonly referred to as "Hollywood", but the term encompasses music and book publishers as well as movie studios.

Chapter 3

Computer security

I have not written this book for the exclusive benefit of full time security researchers—my primary audience is rather one of technically-minded readers with a general computer science background who want to find out about ubicomp security. I
shall therefore use this chapter to introduce some basic topics in computer security,
in particular the three fundamental properties of confidentiality, integrity and availability, together with the cryptographic mechanisms that may help us protect them.
(Despite the fact that this explanation dwells on those mechanisms so as to get the
technical details out of the way, readers should heed the caveat of section 1.2 about
security being more than just cryptography.)

For readers interested in a deeper treatment of such fundamentals, many excellent textbooks will provide further details. Gollmann [123] is one of the best all-
round introductions to computer security; Amoroso [7] concentrates on the theoretical foundations of the discipline; Schneier [227] offers a thorough explanation of
the cryptographic details, for which the monumental Kahn [149] provides the historical perspective; Anderson [11] beautifully illustrates how computer security and
its numerous shortcomings affect the real world, while Rubin [223] gives you an
extremely readable and up-to-date problem-oriented explanation of the security solutions you can adopt in practice. All of these texts are accessible to non-specialists,
particularly the last two. More advanced textbooks include Koblitz [157], which
explains the mathematical foundations of cryptography (particularly public key algorithms), and Menezes *et al.* [187], probably the best mathematical and algorithmic reference for anyone who intends to write crypto code.

3.1 Confidentiality

Confidentiality is the property that information holds when it remains unknown to
unauthorized principals. The threat to confidentiality is known as **disclosure**.

The entity whose confidentiality needs protection typically assumes the form of a *message*, that is to say a sequence of bits m, that is transmitted from a sender A to a recipient[1] B. We wish the message m to be kept secret from any other entities that might (even legitimately) handle the communication between A and B.

3.1.1 Encryption and decryption

The principal mechanism to protect the confidentiality of m is *encryption*. A cipher is a pair of complementary algorithms, one transforming plaintext into ciphertext (*encryption*) and the other performing the reverse operation, called *decryption*. If we denote as P the set of all possible plaintexts and as C the set of all possible ciphertexts, then the encryption function is a bijection[2] from P to C and the decryption function is the inverse bijection from C to P.

Kahn [149, chapter 2, page 84], quoting Suetonius, reminds us that even Julius Cæsar used such a pair of algorithms: for him, the encryption function involved changing every letter of the message with the one three places down in the alphabet (so "a" would encrypt to "d"), and the decryption function was the obvious inverse. It is however apparent that, as soon as the enemy discovers the decryption function, the cipher becomes useless. One would then have to think of a new pair of algorithms (not that this would altogether be a bad idea if the original ones were as weak as Cæsar's).

A more flexible solution is to make the algorithms parametric: by introducing a key K as a parameter, each algorithm describes not one bijection but an entire family of them, and the bijections in a pair parameterized by the same key are of course still inverses of each other. Each bijection is a curried[3] version of the encryption or decryption algorithm with a specific key, and even if the enemy discovers the specific decryption bijection (i.e. key) used for a certain message, we can still safely use the same cipher as long as we choose another bijection pair by selecting a different key.

3.1.2 Security by obscurity (don't)

One of the cornerstones of modern cryptology is a set of principles established in 1883 by Kerckhoffs [155]. In essence, they explain that it is pointless to try to

---

[1] As Hamming [131] remarks, under many respects transmission in space (communication) and transmission in time (storage) are equivalent. The recipient B could just as well be A at a later time, so from this point of view even a file stored on A's system may be viewed as a message.

[2] If you are not too sure what a bijection is (it's basically a one-to-one correspondence between two sets), you will find a review of this and related terms in appendix A. This also contains a brief cheat sheet (page 170) about letters such as $\forall, \exists$ and $\in$ that have been kicked out of shape by mathematicians.

[3] This term is explained in section A.4 on page 173.

hide the cipher algorithm and that all the security should reside in the choice of the key. The algorithm will become known eventually anyway, as it is impossible to guarantee the absence of leaks about the workings of the cipher when people other than the inventor have to use it. It is wiser to assume the algorithm to be public knowledge from the start, and at least reap the benefits of peer review by competent cryptologists.

Incidentally, this is the process that was followed by the American National Institute of Standards and Technology (NIST) to select the Advanced Encryption Standard (AES) cipher: 15 candidate algorithms were submitted by teams of cryptologists from around the world and were subsequently subjected to aggressive peer review from 1998 to 2000. In August 1999, a first round of selection chose 5 finalists [197], and in October 2000 the Belgian algorithm Rijndael created by Daemen and Rijmen [76] was announced as the winner [198]. This open and publicly reviewed selection process is probably the best possible guarantee of the quality of the chosen cipher and the absence of backdoors in it.

Contrast this with the deplorable practice of "security by obscurity", in which the algorithm is guarded as a secret (as was originally done for the infamous "Clipper chip"); this certainly makes the initial cryptanalysis harder for the adversary, but it may hide simple weaknesses that an open peer review process might have revealed—as the pay-TV industry discovered to its dismay after fielding tens of thousands of instances of a closed system that crackers soon learnt to bypass [213].

3.1.3   Brute force attacks

Once the cipher is public, the enemy who gets hold of an encrypted message can in theory decrypt it by applying all the decryption bijections in the family to it and selecting *a posteriori* the one which gives a meaningful result[4]. For this reason it is

---

[4]The alert reader will notice that this requires the nontrivial ability to recognize the meaningful result among all the meaningless ones. While a human reader will have no hesitation in flagging AWEVN4@HBW-CUF as a failed attempt and MEET YOU AT 6 as a successful decryption, things become much harder when the detection has to be performed automatically (which is a necessity when exploring an entire key space) and particularly when the plaintext has no known structure. If the encrypted message contains some integrity-protecting redundancy, this can be checked automatically by the cryptanalyst. Otherwise, the cryptanalyst will have to look out for *cribs*, which are expected items of plaintext such as "Dear Sir", or for statistical properties of the plaintext. But the automatic application of such heuristics, as well as being time-consuming, can only give a probabilistic result. Besides, as the cardinality of the set of keys approaches that of the set of plaintexts (it actually *reaches* it in the one time pad, making the recognition theoretically impossible—see section 3.1.5), the solution space becomes dense, and heuristics that distinguish "plausible messages" from "garbage" stop working: MEET YOU AT 6, while in itself plausible, now competes with many more equally plausible plaintexts such as MEET YOU AT 7, CAN'T SEE YOU TODAY and even EPIMENIDES SUGGESTS NOT TO BELIEVE THIS SENTENCE. It must however be remarked that all these limitations apply only to the most difficult case for the cryptanalyst, the *ciphertext-only* attack. In many other situations it will

important to take into account the size of the family of bijections (i.e. the number of possible keys) when evaluating the safety of a cipher: if the key space is small enough that it can be exhaustively searched, the cipher will be weak regardless of any other consideration. (The reverse implication does not hold: a cipher may be weak due to design flaws, despite having a key space so large that a brute force search would take longer than the age of the universe.)

Under the strict export regulations of the United States known as ITAR[5] [253], for example, which were relaxed in January 2000 [252, 251], ciphers could be freely exported from the USA only as long as their key length did not exceed 40 bits. Even from the point of view of a not very resourceful attacker, any 40-bit cipher is weak, because a space of $2^{40} \approx 10^{12}$ keys can be searched by brute force in a reasonable time; if each decryption attempt takes $10 \ \mu s$, the entire space can be searched in 10^7 seconds, which is about 4 months. Given reasonable assumptions, the ten-microsecond-per-attempt estimate is roughly in the correct ballpark for a modern personal computer implementing the decryption in software[6]; but if the attacker has more resources (such as dedicated hardware to perform the decryption) this estimate could go down by three or four orders of magnitude, bringing the time to try all keys to under an hour—perhaps just a few minutes.

One should also observe that brute force key search is ideally suited to parallel processing, since the problem space can trivially be divided into independent realms down to arbitrarily fine granularity. From March to June 1997, in an effort led by Verser, the idle time of about 70,000 machines across the Internet was harvested for key search; on the 96th day this distributed system succeeded in cracking the first of the DES challenges sponsored by RSA Data Security [222].

DES, or the Data Encryption Standard, created by IBM in the early 1970s and adopted as a US FIPS standard in 1977 [107], is one of the most widely deployed ciphers in the world. No exploitable cryptographic weaknesses have been found in it (although its cryptanalysis prompted the discovery of new techniques such as

be possible to mount a *known-plaintext* attack (where the cryptanalyst knows for sure that a certain plaintext message p maps to a specific ciphertext c) or even a *chosen-plaintext* attack (where the cryptanalyst can feed a plaintext message to the encrypting bijection and observe the result—this might happen if the key and the encryption algorithm had been sealed in a tamper-proof enclosure that could thereafter be accessed freely). In these cases it is of course trivial to verify whether any decryption attempt yielded the correct result or not.

[5]International Traffic in Arms Regulations. ITAR mainly regulates war-grade weapons and parts for tanks, jets and submarines. But encryption software is ranked as "munitions" because of its military intelligence value.

[6]Gladman [116], who implemented all of the 15 AES candidates from scratch based on their published specifications [117], gives performance figures of 1389 cycles for key setup + 352 cycles for decryption of one block for the 128-bit key version of Rijndael (which was neither the fastest nor the slowest of the candidates, or of the finalists). On a 200 MHz Pentium Pro, which was the platform he used, this gives $8.7 \mu s$ to decrypt one block with a new key. Of course this figure will vary with the computer used and the cipher to be cracked, but it gives us an order of magnitude estimate.

Biham and Shamir's *differential cryptanalysis* [34] and Matsui's *linear cryptanalysis* [185]), but it has a 56-bit key. At the time, this was asserted to be adequate for civilian purposes: indeed, in the US, DES used to be the only officially approved method for protecting unclassified data. Diffie and Hellman objected that this key was too short as early as 1977 [91], and in 1994 Wiener [262] presented a design sketch for a DES-specific hardware key search machine, which he estimated could be built for one million dollars and would search the whole space in 7 hours. Between 1997 and 1998 the Electronic Frontier Foundation [94] did actually build a highly parallel DES key search machine out of custom chips for 250 k\$; in July 1998 this machine broke the DES II-2 challenge in 56 hours [95], finally settling the score on the limited security provided by DES even for civilian applications (any major company with valuable trade secrets to protect will expect its competitors to be able to afford a mere quarter of a million dollars for industrial espionage).

In November 2001, while this book was being copy-edited, Bond and Clayton [47, 72] announced their much cheaper (1 k\$) FPGA-based DES-cracking machine that, in the context of a smarter attack, can recover all the DES and 3DES keys of an IBM 4758 running IBM's own CCA cash machine software. The 4758 is the "gold standard" tamper resistant cryptoprocessor (see section 6.2.2) and is widely used in the banking industry. This attack, which combines newly found weaknesses in the CCA software with a smart (i.e. non exhaustive) DES key search that can be run in just a couple of days, would allow a crooked bank manager to forge cash cards and PIN numbers at will and thereby raid the accounts of any of the bank's customers.

As part of the research that lead to this exploit, Clayton also compiled a valuable survey of brute force attacks [71].

3.1.4   The confidentiality amplifier

Having accepted that the security of the cryptosystem must reside in the secrecy of the key rather than in that of the algorithm, one is left with the problem of distributing the key itself. If A wishes to send a message m to B, but wants to encrypt it because she believes the communications channel between them to be insecure, how can she tell B which key to use for the decryption? Traditionally, the solution has been to transmit the key over another channel, deemed to be more secure; the diplomatic courier with an attaché case handcuffed to his wrist is a visual example of this.

In this scenario the cryptosystem acts as a "confidentiality amplifier": once bootstrapped with the help of the secure channel (which may be of insufficient bandwidth, of inadequate latency and of excessive cost to be used for the actual messages), the system ensures the confidentiality of a much larger and cheaper channel.

As noted by Diffie and Landau [92], another remarkable benefit of cryptography is that the robustness and cost of the confidentiality protection it extends over the communications channel do not in any way depend on the length or shape of the channel. Contrast this with other existing ways to secure a channel, such as embedding a data transmission cable inside an armoured and pressurized pipe.

3.1.5 Stream and block ciphers

A cipher of great theoretical importance is the **one time pad**, invented in 1917 by Vernam and Mauborgne [149], which works as follows. *A* wants to send message *m* (a string of bits) to *B*, so she generates a "pad" of completely random bits whose length is at least that of *m*. The ciphertext is obtained bit by bit, by XORing each bit of *m* with the corresponding bit of the pad, which acts as the key. It is trivial to verify that, given any bit p, XORing to it any other bit k twice returns the original bit p[7]. So, to decrypt, one simply XORs again each bit of the ciphertext $p \oplus k$ with the corresponding bit of the pad k; the two copies of the pad bit cancel each other out, yielding the plaintext p.

Since each bit of the pad is random and independent of the others, it contributes one full bit of entropy to the resulting ciphertext bit. (This is only true if the pad is never reused to encipher another bit—hence the "one time" in the name.) It is therefore theoretically impossible to recover the plaintext from the ciphertext without the pad, because any plaintext is equally likely. For every plaintext p and for every ciphertext c, there exists a pad k that will yield c if applied to p—namely the one obtained as $k = p \oplus c$.

The one time pad therefore offers perfect confidentiality with respect to a ciphertext-only attack. Its principal drawback is that the key needs to be as long as the message. If it were easy to send securely such a long pad to the recipient, one might prefer to send the message in the first place, instead of the pad. In other words, as a "confidentiality amplifier", the one time pad does not amplify very much[8].

There is a large family of ciphers that work like a one time pad but replace the pad with a pseudo-random number generator, whose sequence of pseudo-random bits k depends on an initial fixed-length key K. The theoretical unbreakability is lost, because the bits of the pad's replacement are no longer of maximal entropy. If the adversary can predict the pseudo-random sequence, the cipher can be broken. Ciphers like this, that work by XORing each bit of the plaintext p with the

---

[7]This is written $\forall p, k \in \{0, 1\} : p \oplus k \oplus k = p$.

[8]This is not to say it is useless. It may still be useful to time-shift a secure transmission. You send the courier with the one-time tape now, which takes a day or two, and you can then phone the Kremlin later at no notice when something serious comes up.

corresponding bit of a "keystream" k, belong to the class of the **stream ciphers**[9]. A stream cipher E_K^{stream} is a family of bijections from the infinite set S of all possible bit strings onto itself:

$$E_K^{\text{stream}} : S \rightarrow S.$$

It should be obvious that any stream cipher based on a keystream generator will fall to a *known plaintext* attack, i.e. one where the cryptanalyst knows that plaintext p encrypts to ciphertext c and wants to decrypt other ciphertexts encrypted under the same key. In fact, just as for the one time pad (which is itself a special case of stream cipher), the keystream[10] can be trivially recovered as $k = p \oplus c$.

Block ciphers were originally developed to counter this attack. A block cipher E_K^{block} is a family of bijections from the finite set $S_{\text{len}=b}$ of all bit strings of length b (the block size) onto itself:

$$E_K^{\text{block}} : S_{\text{len}=b} \rightarrow S_{\text{len}=b}.$$

Because it is a bijection of a finite set onto itself, a block cipher is a permutation of the set $S_{\text{len}=b}$. In theory it could be implemented as a randomized lookup table, but in practice the table would be infeasibly large[11]. For this reason, the implementation is based on repeatedly stirring bits around in a somewhat more algorithmic fashion. But the point is that, because of their more general structure, block ciphers can be constructed so that even knowing plenty of (p, c) pairs for a given k is insufficient to discover the key itself.

If one needs to encrypt something longer than a block, there exist various *modes of operation* such as "cipher block chaining" to do so in a secure way with respect to the desired properties. Books such as Schneier [227] have all the details.

3.1.6 Public key cryptography

As we move towards a global communications infrastructure where correspondents may be separated by thousands of kilometres, it becomes harder and harder to secure the lower bandwidth channel required for key distribution using physical means. The revolutionary invention that allows keys to be distributed securely over an insecure channel is *public key cryptography*, introduced by Diffie and Hellman in 1976 [90] (the British spy agency CESG claims to have discovered the principle in 1970, but didn't tell anyone until much later [98, 268]). Like many of the greatest ideas, its elegant simplicity allows it to be explained in only a few sentences.

---

[9]There also exist stream ciphers not based on pseudo-random keystream generators—the rotor machines used in World War II [149] being a notable example.

[10]Though not the original key K.

[11]Even for DES, with a block size of 64 bits, the table would have to hold 2^{64} words of 64 bits each, i.e. 2^{72} bytes, i.e. 4 billion terabytes. And this is still peanuts compared to the equivalent figure for AES, whose block size is at least 128 bits.

As before, the cipher is a family of pairs of bijections, with the elements of each pair being the inverse of each other. Now, however, the bijections in a given pair are not indexed by the same key: there is one key to select the encryption bijection and another one to select the decryption bijection, and it is not feasible to derive the decryption key from the encryption key[12]. Each prospective recipient of secret messages chooses her own pair of bijections and makes her encryption key public, while keeping the decryption one secret. Suppose B wants to send a confidential message to A: he can encrypt the plaintext using the encryption key that A made public. This will yield a ciphertext that can only be decrypted by A's secret key, that she never revealed to anyone else. Nobody other than A will be able to read the encrypted reply—not even B who created it. If A wishes to reply, she needs to encrypt her answer under a different key—B's public key in the above case. This construction removes the necessity for a confidentiality-protected channel to transmit the keys: the secret keys never leave their owners, while the public keys, as their name implies, can be distributed to anyone without ill effects. If an eavesdropper acquires A's key, all that he will be able to do with it is to send encrypted messages to her.

There is one remaining vulnerability of this scheme, linked to the fact that B could be tricked into accepting a key as belonging to A when in fact it was manufactured by an active eavesdropper. We shall examine this important point in detail when we discuss man-in-the-middle attacks in section 3.4.3. For the moment, let us simply remark that this same **key distribution problem** exists to an even greater degree in the context of conventional, symmetric-key cryptography, and that it is not a vulnerability *introduced* by the public key construction.

Diffie and Hellman thought of the principle of public key cryptography, but could not at the time suggest an implementation with all the properties they described—this came a couple of years later with the cipher proposed by Rivest, Shamir and Adleman [219], later to be known as RSA. What the two original authors *did* suggest was a "key agreement" scheme, now appropriately known as Diffie-Hellman, allowing two parties to establish a shared secret over a channel subject to eavesdropping. This secret could then be used as the key for a symmetric cipher.

3.1.7 Hybrid systems

Under the hood, public key ciphers are built in a completely different way from their symmetric key counterparts. They require mathematical structure in order to provide the properties of a public key system: the public and the private keys must be mutual inverses, but it must be impossible to derive the latter from the former. To

---

[12]It is however feasible to generate a pair of keys that correspond to mutually inverse bijections.

this end, problems from number theory, based on modular arithmetic over numbers that are several hundred digits long, are used as the core of the cipher. To go into details would lead us well outside the scope of this book; what we want to remark here is that to encrypt or decrypt a given message with a public key cipher is about 1000 times more computationally expensive than with a symmetric key cipher of comparable strength[13]. What is then used in practice is a *hybrid cipher*: the sender generates a random session key, encrypts it under the recipient's public key and transmits it; the rest of the traffic is then encrypted with a symmetric cipher under the session key that the two parties now share. This combines the key management convenience of the public key cipher with the efficiency of the symmetric cipher (at least asymptotically).

It is interesting to observe that this sort of hybrid cipher is no longer a bijection—in fact it's not even a function any more. Since the session key is randomly chosen at each encryption, encrypting the plaintext P under the public key K will yield a different ciphertext every time. (Fortunately, of course, all these ciphertexts will still decrypt to the same plaintext P.) An advantage of this arrangement is that known ciphertext attacks become harder. It is no longer possible for the cryptanalyst who guesses the plaintext to verify the validity of this guess by encrypting it under the target public key, because even the correct guess would encrypt to a different ciphertext than the one observed, unless the random session key were the same. Note the conceptual similarity between this situation and the technique of "salting" described in section 3.4.1.

3.1.8   Other vulnerabilities

Before closing this introductory section on confidentiality-protecting mechanisms we should emphasize that the cost of the brute force attack on a cipher is only an *upper* bound on the cost of breaking the code, sufficient to dismiss a cipher as insecure but insufficient to promote it as safe. Especially in the case of a home-grown cipher, cryptanalysis is likely to find other weaknesses. More importantly, though, from a systems point of view the cipher is rarely the weakest point, and most breaches of confidentiality exploit other weaknesses such as protocol failure,

---

[13]To compare the strengths of two ciphers, one must in fact compare the effort it takes to break them. For a properly designed symmetric cipher with no known shortcut attacks, the effort is that of a brute force search, which is proportional to the cardinality of the key space. With a public key cipher, instead, one does not try all possible private keys but rather tries to derive the private key from the public one. This is of course laborious, by design, and typically proved to be as hard as some well-known difficult mathematical problem, but still not as bad as exhaustive search. For this reason, the key lengths for a public key cipher will be much longer than those for a symmetric cipher of comparable strength. Schneier [227, section 7.3, table 7.9] lists pairs of key lengths of similar resistance for symmetric and public key ciphers.

inappropriate key management, implementation defects (e.g. poor random number generation), physical vulnerabilities and so on.

3.2 Integrity

Integrity is the property that data holds when it has not been modified in unauthorized ways. There does not seem to be a generally agreed upon term in the literature to indicate the threat to integrity; it feels natural to me to suggest **corruption**.

As we saw, protecting the *confidentiality* of a message *m* in transit on a communication channel between *A* and *B* means ensuring that nobody other than *A* and *B* can discover the contents of *m*. Protecting the *integrity* of *m* under the same circumstances means ensuring that, once the message leaves *A*, nobody can alter it until it reaches *B*. In practice it is impossible to prevent an attacker who has control of the channel from altering the message, so what we actually mean is "ensuring that nobody can alter *m* without *B* noticing".

3.2.1 Independence from confidentiality

One might superficially think that confidentiality implies integrity: if you change one bit of a ciphertext *C*, the modified ciphertext will certainly decrypt to garbage and the recipient will notice. Actually this is not always so, and this is particularly evident for additive stream ciphers, where the ciphertext is obtained by the bit-by-bit exclusive-or of the plaintext and a pseudo-random key stream. If the attacker knows the exact format of the message, he will know which bit positions correspond to a specific field. If he also knows or guesses the plaintext, or at least the relevant part of it, for example the second field in "I hereby transfer *<unknown amount of money>* to *<John Smith's bank account number>*", he may manipulate the ciphertext to yield the desired plaintext, such as "I hereby transfer *<amount of money still unknown, but who cares>* to *<the crook's own bank account>*" . The simple algebra behind this is

$$guessedPlaintext \oplus unknownKeystream = knownCiphertext$$

from which the attacker extracts *unknownKeystream*, and

$$alteredCiphertext \oplus nowKnownKeystream = desiredPlaintext$$

from which the attacker works out which *alteredCiphertext* to substitute in the message in transit on the channel. This is called an *attack in depth*. Let us therefore remember that, in general, neither integrity nor confidentiality implies the other.

Do not take this just as an academic warning. The mistaken belief that confidentiality implies integrity is a genuine problem, and people get this wrong all the time, silly as this may seem to you now after having read the trivial boolean algebra in this section. A high-profile culprit, which misused a stream cipher for integrity purposes, is the 802.11 wireless LAN system popularly known as Wi-Fi. This was first pointed out by Borisov, Goldberg and Wagner [48] (see section B.8).

3.2.2 Error-detecting codes

The core idea of integrity protection is to transmit a more robust message by augmenting the payload with some appropriate redundancy which the recipient can check in order to detect modifications. This framework aptly describes the error-detecting codes such as CRCs (cyclical redundancy checks) that should be familiar from information theory [131], but here we have an extra twist: the errors we are trying to detect may be caused not only by random noise but also by malicious forgery. A code that will detect bit errors in 99.9999% of the cases is probably good enough for many communications applications, assuming that bit errors happen randomly; from the security point of view, however, we are in a different scenario: the attacker will *actively search* for that specific 0.0001% of bit errors that the code cannot detect, looking for any that he might turn to his advantage. Suddenly, the probability of failure becomes much higher than 0.0001%.

3.2.3 Hash

An error-detecting code with an external interface similar to that of a CRC, but suitable for integrity protection, is the *cryptographic hash function*, sometimes indicated as *one-way hash* to convey the intuitive meaning that it is easy to compute the function in the forward direction, but practically impossible to compute it in the reverse direction. It is a surjection[14] from the infinite input set S of all possible bit strings to the finite set $S_{\text{len}=n}$ of all possible bit strings of length n, where n is the output size of the hash function (e.g. 160 bits for the Secure Hash Algorithm SHA-1).

$$h : S \to S_{\text{len}=n}$$

Its fundamental property is *non-invertibility*: given any hash output $y \in S_{\text{len}=n}$, it is computationally infeasible to find an input $x \in S$ such that $h(x) = y$ (despite the fact that there will usually be an infinite number of items x with this property). The idea here is to produce a representative "fingerprint" of any input message; this way, if the hash output is secure from modifications, it will not be possible for the attacker to modify the message in a way that still matches the hash.

---

[14]Well, at least conceptually it is. Theoretically, though, there is no guarantee that *all* elements of the domain will have a preimage. Most elements of $S_{\text{len}=n}$ will have infinitely many preimages, but there could be lonely elements of $S_{\text{len}=n}$ that no input string generates.

An even stronger requirement for a hash function is *collision resistance*[15]: it is infeasible to find two inputs with the same image (no matter what it is). If one could do that, then it would no longer be possible to consider hashes as representative fingerprints of longer strings, and "birthday attacks" such as the one famously described by Yuval [269] would become possible. Without going into details, that's where someone makes you sign an unfavourable document while making you believe that you are signing a favourable one, thanks to the fact that they both have the same hash.

We recognize the hash as an "integrity amplifier" in the same sense as we saw the cipher as a "confidentiality amplifier" in section 3.1.4: securing the integrity of a small bit string, for example by publishing it as a line ad in a newspaper, has the effect of similarly protecting an arbitrarily long message, like a 10 MB transaction log that you published on your web page.

One of the canonical warnings that accompany the introduction of error-detecting codes is that we cannot expect errors to concentrate only on the payload, ignoring the added redundancy. The equivalent observation in the security domain highlights that the hash works as an integrity amplifier only given a high integrity channel for bootstrapping purposes; if the attacker is able to modify the hash as well as the payload, it will be trivial for him to calculate a new hash that matches the modified message. There exist however two other cryptographic primitives, the MAC and the digital signature, capable of withstanding that type of attack.

3.2.4 MAC

The MAC, or *message authentication code*, is a bit like a hash parameterized with a secret key—each key you apply to the MAC gives you a different hash function. We saw a similar situation with ciphers in section 3.1.1: the hash is a surjection, while the MAC is a family of surjections. You might conceptually view the hash as a MAC whose key has been curried away with a well-known constant[16].

Both sender and recipient need that key: the former to calculate the MAC from the payload in the first place, the latter to recompute it for verification. Now the attacker who wants to modify the message can no longer generate a new MAC for the forgery, because he does not know the key. For the same reason, he cannot even *check* whether his forgery matches the old MAC. So this solution does away

---

[15]Commonly, but less accurately, also referred to as *collision-freedom*. The literal interpretation of this locution is of course an impossibility given the cardinalities of the input and output sets.

[16]What happens in practice is usually the reverse: the MAC is implemented from the hash by combining the key and the payload in a complicated way, as in the HMAC construction [162]. Another way to obtain a MAC from a hash is to encrypt the hash value using a symmetric cipher—this is simpler to understand but may be more costly to implement in terms of code size and running time, because one uses both a hash and a cipher.

with the need for the low bandwidth, high integrity channel—but note that it now requires a mechanism to allow sender and recipient to establish a shared secret key[17].

3.2.5 Digital signature

The digital signature is a development of public key cryptography. It attempts to recapture some of the defining properties of the written signature, namely that (at least in theory) nobody other than the signer may generate it, and anybody can verify its validity. Additionally, to avoid cut and paste attacks that are trivial on bit sequences even if they take some effort on paper artefacts, the digital signature must depend on the document being signed.

The construction originally proposed by Diffie and Hellman [90] to achieve this is simple and elegant, and was invented before a mathematical primitive to implement the underlying cipher could be found (the solution to that came two years later thanks to Rivest, Shamir and Adleman [219]).

Assume the availability of a public key cipher, as described in section 3.1.6 above: user A publishes a public key K_A and holds a private key K_A^{-1} known only to herself. Assume furthermore that $P \equiv C$, that is to say that the set P of all plaintexts coincides with the set C of all ciphertexts, so that it is possible to apply the decryption bijection to elements of P. It is then possible for A to produce a "signed" version of message $M \in P$ by exhibiting the following pair:

$$M, \mathrm{D}_{K_A^{-1}}(M)$$

which consists of the message accompanied by its image through the decryption bijection[18]. Nobody other than A knows the decryption bijection, so nobody else could have generated the signature; at the same time, though, anyone can check its validity by applying the publicly known encryption bijection E_{K_A} to $\mathrm{D}_{K_A^{-1}}(M)$, and verifying that it yields M.

This core idea is susceptible of refinements. For a start, there are clear performance advantages[19] in signing $\mathrm{h}(M)$ rather than M. It is also beneficial to keep a

---

[17]Not as bad as it sounds, because the key can be reused many times to protect the integrity of different messages. So we are not simply trading the requirement for a low bandwidth, high integrity channel with that for a low bandwidth, high confidentiality channel, but rather with the requirement for a *once-only* high confidentiality channel. Maybe not even that, if the shared secret were established through a key agreement scheme like Diffie-Hellman. However, the integrity properties of the mechanism used to establish the shared secret, whether it is the confidential channel or the DH exchange, must (almost recursively) be taken into account.

[18]Recall that, as explained in section 1.4, my notation for decryption is $\mathrm{D}_{KEY}^{CIPHER}(ciphertext)$.

[19]Without loss of security as long as it is infeasible to find collisions for the hash function.

clear separation between encryption and decryption on the one hand, and verification and signature on the other, despite the fact that the above construction shows that the second pair of functions can be implemented with the first. Interesting threats come about when a user makes no distinction between signature and decryption, from the "chosen protocol attack" (someone runs a challenge-response protocol with you, as in section 3.4.3, asking you to decrypt something that they claim is a random number encrypted under your public key, but in fact they are making you sign a message saying that you'll pay them lots of money) to the risks of legal seizure (the police force you to reveal your secret key under court order to decrypt messages you received, and can now forge your signature on fake incriminating documents[20]). A convenient way to enforce the separation is to have different key pairs for encryption/decryption and for signature/verification. There are also algorithms of a different design where signature is implemented without resorting to decryption.

3.2.6 Integrity primitives compared

Whenever I explain all this, I find it useful to summarize the differences between these three integrity-protecting constructions by lining them up in a matrix[21] like table 3.1. The main distinction between the various primitives stems from identifying who can generate the code and who can verify it. This in turn determines the suitability of the construction for a given purpose, and one could add further columns to list what the extra requirements would be (e.g. a shared key in place) to achieve given goals.

	Who can generate it	**Who can verify it**
Hash	Everyone	Everyone
MAC	Holders of secret	Holders of secret
Signature	Holder of secret	Everyone

Table 3.1. A comparison of integrity-protecting primitives.

A subtle point highlighted by this comparison regards the transferability of the beliefs held by the verifier of the code. Assume that B receives a pair (m, c) over

---

[20]This cuts both ways, and to some principals this will be a feature, not a bug, in so far as it provides them with *plausible deniability* [221].

[21]The æsthetically-minded reader, seeking an elusive symmetry, may now be wondering about the missing fourth combination in the table—the one describing an item that everyone can generate and that only the holder of the secret can verify. A moment's thought shows that, with some flexibility in the interpretation of "verify", this primitive is simply public key encryption. It does not appear in the table because it is not an integrity primitive.

an insecure channel; m is a message purporting to be from A, while c is an integrity protecting code; assume furthermore that, upon verification, B finds that c matches m. What can B deduce about the genuineness of m, and can he transfer this belief to a third party C?

In the case of the hash, B has no guarantees at all: the message could be a fake and the hash might have been recalculated by the forger. (The hash is only useful when its own integrity is guaranteed.)

In the case of the MAC, if B is correct in assuming that only he and A know the secret key K, then he can deduce that the message is genuine. However—and this is the interesting bit—he cannot transfer this belief to anyone else. He certainly cannot convince an outsider C that the message is genuine: B would have to divulge the key to allow C to check the MAC, but since C does not know the real K, as far as he is concerned B could have easily made up both message and key, and calculated a new MAC before showing the pair to C. So the fact that the MAC checks proves nothing to C.

But there's more: even if we assume that A, B and C all shared the secret key K from the start, it is still impossible for B to prove to C that the message he is showing has not been changed from what A sent. Since C gets both message and MAC from B, B could still have made up the message and recomputed the MAC with the common key. The same holds in reverse: in fact, as soon as the key is shared by three parties instead of two, even B himself can no longer be sure that the message he received from A was not modified in transit by C.

The situation changes with the digital signature: the key that A uses to sign messages is never shared with anyone, since all that is needed for verification is the public key. Therefore, if the signature matches the message, it must perforce have been produced by A[22], and this argument is just as convincing to the first recipient B as to any subsequent principal who obtains the signed message.

In other words, unlike what happened with the MAC, B can show message and signature to a third party C and convince him that the message is the one originally generated by A. This property of digital signatures is often indicated as **non repudiation** to indicate that, once A signs a message, she cannot later deny to have done so, because nobody else could have generated that signature.

---

[22]We are sweeping under the carpet a number of problems that may occur in the real world, such as A temporarily "losing control" of her purse with the signing smartcard; but for this first order description let's stick to the idealized behaviour where principals are assumed to be able to keep keys secret.

3.3 Availability

Any system that performs its advertised service in a timely fashion when requested to do so by an authorized user enjoys the property of **availability**. The threat to availability is called **denial of service**.

An influential analysis of the problem of denial of service is due to Gligor [118, 119], who introduced the concept of **maximum waiting time** (MWT). The system should advertise the intended MWT for each of the services it offers. Whenever a user who issued a legitimate request has to wait for longer than the corresponding MWT, that user is being denied service.

Gligor observes that, while confidentiality and integrity are essentially concerned with what a user is allowed to do ("May she read? May she write?"), availability is concerned with what the authorized user is actually *able* to do ("Okay, she is allowed to write, but will it work if she tries?"[23]).

3.4 Authentication

Authentication is the process of verifying a principal's claimed identity. It is the logical step that follows **identification**, i.e. establishing who that principal claims to be. Both steps are necessary to convince the verifier of the identity of her interlocutor. (The familiar two-step interrogation of "userid? password?" is the perfect illustration.) It should be apparent that identification is the easier activity of the two (one just listens), while authentication is the one where some detective work is required of the verifier.

Authentication is by necessity a frequent event in distributed systems. Every day, many times a day, a computer M in your organization will receive an access request from an entity claiming to be legitimate user A, and M will have to decide whether to accept or reject the request based on its assessment of whether the bits that come out of the channel are sufficient proof that the principal at the other end really is A.

A basic taxonomy of authentication methods is neatly summarized in the traditional suggestion to check "something you know, something you have or something you are", examples of which might respectively be a password, a passport and a fingerprint. This classification is not exhaustive: Gollmann [123], for example, also lists "what you do" (e.g. keystroke patterns) and "where you are" (potentially of interest for ubiquitous systems). Imaginative readers may come up with further suggestions.

---

[23]Language purists will delight at the chance of being able to express this as: "She may write, but can she?".

As far as this introductory survey is concerned, though, we shall concentrate on the "something you know" approach: verifying knowledge of a shared secret is by far the most widely used foundation for authentication in computer networks today.

3.4.1 Passwords

Let us therefore assume that a principal A wishes to authenticate herself to a machine M; A is known to M by her name "A" (this could be the login name) and can prove her identity by demonstrating knowledge of a secret password p that she previously agreed with M.

The simplest way to demonstrate knowledge of the password p is simply to say it. This is what users normally do to log into a local computer.

The problem here is that, if M keeps a list all the passwords of its users, this password file becomes a valuable target for an attacker. Encrypting the file would bring little benefit, since M itself would need the key to decrypt it in order to be able to check any supplied password; so the attacker who managed to break into M could simply steal both the file and the key.

To address this, M may record a hash of A's password instead of the password itself—a technique pioneered by Needham at Cambridge [263] in the 1960s, later adopted by UNIX and now standard on most modern systems. This means that an attacker grabbing the list stored on M does not have access to any passwords.

But, despite this improvement, the system still isn't invulnerable: a more sophisticated adversary will mount a **dictionary attack**. Banking on the fact that many users will choose passwords that are easy to guess (e.g. names of loved ones, swear words, lines from favourite songs or movies ...), the attacker generates hashes of such candidate guesses and checks whether the result matches any entry in the list stolen from M. If it does, a password has been found. The guesses may even be precomputed once and for all and stored in a lookup table indexed by the hash value; then the attacker can crack on sight any account that used one of the guesses as its password. Safeguards against this kind of attack, other than educating users about the choice of proper passwords, include salting (see below) and artificially slowing down the hash function in order to increase the attacker's workload. Morris and Thompson [195] discuss those issues in detail, while a recent study by Yan *et al.* [267] provides experimental results on the (poor) choice of passwords even by users who have received specific training.

Salting is the practice of adding random bits to the user-supplied password before hashing it. These random bits have to be stored on M in the password list next to the hash value, otherwise the system itself would not be able to regenerate the hash for comparison even when supplied with the correct password. So this technique does not prevent the attacker from verifying the validity of a guess, but it does frustrate precomputation and parallel search. Furthermore, two users might choose the same (poor) password, e.g. "samantha"; without salting, their hash values would be identical, telling an attacker that the penetration of one account also opens the door to the other, and also highlighting that the password is so easy to guess that those two users thought of it independently. Even more interestingly[24], if one of the users with the poor password noticed this circumstance, it would be trivial for him to abuse the other user's account.

Whether A exhibits p or $h(p)$, if this happens in cleartext across the network (as in Telnet, Rlogin, FTP and in the HTTP Basic Authentication that most web sites use to password-protect a page) then an eavesdropper can record what A says and replay it later to impersonate her. Note that the hash offers no protection here: the attacker won't know the actual password, but won't need it to impersonate A. To defeat this **replay attack** it is necessary to ensure that A's authenticators can not be predicted from previous ones. This implies, among other things, that they will have to be always different.

3.4.2   One time passwords

An elegant way to do this using a chain of hashes was originally devised by Lamport [167], then implemented as a product (S/KEY) by Bellcore [130] and finally released as an open specification via a series of Internet RFCs [127, 128, 129]. The essence of the idea is for A to generate a series of passwords $p_0, p_1, \ldots, p_n$ linked by the recurrence relation

$$p_i = h(p_{i+1}).$$

These are computed by A in reverse order, starting from a randomly chosen value for p_n. A keeps the entire list to herself and bootstraps by securely sharing p_0 with M. At the first authentication, A presents p_1 to M. M doesn't know p_1, but he can verify that it is genuine by checking whether $h(p_1) = p_0$. This procedure extends by induction to all other passwords in the chain: A just shows p_i at the ith authentication, and M will know its hash p_{i-1} from the previous round. Eavesdropping attacks are defeated and so are attempts at stealing the "password file" from M. The information held by the server refers only to the past: it cannot be used to reconstruct the portion of the chain that has not yet been used, and therefore it can be used for verification but not for impersonation.

Among the disadvantages of the scheme are the need to "reload" after n authentications, the need for A and M to maintain synchronization (the protocol is not stateless) and the need for A to store the whole chain of passwords (though, of course, used passwords can be thrown away). This last requirement might be

---

[24]Taking insider fraud into account is still, to some extent, a paradigm shift. Needless to say, this is a problem. Major security holes go undetected for a long time because of this mindset.

traded off against extra computation in the unlikely case that A prefer to recalculate
the chain from p_n at each authentication.

3.4.3   Challenge-response and man-in-the-middle attacks

Authentication can be performed in a stateless manner by using a **challenge-response** strategy. M sends A a random number n which A must return encrypted
under the shared secret key K_{AM}.

$$M \rightarrow A : \quad n$$
$$A \rightarrow M : \quad E_{K_{AM}}(n)$$

Note that in this case a MAC, which is not invertible, would serve the same purpose
as the encryption, since there is no need ever to decrypt the result; to verify, M
simply performs the same encryption and compares the result, as per Needham's
technique described in section 3.4.1.

   This is the model originally used for air force IFF (identify friend or foe) systems, which led to the development of block ciphers. Jet fighters move at such
speed that it is not possible to rely on visual identification to decide whether the dot
on the radar is one of ours that should be protected, or one of theirs that should be
shot down. If the fighters from the same side share a secret key, they can challenge
each other by radio using the above protocol, and fire at those who can't prove
ownership of the key.

   The method is safe from passive replay attacks, but it remains vulnerable to
more sophisticated *active* attacks, such as "man-in-the-middle". Anderson [11,
section 2.2.2] relates of such an attack in the course of a battle between the South
African and Cuban air forces at the border between Namibia and Angola and, with
characteristic wit, labels it "MIG-in-the-middle". (The story later turned out to be
apocryphal, but it still makes the point nicely.)

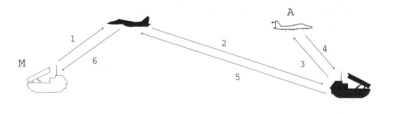

Figure 3.1. Anderson's "Mig-in-the-middle" attack.

   Assume that the white side has an aircraft A and an anti-aircraft gun M that
share a key. When M sees any aircraft it challenges it, and fires at it unless it responds correctly. The black side waits until the white plane attacks black territory

and at that point it sends a black plane to raid the white headquarters (figure 3.1). The black plane gets challenged (1) by the white gun M, so it relays (2) the challenge to the black anti-aircraft gun that spotted A; the black gun, in turn, challenges (3) A, who provides (4) the correct response. This is relayed (5) back to the black plane, who answers (6) M's challenge correctly, is let through unharmed and proceeds to carpet-bomb the white headquarters.

Similar attacks apply to many other situations, such as the one described in section 3.1.6 where two users who do not share a secret establish a confidential communications channel using public key cryptography. Here A and B are the honest players, who believe they are having the exchange pictured in figure 3.2, which is safe from passive eavesdropping attacks.

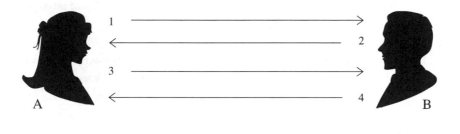

(1) $A \rightarrow B$: K_A;   *A enables B to send secret messages to her.*
(2) $B \rightarrow A$: K_B;   *B returns the favour.*
(3) $A \rightarrow B$: $E_{K_B}(m_A)$;   *A sends secret message m_A to B.*
(4) $B \rightarrow A$: $E_{K_A}(m_B)$ *B replies with secret message m_B.*

Figure 3.2. What A and B think is happening.

Unfortunately for them, the malicious network operator N intercepts their messages and substitutes them with forgeries. He manufactures two fake key pairs, $(K_\alpha, K_\alpha^{-1})$ and (K_β, K_β^{-1}), the first to pretend to B that he is A, and the second to pretend to A that he is B. While A and B believe that they are having the exchange pictured in figure 3.2, N sits between them like the two-faced god Janus and what actually happens is shown in figure 3.3.

To avoid this problem, A and B need to ensure that the public keys they receive from each other are genuine. One way to do this is for each principal to disseminate a hash of her public key using a higher integrity channel. Some people, for example, myself included, list the hash of their public key (known as the key's *fingerprint*) on their business card; of course this only helps if your interlocutor receives your business card before having to send you a secret message. It doesn't work if someone you never met wishes to contact you in confidence after having

A   N   B

(1.1) $A \rightarrow N : K_A$; A thinks she is sending her public key to B. Actually, the
                                   key is intercepted by N.

(1.2) $N \rightarrow B : K_\alpha$; N saves away A's key and sends B another public key he
                                   made himself, for which he has the matching private key.

(2.1) $B \rightarrow N : K_B$;   The same thing happens ...

(2.2) $N \rightarrow A : K_\beta$;   ... in the opposite direction.

(3.1) $A \rightarrow N : E_{K_\beta}(m_A)$; A thinks she is sending B a secret message, so she encrypts
                                   it under what she believes to be B's key. But this is in fact
                                   one of N's fake keys, so N can decrypt what he gets and
                                   read m_A.

(3.2) $N \rightarrow B : E_{K_B}(m_A)$; N re-encrypts m_A under B's genuine key and sends it along
                                   to the intended recipient, to whom everything appears as
                                   normal.

(4.1) $B \rightarrow N : E_{K_\alpha}(m_B)$;   The same thing happens ...

(4.2) $N \rightarrow A : E_{K_A}(m_B)$;   ... in the opposite direction.

Figure 3.3. What is actually happening.

read your web page.

A high integrity channel with more widespread distribution than one's own
business card is a book[25]; banking on this, a group of researchers at Cambridge,
led by Anderson, produced a book, *The Global Trust Register* [20], containing a
list of public key hashes[26]. Of course such a book has little hope of containing the
keys of all the users in the world, but it may be helpful in bootstrapping a "web
of trust", as used by Zimmermann's PGP[27] [270]. In PGP's model all the users,

---

[25]This is the reason why I listed the fingerprints of my keys on page xx.

[26]This had been theorized even in the original Diffie-Hellman paper [90], but doing it in practice
raised a number of interesting issues. The act of publishing this book was meant by its authors to be
as much a provocation as a useful service.

[27]PGP, which stands for *Pretty Good Privacy*, is a public key cryptography program that is the de
facto standard for email encryption. Originally released as open source for MS-DOS in 1991, and at

as peers, mutually certify the validity of the keys of their interlocutors. Users may thus obtain unreliably certified keys over insecure channels, as long as they can build "chains of trust" starting from people they know and leading to those keys.

The "signature of Alice on Bob's key" is actually a signature on the combination of Bob's public key and Bob's name. It means: "I, Alice, solemnly certify that, to the best of my knowledge, this key and this name do match". To Charlie, who must decide on the validity of Bob's key, this statement is only worth as much as Alice's reputation as an honest and competent[28] introducer; in fact, PGP lets you assign a rating (denoted as "trust level") to each introducer, as well as a global confidence threshold that must be reached (by adding up the ratings of all the introducers) before a key can be considered as valid as one that you signed yourself[29]. For example you may require two signatures from marginally trusted introducers, or just one from a fully trusted one; but someone with a higher paranoia level might choose five and two respectively. The supremely paranoid PGP users (I am one, and I know several others) do not place any great deal of trust in the competence of external introducers and truly rely only on keys whose validity they personally verified.

In this model *The Global Trust Register* acts as a supplementary introducer, with the scientific reputations of its authors as guarantees of honesty and competence. Because it certifies a number of "important" keys (e.g. keys of crypto pioneers and activists who are likely to have signed many other keys in their respective communities), there is a non-zero chance that, with only a couple of degrees of separation, it will be possible to form chains connecting the desired key with one or more of the ones listed in the book.

---

the time the only military-grade encryption software widely available to civilian users, it was quickly ported to every imaginable platform and is now sold as a commercial product by Network Associates.

[28]These two qualities are completely independent, and both are required for the introducer to be trustworthy. A dishonest introducer might intentionally sign a falsehood such as "This key belongs to the president of ABC Bank" in preparation for a fraud, while an incompetent one might be conned into signing that same falsehood because he is insufficiently careful in his verification of the supporting credentials of the principal who requests his signature.

[29]Note also that the fact that a key is valid does not imply that it is trusted. To believe that Alice's key is valid is to believe that it really belongs to Alice. To believe that it is trustworthy (for introductions) means to believe that Alice is honest and competent at key management. It will be easy for the reader to come up with examples of cryptographically illiterate acquaintances whose keys should be taken as valid but untrusted.

3.5 Security policies

3.5.1 Setting the goals

In most engineering disciplines it is useful to clarify the requirements carefully before embarking on a project. Such advice may sound so obvious as to border on the useless, but it is of special relevance to computer security. Firstly because, as shown by Anderson [8], it is all too often ignored: diving straight into the design of crypto protocols is more fascinating for the technically minded. Secondly because security is a holistic property—a quality of the system taken as a whole—which modular decomposition is not sufficient to guarantee[30]. It is thus important to understand clearly the security properties that a system should possess, and state them explicitly at the start of its development. As with other aspects of the specification, this will be useful at all stages of the project, from design and development through to testing, validation and maintenance.

The security policy is a set of high-level documents that state precisely what goals the protection mechanisms are to achieve. It is driven by our understanding of threats, and in turn drives our system design. Typical statements in a policy relating to access control describe which subjects (e.g. users or processes) may access which objects (e.g. files or peripheral devices) and under which circumstances. It plays the same role in specifying the system's protection properties, and in evaluating whether they have been met, as the system specification does for general functionality. Indeed, a security policy may be part of a system specification, and like the specification its primary function is to communicate.

Because the term "security policy" is widely abused to mean a collection of vapid managerial platitudes, there are three more precise terms which have come into use to describe the specification of a system's protection requirements.

1. A *security policy model* is a succinct statement of the protection properties which a system, or generic type of system, must have. Its key points can typically be written down in a page or less. It is the document in which the protection goals of the system are agreed with an entire community, or with the top management of a customer. It may also be the basis of formal mathematical analysis.

2. A *security target* is a more detailed description of the protection mechanisms which a specific implementation provides, and of how they relate to a list of control objectives (some but not all of which are typically derived from the policy model).

---

[30]Connecting secure components together does not necessarily yield a secure system.

3. A *protection profile* is like a security target but expressed in an implementation-independent way to enable comparable evaluations across products and versions. This can involve the use of a semi-formal language, or at least of suitable security jargon. The protection profile forms the basis for testing and evaluation of a product.

3.5.2   The Bell-LaPadula security policy model

The first and most influential security policy model was proposed in 1973 by Bell and LaPadula [29]. The US military had developed a system for the classification of sensitive documents (based on the well-known hierarchy of OPEN, CONFIDENTIAL, SECRET and TOP SECRET) and rules that prevented officers with a lower clearance from reading data in documents of higher classification. Bell and LaPadula were trying to enforce this information flow policy, also known as "multilevel security", in computer systems. They boiled everything down to two rules that every object access should obey:

1. (No Read Up, or "simple security property".) No process may read data at a higher level.

2. (No Write Down, or "*-property".) No process may write data to a lower level.

The first rule, as the name suggests, is simple to understand: the cleaner is not allowed to read the documents in the general's safe. But the second rule, despite being less intuitive, is also necessary. It prevents the general from leaving his important documents on his desk (a "lower level" area compared to his safe) whence the cleaner could obtain them without violating the simple property.

This simple formalization captures the essence of "multilevel security". But the methodology itself merits attention. Once appropriately modelled, the system can be represented as a state machine. Then, starting from a secure state, and performing only state transitions allowed by the rules of the policy model, one is guaranteed to visit only secure states for the system. This allows one to derive security proofs. (Amoroso [7] gives a good description of this process, with worked examples.)

This process can be applied independently of the particular policy, as long as the policy itself is consistent. This idea of how to model a security policy formally was a significant and influential contribution from Bell and LaPadula, perhaps as important as the introduction of the BLP policy model itself.

An important concept associated with this modelling strategy is that of *trusted computing base* or TCB, which is the controlling core of the system that makes sure that only the allowed transitions ever occur. More formally, the TCB is defined as the set of components (hardware, software, human, ...) whose correct functioning is sufficient to ensure that the security policy is enforced—or, more vividly, whose failure could cause a breach of the security policy. The goal of formalization is to make the security policy sufficiently simple, in order for the TCB to be amenable to careful verification.

3.5.3 Beyond multilevel security

It must however be appreciated that not all security policies are sets of rules about access control. There are many contexts in which the aspect of greatest interest in the system is not access control but authentication, or delegation, or availability—or perhaps a combination of those and other properties. The Biba [33] and Jikzi [16] policies, for example, and several others that I discuss at greater length with Anderson and Lee in [17], are cases where integrity matters more than access control. These are not just a matter of controlling write access to files, as they bring in all sorts of other issues such as reliability, concurrency control and resistance to denial-of-service attacks. Policies for key management and certification, which we shall encounter in section B.3, are further examples that have no relationship to multilevel security or access control.

On a more general level, we may speak of "security policy" whenever a consistent and unambiguous specification is drawn stating the required behaviour of the system with respect to some specific security properties.

A security policy is a specification of the protection goals of a system. Many expensive failures are due to a failure to understand what the system security policy should have been. Technological protection mechanisms such as cryptography and smartcards may be more glamorous for the implementer, but technology driven designs have a nasty habit of protecting the wrong things.

There exists a spectrum of different formulations for security policies, from the more mathematically oriented models that allow one to prove theorems, to informal models expressed in natural language. All have their place. Often the less formal policies will acquire more structure once they have been developed into protection profiles or security targets and the second- and third-order consequences of the original protection goals have been discovered.

Chapter 4

Authentication

When I started this research work, I thought that confidentiality of communications would be the most important issue that I would have to deal with, as the prime concern for any system relying on wireless transmission. I later realized that this was not so: the real problem is actually authentication. Without being sure that you are speaking to the correct party, there is little point in encrypting the secrets you want to communicate; whereas, if you have successfully authenticated your interlocutor and established some key material, protecting communications confidentiality with strong and efficient encryption is nowadays a solved problem.

We already saw in section 1.3 that authentication is in fact a prerequisite not only of confidentiality but also of integrity and availability: excellent ways to threaten those properties include respectively sending confidential information to, accepting state modifications from, and granting resources to, a principal whose identity has not been adequately verified.

As it turns out, authentication is also one of the most interesting security problems in ad hoc networking, because much of the conventional wisdom from distributed systems does not quite carry over. This leads to one of my original contributions, the *Resurrecting Duckling security policy model*. It therefore seems appropriate to place this chapter before the ones about the three security properties.

4.1 New preconditions

4.1.1 The absence of online servers

Many authentication protocols have been developed to verify the identity claimed by a principal. We saw the basic mechanisms in chapter 3 and some more substantial examples may be found in appendix B. However, the ad hoc network environment introduces a fundamental new problem: the *absence of an online server*.

Take for example Kerberos, discussed in section B.2: when a new node comes within our range, we have no assurance that we (or it) will be able to connect to an authentication server to obtain a ticket.

An authentication protocol based on public key cryptography would at first appear to be preferable: every node initially receives a certificate of identity signed by an appropriate authority[1] and the verifier only has to check the signature of that authority, without having to interact with it in real time.

The problem of online access to the server, however, reappears from the back door. If we want the authority to be able to revoke certificates, then the fact that its signature verifies correctly is not sufficient to guarantee the validity of the certificate: the verifier also needs to check whether that particular certificate has been revoked. Either the verifier will have to contact the authority (thereby requiring online access during the authentication procedure), or the certificate will have to specify a validity interval. This in turn opens two new problems.

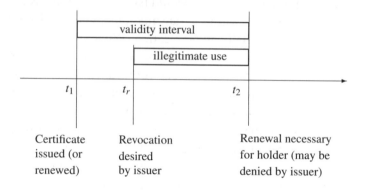

Figure 4.1. The validity interval of a certificate.

Firstly (see figure 4.1), if at time t_r the authority has reason to revoke a previously issued certificate which is valid from t_1 to t_2, it will certainly refuse to renew it when it expires at t_2; but, since we assumed disconnected operation, it has no way to prevent the certificate from being illegitimately used for the remainder of the validity interval between t_r and t_2. This can be mitigated by shortening the validity interval, but this in turn increases the administrative burden because certificates will have to be renewed more often; and, in the hypothesis of disconnected operation, this may mean physically bringing the nodes back to the authority. There is therefore a trade-off between timeliness and convenience.

---

[1]This may be a company-wide certification authority, a household-wide one, a personal one, one for an entire nation or one for a group of friends. We just note the importance of this scoping issue here, but we won't discuss it in depth for the moment. See section B.3.

Secondly, and more subtly, relying on expiration dates imposes on the nodes the extra cost of running a secure clock—otherwise the holder of an expired certificate might reset a node's clock to a time within the validity period. Many ubiquitous computing nodes would not normally have an onboard real time clock, let alone a secure one. Providing a secure clock involves a certain amount of tamper resistance of the node and a time distribution protocol explicitly designed to withstand malicious attacks. (Note the suspicious recursion in the fact that the source of authoritative time will have to be *online*, and will require *authenticating*.) All these problems are soluble, but let's remark that "just adding expiration dates" is not as trivial a fix as it may sound at first.

4.1.2 Secure Transient Association

The authentication problem of greatest relevance in this new context is itself new. We shall call it **secure transient association**.

If a householder owns a device, say a universal remote control, that lets her control various other devices in her home (such as hi-fi and television components, the heating system, lights, curtains and even the locks and burglar alarm) then she will need to ensure that a new device she buys from the shop will obey her commands, and not her neighbour's. She will want to be assured that a burglar cannot take over the heat sensing floodlight in the garden, or unlock the back door, just by sending it a command from a remote control bought in the same shop.

The threat is realistic: cordless telephones have long been a prime example of *insecure* association between the portable handset (the controller) and the base (the device that gives you access to the wired network, and therefore to the actual service). Criminals used to drive around posh neighbourhoods with a handset until they got a dial tone, at which point they'd enjoy free and untraceable phone calls. In 1992 the problem got so serious that France Télécom had to issue a public warning about it [163]. I have personally witnessed a relative's phone being "used", hopefully only by an innocent and unsuspecting neighbour, while nobody in the house was even near the handset. This was with analogue cordless phones, but Anderson [11, section 17.2.1] reports that current DECT phones are little better, in that the handsets simply transmit their identifiers to the base station in plaintext, despite the provision for challenge-response in the standard. This may stop accidental interference between neighbours, but not determined attacks by crooks.

As well as being *secure* (whatever we decide that to mean), the association between the controller and the peripheral must also be *transient*. When a householder resells or gives away her television set or hi-fi or fridge, the appliance will have to obey another controller; when her controller breaks down (or she decides to replace it or upgrade its operating system), she must be able to rebind to a new one all the gadgets she already owns.

A central authentication service is possible for expensive consumer durables; most governments run such services for houses and cars. But there is no prospect that this will be extended to all durable consumer goods; the UK government abandoned dog licensing some years ago as uneconomical. In any case, there would be very grave civil liberties objections to the government maintaining lists of all PCs, hi-fis and DVD players in the country; the outcry over the Pentium III processor ID [97] indicates the likely level of political resistance. Even the existing registration services stop short of managing keys; the replacement of car keys is left to the motor trade, while house locks are completely uncontrolled. So it is desirable that key management be performed locally: the last thing we want is to impose an expensive and unpopular central solution. Yet it would be nice if we could still provide some means of making a stolen DVD player harder to resell.

Another insight comes from scenarios where we have a pool of identical devices, such as a bowl of disinfectant in a hospital ward containing ten electronic wireless thermometers that can report temperature readings to a doctor's PDA. The doctor does not really care which thermometer she gets when she picks one up, but she does care that the one her palmtop talks to is the same one she is holding and not any other one nearby.

Many more potential applications of wireless devices require establishing a secure transient association between two principals (typically, but not necessarily, a user and a peripheral). For example, there has been significant interest in the possibility of a police pistol that can only fire when held by the officer to whom it was issued, who for this purpose might be wearing a very short range radio ring: some claim that, in the USA, a large number of the firearm injuries sustained by policemen come from stolen police guns. Similar considerations might apply to more substantial weapon systems, such as artillery, that might fall into enemy hands.

4.2   The Resurrecting Duckling security policy model

4.2.1   Imprinting and reverse metempsychosis

A metaphor inspired by ethology will help us describe the behaviour of a device that properly implements secure transient association.

As Konrad Lorenz beautifully narrates [174], a duckling[2] emerging from its

---

[2]Actually Martina, the web-footed bird of the family *Anatidæ* lovingly raised by Dr. Lorenz, was not a duck but a goose. The "duckling" of the title comes from my having read his book in Italian as a kid and having incorrectly translated "ochetta" into English in my original presentation for the Protocols workshop (1999-04-20), perhaps with subliminal influence from the Barks ducks to which I am attached. The mistake was carried over to the paper [240], its later revision [238], an appearance on Slashdot [232] and several more talks on both sides of the Atlantic, until the day (2000-02-03) when an anonymous member of the audience at Telcordia in Morristown, New Jersey, USA raised his hand to point it out. By that time it was unfortunately too late to rename the policy.

egg will recognize as its mother the first moving object it sees that makes a sound, regardless of what it looks like: this phenomenon is called **imprinting**. Similarly, our device (whose egg is the shrink-wrapped box that encloses it as it comes out of the factory) will recognize as its owner the first entity that sends it a secret key. As soon as this imprinting key is received, the device is no longer a newborn and will stay faithful to its owner for the rest of its life. If several entities are present at the device's birth, then the first one that sends it a key becomes the owner: to use another biological metaphor, only the first sperm gets to fertilize the egg (but see section 4.2.4).

We can view the hardware of the device as the body, and the software (particularly the state, which includes the imprinting key) as the soul. As long as the soul stays in the body, the duckling remains alive and bound to the same mother to which it was imprinted. But this bond is broken by death: thereupon, the soul dissolves and the body returns in its pre-birth state, with the resurrecting duckling ready for another imprinting that will start a new life with another soul. Death is the only event that returns a live device to the pre-birth state in which it will accept an imprinting. We shall call this process **reverse metempsychosis**. Metempsychosis refers to the transmigration of souls as proposed in a number of religions; this policy is the reverse of this as, rather than a single soul inhabiting a succession of bodies, we have a single body inhabited by a succession of souls[3].

With some devices, death can be designed to follow an identifiable transaction: in medicine, a thermometer can be designed to die (and lose its memory of the current patient's temperature history) when returned to the bowl of disinfectant at the nursing station. With others, we can arrange a simple timeout, so that the duckling dies of old age. With yet other devices (and particularly those liable to be stolen) we will arrange that the duckling will only die when so instructed by its mother: thus only the currently authorized user may transfer control of the device. In order to enforce this, some level of tamper resistance will be required: assassinating the duckling without damaging its body should be made suitably difficult and expensive.

4.2.2 Recovery of the imprinting key

Sometimes the legitimate user will lose the imprinting key (e.g. when the password is forgotten or the remote control is broken beyond repair).

To be able to regain control of the duckling, an easy solution is **escrowed seppuku**[4]: someone other than the mother, such as the manufacturer, holds the role of Shōgun and can order the device to commit suicide. Technically, this might be

---

[3]Prior art on this technique includes Larry Niven's science fiction novel *A World Out of Time* (1977) in which convicted criminals have their personalities "wiped" and their bodies recycled.

[4]Seppuku was the ritual "honourable suicide" (by disembowelment) of the samurai, which took place in several circumstances, including on request from the samurai's lord.

performed using *key diversification*: each device accepts a different seppuku key KS_i, burnt into its ROM during manufacturing, which is obtained by encrypting the device's serial number i with the Shōgun's master key KM:

$$KS_i = \mathrm{E}_{KM}(i).$$

But this reintroduces centralized control: the Shōgun can always take over any device and, more worryingly, he is forced to keep a global database (built from warranty cards sent in by the owners as they purchase the ducklings) mapping serial numbers to legitimate owners, lest he give out the seppuku key to the thief of the DVD player.

The experience of the motor industry shows that the manufacturer, whose profits come from sales, often has little incentive to make its products hard to steal. This makes us suspicious about how careful or scrupulous the Shōgun would be in managing such an escrow database.

To keep key management local, a better solution is for the mother duck to back up the imprinting key, and even split it into shares[5] if necessary; this gives her better privacy guarantees, at the cost of transferring the key management burden from the Shōgun to her.

A key recovery facility may be genuinely beneficial to the mother, as long as she is free to choose local escrow parties that she trusts instead of global ones imposed from above. Most of us are happy to leave a copy of our home keys with the neighbours, but would feel uneasy about being compelled to leave them with the police.

4.2.3 Multilevel souls

There are also applications in which only part of the duckling's soul should perish. Our medical thermometer might be calibrated every six months, and the calibration information must not be erased along with the patient data and user key when the device is disinfected, but only when it is plugged into a calibration station. So we may consider the device to be endowed with two souls—the calibration state and the user state—and a rule that the latter may not influence the former. So our Resurrecting Duckling security policy may be combined with multilevel security concepts. In fact, "multilevel secure souls" are a neat application of the Biba integrity policy model[6].

---

[5] *Secret sharing schemes* such as Shamir's [230] allow you to split a secret into n shares, of which any $k \leq n$ will be necessary and sufficient to reconstruct the secret. So you can split your key among n mildly trusted friends and be confident that it won't be misused unless at least k of them conspire against you.

[6] We discussed multilevel security in section 3.5.2 with the Bell-LaPadula policy, where information is not allowed to flow down; but that was from the point of view of confidentiality. Biba [33]

4.2.4 Bootstrapping

During the imprinting phase, as we said, a shared secret is established between the duckling and the mother. One might think that this is easy to do: the mother generates a random secret and encrypts it under the public key of the duckling, from which it gets back a signed confirmation.

But many ubiquitous computing nodes, due to their peanut-sized CPU, lack the ability to perform expensive modular arithmetic operations, and even if they did it would still not help much. Suppose that a doctor picks up a thermometer and tries to get his palmtop to do a Diffie-Hellman key exchange [90] with it over the air. How can he be sure that the key has been established with the right thermometer and not one of the others sitting in the bowl of disinfectant? If both devices have screens, then a hash of the key might be displayed and verified manually; but this is both tedious and error-prone, in an environment where we want neither. Besides, we do not want to give a screen to every device: sharing peripherals is one of the goals of ad hoc networking.

In many applications there will only be one satisfactory solution—physical contact. Anderson and I advocate its use generally, as it is effective, cheap and simple. When the device is in the pre-birth state, simply touching it with an electrical contact that transfers the bits of a shared secret constitutes the imprinting. No cryptography is involved, since the secret is transmitted in plaintext, and there is no ambiguity about which two entities are involved in the binding.

4.2.5 The policy's principles

After a narrative illustration of the policy, we now formally and concisely list its four principles for reference.

1. **Two State principle.** The entity that the policy protects, called the **duckling**, can be in one of two states: **imprintable** or **imprinted** (see figure 4.2). In the imprintable state, anyone can take it over. In the imprinted state, it only[7] obeys its mother duck, *q.v.*

2. **Imprinting principle.** The transition from imprintable to imprinted, known as **imprinting**, happens when a principal, from then on known as the **mother duck**, sends an **imprinting key** to the duckling. This must be done using a channel whose confidentiality and integrity are adequately protected. As part

---

introduced a multilevel integrity policy, isomorphic to Bell-LaPadula but "reversed", in which information is not allowed to flow up—otherwise the low integrity levels would pollute the high integrity ones.

[7]Unless the mother duck herself tells the duckling to obey someone else as well; but let's not jump ahead of ourselves (see section 4.3.3).

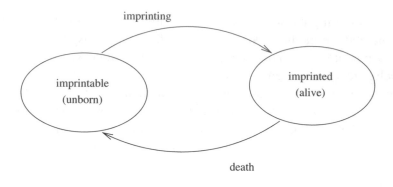

Figure 4.2. A state diagram for the Resurrecting Duckling.

of the transaction, the mother duck must also create an appropriate backup
of the imprinting key.

3. Death principle. The transition from imprinted to imprintable is known as
   death. It may only occur under a very specific circumstance, defined by
   the particular variant of the Resurrecting Duckling policy model that one has
   chosen. Allowable circumstances, each corresponding to a different variant
   of the policy, include the following.

- Death by order of the mother duck (default).
- Death by old age after a predefined time interval.
- Death on completion of a specific transaction.

4. Assassination principle. The duckling must be constructed in such a way that
   it will be uneconomical for an attacker to **assassinate** it, i.e. to cause the
   duckling's death artificially in circumstances other than the one prescribed
   by the Death principle of the policy.

Note that smashing the duckling with a sledgehammer is not a way to cause
its "death" in the technical sense, since this is not a transition from "imprinted" to
"imprintable" but rather from "imprinted" to "broken"!

Note also that implementation of the Assassination principle generally requires
some suitable level of tamper resistance in the duckling, but the precise amount
depends, among other things, on the value of the duckling and on the cost of a

successful tampering attack. This, in turn, depends to some extent on the attacker: for some attackers, the value of your particular duckling may be so high that they may be willing to spend millions[8] to violate its security; while most other attackers not only will not *have* the millions to spend, but they would not spend them on cracking your duckling even if they had them, because to them the return would not be that great.

Quite deliberately, the policy only says "uneconomical for the attacker" and leaves you with the task of performing this assessment. What this really means is therefore "uneconomical for all the attackers from whom you want to be protected", with the understanding that you will still—as always—be vulnerable to attackers outside the threat model you considered.

A similar remark applies to the clause in the imprinting principle that says that the imprinting key must be transferred to the duckling under a channel with "adequate" confidentiality and integrity protection. This is a more formal way of expressing the suggestion made in section 4.2.4 that one should bootstrap using an electrical contact rather than radio. The adequacy will depend on the value of the duckling being protected.

Yet another note of the "it depends" variety concerns the mandatory backup of the imprinting key. As we saw in section 4.2.2, there is a tension between convenience and liberty which gives rise to a continuous spectrum of key recovery solutions, from the completely centralized where the user has no key management burden but where the Shōgun is all-powerful, to the completely decentralized where the advantages and disadvantages are reversed. I have a definite preference for the decentralized end of this spectrum, but the choice of an appropriate key recovery policy for the application at hand is technically orthogonal to the Duckling and it would therefore be inappropriate for the Duckling policy to dictate how the imprinting key should be backed up, as long as it is.

4.2.6 Anonymous authentication

We developed the Duckling policy from the premise of the unavailability of an online server that could certify the identity of the unknown principal who needed to be authenticated. It is interesting to observe how, in the Duckling case, the identity of the principals involved actually becomes irrelevant. To whom is the duckling imprinted? The duckling doesn't know. It knows that Mother is "whoever

---

[8]In the words of Bob Morris during the discussion that followed the first public presentation of the Resurrecting Duckling policy model, as transcribed in [68, p. 191]:

> every time he's used the word thermometer I have assumed he really meant thermonuclear warheads, that's the kind of guy that I am, and now I think you have to rather rethink and reword your notions of budgets on both sides.

sent me the imprinting key when I was born", but it doesn't have a clue who she is in absolute terms, and would get no benefit from knowing it anyway.

The globally unique X.509 "distinguished names" (see section B.3) are unnecessary luggage in this context. In fact we may recognize the Duckling as promoting **anonymous authentication**, which is not as oxymoronic as it may sound at first. As Ellison [99] remarks in the context of SPKI/SDSI, and as Blaze *et al.* [39, 38] remark in the context of PolicyMaker and KeyNote, you don't really care who your interlocutor is, so long as she carries the right credentials. "I'm ABC's lawyer" will in many cases be a much more useful introduction than "I'm Laura Smith". Similarly, "I'm your mother duck", and not "I'm `host.domain.org`" or "I'm `01:23:45:67:89:AB:CD:EF`", is all the duckling needs, and all it should care about.

4.2.7   Other uses for the Duckling model

The model so far presented expressively describes a great variety of interesting situations, not just the relationship between a remote control and an array of household appliances.

- It also describes, as we have seen, the bond between a wireless thermometer and the doctor's PDA that records graphs of the temperatures of the various patients; and the bond between a handgun and its owner's signet ring.

- It even describes a possible mode of interaction between an e-wallet (mother duck) and an e-ATM (duckling): as the banking customer gets near the e-ATM, the machine gets imprinted to her e-wallet and to no one else's; but, at the end of the transaction, the e-ATM duckling dies and is again imprintable to any other customer.

  The establishment of this bond allows the e-wallet's keyboard and display to be used instead of those normally found on the ATM; in fact the e-ATM might have nothing more than an output slot for the cash (e-cash is an obvious further development—but then the physical ATM itself would hardly be necessary). Note however that there will have to be a separate layer of non-Duckling authentication to persuade the bank that it is talking to one of its customers. But a "traditional" authentication protocol is adequate here, because the e-ATM will have access to an online server as its back-end.

- The car keys of my colleague Richard Clayton unlock the engine management unit via a radio link. The bond between the keys and the car unit is established once and for all in the course of an irrevocable operation very similar to imprinting. The assassination principle, too, appears to be respected:

customers buying this car must sign a form declaring that they understand that the entire engine management unit will need replacing, at substantial expense, if they ever lose their keys. The only discrepancy from the Duckling policy appears to be the absence of a legitimate Death transaction—there is no way to force the car to forget the current imprinting, even if you are the holder of the key that is currently mother duck.

- The Cooltown project at HP (section 2.4) envisages a situation where, for example, the data projector of a meeting room is a shared resource onto which today's presenter can teleport her data as required. Many visions of ubiquitous computing put forward a similar scenario of serialized shared use of common infrastructural resources. This is an ideal application for the Duckling, being as it is a textbook example of secure transient association. In particular, wiping out all user state on death provides a much needed insulation against accidental inter-user leaks. (Think of the next user checking the history of visited URLs on the meeting room web browser you just used. We shall come back to this in section 5.2.2.)

- Jerry Saltzer suggested that the Pentium III can also be viewed as a duckling, in so far as it uses a state machine with a trapping state to address a security problem. He quotes from [112] that the infamous "processor serial number", which raised vocal concerns owing to its privacy-intruding implications [97], is now accompanied by a "sticky bit" which, if set to one, prevents reading of the serial number register. This bit can only be set back to zero by rebooting the chip.

- Yet another interaction that matches the Duckling model is that between a computer and its administrator. Since it provides several useful insights and was in fact inspirational for the invention of the policy model itself, we shall dedicate the entirety of the next section to it.

4.2.8 The computer as a duckling

Like many other more influential security policy models such as Clark-Wilson [70] and Chinese Wall [50], the Resurrecting Duckling was an attempt to capture the essence of an existing practice and to codify it formally in order to obtain a coherent model with definite security properties. The practice that the Resurrecting Duckling originally attempted to codify is that of binding a personal computer to its owner by way of a password.

It is interesting to note how in many cases the practical implementation of this idea lacks some of the elements described in the formalized policy it predates, and therefore fails to guarantee the corresponding security properties.

At the lowest level, for example, we recognize something very similar to the Duckling policy in the practice of locking the BIOS with a password. Depending on the chosen settings, it will be necessary to enter that password in order to change the BIOS settings stored in battery backed-up memory and possibly also in order for the machine to bootstrap after a reset. The machine is shipped with the password disabled, which corresponds to the imprintable state; but, once a password is set, only someone who knows it can enter the setup program to remove it and make the computer imprintable to someone else again.

The discrepancy between this arrangement and our policy is that the Assassination principle is not respected. It is usually possible to reset the BIOS settings by disconnecting the backup battery for a suitably long period; some motherboards even have a jumper that will immediately erase that memory if short-circuited. This is not a design flaw but a purposeful decision meant to prevent the embarrassing situation where forgetting the password makes the computer inoperable because its BIOS settings can no longer be reconfigured (or because the computer cannot even be *started*, if a boot password was also set). The unstated underlying rationale is a sound design principle which I formulate as follows:

Big Stick principle

Whoever has physical control of the device is allowed to take it over.

In many cases this makes perfect sense, especially because whoever has physical control of the device has so many devious ways to take it over anyway (regardless of whether he is allowed or not) that it is simply more honest to admit this explicitly at the policy level and grant him the permission that he would otherwise take by himself. At least this prevents catastrophic failures due to users storing valuable data on the computer and assuming that the BIOS password will protect them unconditionally while in fact it cannot resist an attacker with physical access to the machine (who might, for example, take out the hard disk and read or write it in another computer).

The Resurrecting Duckling policy explicitly chooses to go against the Big Stick principle in order to safeguard items over which the owner may not have physical control at all times. Without doing that, the policy would not for example be able to protect your PDA if it were lost or stolen. Ubiquitous and wearable gadgets, which will often hold personal information and which will often be left unattended, require stronger protection than the Big Stick principle. The same holds for a vending machine. The price to be paid is that of adequate tamper resistance.

If the policy did not explicitly require the imprinting key to be adequately backed up (see the Imprinting principle), there would be also another serious penalty to pay, since the loss of the imprinting key would lock up the duckling[9].

To build a PC—or, more to the point, a laptop—that implements the Resurrecting Duckling policy, we need to ensure that it be impossible to reset the password, even by physical means, without knowing it. For example we could place the password and the rest of the BIOS configuration data in a flash ROM (so that there would be no backup battery to disconnect) and we would not provide any special jumper to reset it. However, an attacker could remove the flash chip from its socket and read it out or even rewrite it in an external ROM programmer. To counter this, we could solder the chip to the motherboard instead of socketing it, but it would not take inordinate amounts of extra effort for an attacker to unsolder it. We could go on for several more rounds in this arms race, moving the memory inside a bigger chip or even adopting armoured tamper resistant chips such as the Dallas iButton [78]. What is important to point out is that the policy model does not contain any a priori definition of a required level of tamper resistance, and the appropriate level must be decided on an application-specific basis after a risk assessment of the use to which the duckling will be put.

We also recognize another incarnation of something closely resembling the Duckling policy at a higher level than the BIOS—for example the password protection at the OS level. There, too, you can decide on a root password when you first install the OS, and you can later change it only if you know the then-current one.

There is no immediate equivalent of an unborn state into which the system could return after the mother orders suicide (the root password can be changed to a new value in a handover from one owner/administrator to another, but there is no intervening transition to a state with no password, similar to the one that existed on installation). But a functional equivalent to this missing state can be obtained by having the abdicating administrator stick on the computer a piece of paper with the password in cleartext, with the intended semantics of "anybody who walks up to this computer is welcome to take over as administrator by changing this password to something else".

Having thus simulated the unborn state, do we now have a system that complies with the Duckling policy? Well, not yet, because the Assassination principle has not been satisfied. The attacker could still boot from floppy, bypassing the OS which provides the password protection, and access the raw hard disk volume to

---

[9]Note that a "locked up" duckling, i.e. one for which the imprinting key has been lost, may or may not continue to be perfectly usable, depending on which of its functions may only be performed by the mother duck. Using the BIOS password example, if the only active password were that for "BIOS setup", then its loss would make it impossible to reconfigure the computer, but would not prevent usage of the computer in the then-current configuration. If, however, the "boot" password were also active, then its loss would make the computer totally unusable. This hierarchy between the two passwords is not entirely unrelated to the multilevel secure souls we mentioned in section 4.2.3.

violate its confidentiality (read) or integrity (write). Combining the OS level protection with the previously discussed BIOS level protection will prevent booting
from floppy, but the attacker could still physically take out the hard disk and read
or write it in another machine. Adopting an encrypted file system would protect
the confidentiality (but not the integrity) of the data regardless of any indirect ac-
cesses to the disk. This would indeed implement a Duckling policy, but only—this
is an interesting point—if the value of the duckling is defined to be the confidentiality of its data. If we instead consider the hardware itself to be valuable (not
unreasonable for a high-end laptop), then the combination of OS level password
and encrypted file system still doesn't implement the Duckling policy, because the
thief can simply reformat the disk (without being able to read the data on it, but
who cares?) to obtain a virgin imprintable machine that can be resold, in violation
of the Assassination principle.

To make a laptop Duckling-compliant with respect to the threat of its hardware
being stolen we must return to hardware tamper resistance safeguards. The BIOS
boot password (without an escape mechanism to reset it) is a good start towards the
goal of making the stolen laptop unusable, but given the modular construction of
modern machines it will probably still be possible to resell the individual components such as the RAM, the processor, the hard disk and the DVD drive.

Since our aim is not really to show how to build a secure laptop but simply to
explore some of the subtleties involved in instantiating the Resurrecting Duckling
policy in a physical implementation, we shall stop this discussion here. The interested reader should feel free to pursue it and devise appropriate mechanisms to
make the individual components inoperable for someone to whom the laptop is not
imprinted.

4.3   The many ways of being a master

There are however a number of other equally interesting situations that the model
so far described does not adequately cover.

All the cases seen so far involved a definite master-slave relationship between
the mother and the duckling, but we can envisage cases of ad hoc networks between
devices that it would be more natural to consider as peers. If the components of
your hi-fi and video system talk to each other, for example because the timer wants
to start the satellite TV tuner and the VCR in order to record something off air,
or because the DVD player wants to tell the TV that it should set the aspect ratio
to widescreen for this programme, does it make any sense for the DVD player to
become the mother duck of the television?

Let's see how the model can be extended to handle those other cases as well.

4.3.1 Human or machine?

The first interesting remark concerns the nature of the principals. The master-slave model so far presented seems to make sense primarily when the mother duck master is a person and the duckling slave a peripheral that the person wishes to use. The master initiates imprinting of the slave (including the key backup and the bootstrapping step usually based on physical contact) and then starts giving it orders. In the case of the password-protected computer duckling seen in section 4.2.8, the mother duck is a genuine human. In other cases, where the master is a physical device (the remote control), we notice that the device is actually only the cyber-representative of a sentient being (the person who owns the remote control, the television, the fridge and all the rest of the equipment).

Blurring the distinction between the person and the computer that represents it is a common sin, which may sometimes have unexpected consequences. We shall remedy it by being more precise and identifying two separate interactions. The one between the remote control as master and the DVD as slave is one where the principals are both computing devices; but on top of that there is another relationship between the owner as master and the remote control as slave, in which one principal is a human and the other is a machine. The interesting point is that this second relationship, too, can be modelled with the Resurrecting Duckling: the virgin remote control gets imprinted to its owner on purchase when the owner types in a PIN. We thus have a hierarchy of master-slave Duckling relationships: the human is mother duck to this remote control and possibly other cyber-representatives (for example the e-wallet, to use another one of our previous examples), while the remote control is in turn mother duck to a number of devices (DVD, hi-fi, garage door etc.). Each principal (whether man or machine) has control over all the principals in the subtree of which it is root[10]—but such control can only be exerted with the co-operation of all the principals down the relevant chain of command: I may be the mother duck of my remote control, which is in turn mother duck of my DVD player, but if I break the remote control I will not be able to play any DVDs despite being the grandmother duck of the player (unless I restore the relevant imprinting keys from the backups into a new remote control).

4.3.2 Smart dust

Before going any further we should introduce the application scenario that originally inspired me to extend the Duckling model to peer-to-peer interaction.

Take a wireless network not of a few nodes but of several thousand; scale the

---

[10]Since the link from a node to its parent is indeed a representation of a duckling-to-mother relationship, this graph can be viewed as a duck family tree. So each principal has control over all its offspring.

nodes down in volume by four orders of magnitude, from a few cm across to 1 mm^3; throw in some extra science fiction such as laser-based optical communications between those microscopic gizmos; what you get is a rough approximation to what scientists at Berkeley are developing under the heading of "smart dust".

Kahn, Katz and Pister [150] describe a system consisting of autonomous milli-metre-sized sensor nodes, the "dust motes", that can be scattered in great quanti-ties over the area to be monitored. Each dust mote consists of battery, solar cell, sensors, micromachined catadioptric mirror (which can reflect or not reflect an in-coming laser ray towards its sender, thus passively transmitting one bit) and some digital computing equipment, plus extra optionals such as an active transmitter and a receiver (in their absence, the node consumes less power and lasts longer, but it can only talk to a larger entity such as a better equipped dust mote or a base station).

In one example scenario, a cloud of dust motes is dumped on the battlefield from a military aircraft; later a base station with a laser and a high-speed video camera acquires the sensor results from a safe distance, for example to detect the passage of vehicles or the presence of toxic gases. It is also envisaged that the better endowed dust motes might talk to each other in order to route data from motes that don't have direct line of sight to the base station.

At this early stage in the project, manufacturing the devices and devising the appropriate low-level communications and routing protocols so that they work at all are, quite reasonably, the primary concerns, and the security issues appear not to have been tackled yet. If the White general deploys his dust motes, how can he be sure that the sensor readings he gets are good ones from his own White dust motes and not fake ones from the much more numerous Black dust motes that his adversary has cunningly deployed over the same area? And, for dust motes that have the capability of talking directly to their neighbours, how is the mutual authentication problem solved?

Once we realize that this is, in fact, a low-power ad hoc wireless network, only with some of the numbers off in unexpected directions by several orders of magni-tude, it becomes plausible to think that the Resurrecting Duckling might be of help. But something is still missing. The dust motes are certainly peers, and it would not feel right for one of them to have to become master of another in order to be able to communicate securely with it, especially given that the individual dust motes are neither self-propelled nor cyber-representatives of hypothetical humans that could physically help them perform the initial contact-based bootstrapping phase of im-printing.

4.3.3   *Mater semper certa...*

You always know who the mother is, the Romans used to say in their wisdom, but you can never be sure about the father, where there may be several candidates. In the Duckling model we don't care about the father at all, but we may have got somewhat carried away on the subject of the uniqueness of the mother.

OK, granted: after imprinting there is one and only one very special principal that the duckling will recognize as mother, and obey to the death; but do we really need to forbid the duckling from ever interacting with anybody else? In particular, would it not be possible for the duckling to accept orders (at least *some* kinds of orders) from other principals too? An affirmative answer to these questions leads the way to the announced extension of the Resurrecting Duckling model to peer-to-peer interaction.

There are two distinct ways of being master that we have so far confused and that we shall now distinguish. Firstly, you can be master because the slave is imprinted to you and will be faithful to you for all its life; this is a long-term relationship. Secondly, you can be master on a much more temporary basis, just for the duration of a brief transaction: you ask your dining neighbour to pour you some wine and you assume the role of master for a moment, only to become slave later when it's your turn to pass on the vegetables. So far we implied that, in order for one principal to be master of another, the second principal had to be imprinted to the first. We now repudiate this view: the two devices can establish a very temporary master-slave relationship without either being imprinted to the other.

The imprinted duckling is indeed faithful for life to its unique mother duck; but it is happy to talk to others, and even obey their requests, as long as the mother duck said it was OK to do so.

Let's model the duckling as an object[11] with a series of methods, i.e. actions that the duckling can perform on itself, possibly changing its own state. A *policy*[12] for the duckling shall be an arbitrarily complex statement specifying, for each of the available actions, which credentials a principal should exhibit in order to persuade the duckling to perform it. The policy can grant or deny any privileges it wants over the possible actions for the duckling; the only fixed rule, which is in some sense a bootstrapping base, is that if a principal can demonstrate knowledge of the imprinting key of the duckling, then it can upload a new policy into it.

Note that this implication is only one way: I see no reason to also dictate that one can only upload a new policy if one knows that imprinting key. As a matter of

---

[11] In the "object oriented programming" sense.

[12] We appear to be guilty of semantic overloading here, since we have until now described the whole Resurrecting Duckling construction as a *security policy model*. We do in fact distinguish the two uses. A "security policy model" is a general security specification that gives overall guidelines for the behaviour of a certain class of systems: typical examples would be Bell-LaPadula [29], Clark-Wilson [70] and Chinese Wall [50]. Actual policies (sometimes referred to as "security targets") may be derived from it by specialization to a particular application and implementation. The reason why we decided to reuse the word "policy" here is to emphasize that this is the same type of entity as those mentioned in trust management systems such as PolicyMaker [39] and KeyNote [38].

fact, for the duckling "downloading a new policy" (and even "committing suicide") are just two of the many possible actions: whether any given principal is allowed to invoke them is something that depends on the specific policy that currently resides in the duckling.

It is conceivable for the original mother duck to upload a policy that would allow other principals to upload a new policy or even kill the duckling. This may effectively be a functional alternative to backing up the imprinting key: it amounts to designating a "godfather" that may at any time take over the role of mother duck.

It should be clear that this power of delegation should be exercised with care, since the designated godfather(s) will be able to kick out the original mother at will: a godfather who can upload a new policy can also kill the duckling (by making that action possible for himself), then re-imprint it and ensure that the original mother is no longer recognized.

Without pursuing the matter in great detail, we hint at the fact that the above problem might be kept under control using a multilevel integrity system, à la Biba [33]. The various parts of the policy would be ranked at different integrity levels, so that one could allow the low integrity items to be rewritten but not the high integrity ones, which would include the most sensitive actions such as killing the duckling and, recursively, rewriting the high-level portions of the policy.

To sum up the important extension to our model, being mother duck allows one to perform the special action of uploading a new policy in the duckling; but, apart from that, any action can be invoked by any principal who presents the required credentials, as required by the duckling's then-current policy.

This enables peer-to-peer interaction. The remote control will give all the components of the hi-fi system the necessary credentials so that they can ask each other to perform the appropriate operations. The White general will be mother duck to all his dust motes (probably via a cyber-intermediary) and will give them the credentials that allow them to talk to each other—credentials that the dust motes from the Black army won't have, even if they come from the same manufacturer.

4.3.4   Further indirection issues

I have chosen a question and answer format to explore some of the subtle points of the separation between ownership and control.

Many of these questions and answers are genuine, in that similar ones were actually uttered on 2000-04-05 during the discussion that followed my presentation at the 8th Security Protocols workshop [236]. I am grateful to the attendees, in particular to Virgil Gligor, Markus Kuhn and Pekka Nikander, for their active participation. Their contributions and stimuli have significantly enriched this section.

I am also grateful to Stuart Wray for his offline suggestion about apoptosis.

Interoperability

If you take me for a ride in your GPS-equipped car, where the GPS is imprinted to you, can my camera obtain the current geographical position from your equipment to stamp the pictures I take while you are driving? More generally, is a duckling limited to talk only to its siblings? If so, there would be no interoperability.

The interoperability problem is solved by appropriate clauses in the policy.

Firstly, there may be innocuous actions (e.g. giving out the current position for a GPS unit) that a duckling is happy to perform for anyone[13]. This is obtained by not requiring any credentials for the initiators of such actions in the policy of the GPS duckling.

Secondly, my camera still must have some assurance that the positions given out by your GPS unit are trustworthy, otherwise anyone could fool it into stamping the pictures with bogus geographical coordinates. This is obtained by defining your GPS as a valid source of geographical coordinates in the policy of my camera duckling. At the implementation level this may be performed in many ways whose relative advantages will have to be assessed. For example the GPS might be given a "this device can be trusted to give out valid position information" certificate by some standards body, and the camera might recognize and accept this[14]. Alternatively, the mother duck of the camera might issue such a credential herself for that GPS ("I tell you, my son, that you can believe the coordinates sent to you by this specific GPS unit") and store it in the camera duckling as part of its policy.

Thirdly, there may even be cases where we *want* the duckling to be able to talk only to its siblings, as with the White vs. Black dust motes.

Control interface

If I go abroad and forget at home my PDA, which is mother duck to all my other gadgets, is it now impossible for me to control them until I get back?

No. One should not make the mistake (induced by the primary example of the universal remote control) of identifying the mother duck with the control interface for the duckling. As soon as I buy a new gadget, I imprint it to my cyber-representative (which might well be my PDA for illustration purposes), but the policy I upload into it may specify that any other gadget of mine is allowed to control it, as long as it has a user interface that is suitable for issuing the appropriate commands. I may then use any available gadget for controlling any other, and I could conceivably imprint my MP3 player to my PDA but control it from my wristwatch. As a matter of fact I might even keep my cyber-representative in a safe and

---

[13]But note the denial of service problem, and the *sleep deprivation torture* mentioned in section 7.2.1.

[14]The validity of such a certificate is linked to the tamper resistance of the device.

only ever take it out to imprint my other gadgets.

Tamper resistance

What happens if the Black general captures a White dust mote, dissects it à la Markus Kuhn [14] and steals its credentials? Can it now impersonate it to all the other White dust motes?

Yes, unfortunately. If we decide to put credentials inside the ducklings, we must rely on the ducklings being tamper resistant to some extent. The Assassination principle already stated that breaking the tamper resistance ought to cost more to the attacker than legitimately acquiring an imprintable duckling. We now add that it also ought to cost more than the value obtained by stealing the duckling's credentials.

The cost to the White general, as well as that of the direct loss of any valuable secrets, would have to include that of revoking those compromised credentials and replacing them by new ones in all the dust motes—a costly operation if they cannot all be easily contacted once deployed.

This in fact highlights a non-trivial conceptual problem: once we introduce delegation as we just did, we also reintroduce, in its full glory, the problem of revocation in the absence of an online server. Since we make no a priori guarantees about the connectivity status of the duckling, there may be circumstances where not even the mother duck (let alone a central authentication server) is contactable. From a theoretical point of view, this is probably just as bad as the original starting point. In practice the problem is somewhat mitigated by the fact that the authority issuing those credentials is now less centralized.

Trust management

How shall the duckling decide whether the credentials exhibited by another principal are sufficient to grant the principal permission to execute the requested action?

This is a general problem for which, fortunately, a general solution has already been developed. Ducklings may embed a generic trust management engine such as KeyNote [38]. Policies and credentials shall be expressed in a common language and any duckling will be able to just feed its own policy, the external request and the supplied credentials to its engine which will return a boolean answer as to whether the requested action is allowed or not.

Policy specification

How will the owner of a device be able to specify a sensible policy for it? It looks as if doing this properly will be a job for a security expert.

Writing a policy will indeed require competence in security and will be no less complicated than programming. End users will not be expected to write their own policies; instead, devices will come with a portfolio of "sensible policies" (hopefully with explanations), that the user will be able to parameterize. Power users will be able to write their own policies if they wish, or edit the supplied ones, and probably web sites will appear that archive the best of those homebrew variants.

Trojan policies, containing subtle intentional flaws that their author plans to exploit, are of course a danger in such a scenario. But the same concern applies to any software that will run inside the Trusted Computing Base. You can't write all such software yourself, so in the end you are forced to trust another author axiomatically. As Bob Morris once famously remarked, the TCB is by definition the portion of your system that can violate your security policy.

Family feelings and apoptosis

Wouldn't it be possible to exploit the fraternal love among sibling ducklings as an additional security feature?

Sure, neat idea! The policy for the ducklings in your home might say that they should stop working when they feel lonely, because in normal operation it is reasonable for them to expect that they will be surrounded by at least n siblings. This is a case in which we make explicit use of the *short range* of our wireless communications, inferring proximity from connectivity. If they are not in range of their siblings, it may be because they were stolen, so they should refuse to work. (Of course this heuristic fails if the thieves steal the whole lot. . .)

This is reminiscent of **apoptosis**, or "programmed cell death"—a process through which cells commit suicide and which may be triggered by the lack of positive reinforcing signals from neighbouring cells [189]. As the human fœtus develops, for example, apoptosis is responsible for the orderly death of the membrane between the fingers. Under other circumstances, when an organism is attacked by a virus, apoptosis of the infected cells prevents the infection from spreading. The importance of apoptosis can also be appreciated by the consequences of its malfunctioning: if apoptosis is insufficient it may result in cancer; if it is excessive, some scientists believe it may be cause for Alzheimer's.

The fraternal ducklings may be viewed as the individual cells of a larger organism whose self-defence countermeasures (here against the threat of theft) include apoptosis. This is also similar to the case of the brave outnumbered warriors who prefer to burn down their own village rather than having it pillaged by the enemy invaders.

Chapter 5

Confidentiality

We have explained that the hard part of providing communications confidentiality is authenticating the interlocutor. The typical side effect of authentication (either the establishment of a shared secret or the validation of a public key) is sufficient to bootstrap the cryptography and protect communications using well known techniques. At the dawn of the 21st century, the state-of-the-art ciphers are for all practical purposes unbreakable—or, to use a less Manichæistic terminology, they are no longer the weakest link in the chain, by a wide margin.

There is little else to say on communications confidentiality *per se* other than noting that the available cryptographic primitives depend on the computational capabilities of our ubiquitous gadgets, which in most cases exclude public key cryptography. We shall briefly examine this aspect of the question.

From the point of view of ubiquitous computing, though, it is interesting to go beyond the confidentiality *of transmitted messages* and to look also at the confidentiality of any secrets that may be *held in the devices* themselves.

One of the promises of ubiquitous computing is that of an intelligent, sentient environment that detects our presence, remembers our preferences and acts as our invisible butler. However, just as a butler is privy to sensitive information about his master, so our gadgets become repositories for all sorts of information about us that we may wish to keep private. This point needs further attention.

Going back to communications, another kind of information that we may wish to keep confidential is the metadata describing *who*, *with whom* and *when* (as opposed to *what*, which encryption can adequately protect). We shall postpone this discussion until chapter 8.

5.1   Cryptographic primitives for peanut processors

5.1.1   Asymmetric asymmetric cryptosystems

Public key ciphers, typically based on modular arithmetic operations on integers whose length is currently around one or two thousand bits, are several orders of magnitude slower than symmetric ciphers of comparable security. This makes them generally unsuitable for the smaller and slower CPUs ("peanut processors") that are common in embedded systems. Asymmetric asymmetric ciphers[1], described next, are one way to make the situation more bearable, albeit with some limitations.

In the widely deployed RSA public key cryptosystem [219] one may choose a small encryption exponent which will make encryption (and signature verification) much faster and decryption (and signature generation) much slower compared to the standard case where they take comparable amounts of time. Careful system designers will exploit this asymmetry by adopting protocols such that the peanut devices mostly perform cheap operations, while the expensive operations are left to large servers.

As an aside, we remark once more that "careful" is the pivotal word here, since it is easy to overlook details that may lead to dramatic security holes. The classical example comes from the protocol developed by Tatebayashi, Matsuzaki and Newman [246] to allow two mobile phones to establish a shared key with the help of the powerful server in the network centre.

(A word of advice. If you are not comfortable with the crypto protocols and the mathematics that you see below, feel free to skip to the next section on page 110. The details we are about to explore are interesting and instructive, but not needed to understand the rest of the book. Just remember that one word, "careful".)

The server publishes his system-wide RSA public key with an encryption exponent of 3. Encrypting (modular cubing) is inexpensive and can easily be done by the peanut devices, but decrypting (taking the modular cubic root, which is done by raising the argument to a secret exponent whose length in bits is comparable to that of the modulus N) is expensive even with knowledge of the secret key, and of course infeasible without. The protocol runs as follows[2], with each of the two peanut devices Alice and Bob sending an encrypted secret random number to the server Sam, and with Sam handing out to Alice the XOR of the two secrets, to which Alice can XOR her own secret again to recover Bob's. At the end of the protocol run, Alice and Bob share the secret that was invented by Bob.

---

[1] See footnote 13 on page 189.

[2] We omit practical details of no cryptographic relevance such as handshaking between the server and the second device to solicit the second secret r_B.

$$A \to S: \quad \mathrm{E}_{K_S}^{\mathrm{RSA}}(r_A) \triangleq r_A^3 \quad \mathrm{mod}\, N$$

$$B \to S: \quad \mathrm{E}_{K_S}^{\mathrm{RSA}}(r_B) \triangleq r_B^3 \quad \mathrm{mod}\, N$$

$$S \to A: \quad r_A \oplus r_B$$

This apparently simple and elegant protocol was broken by Simmons [231] who pointed out that an attacker may use Sam as an oracle, conning him into decrypting messages that the attacker previously intercepted.

Assume that the two co-operating attackers Carol and Dave eavesdrop on the messages in the exchange above. If only they could extract the cubic root of the second message, they would own the shared secret r_B established between Alice and Bob at the end of the protocol. Similarly, if they could extract the cubic root of the first message, they would get r_A which, XORed into the third message, would again yield the desired r_B. They observe that Sam sits there extracting cubic roots on demand, so they run the following exchange.

Carol does not invent an r_C which she later cubes; instead, she sends out the already-cubed r_A^3 she overheard from Alice, pretending to have cubed it herself out of an original value which she in fact does not know. Sam unwittingly helps by extracting the cubic root and sending her the result, only obfuscated by a value r_D of Dave's choosing. Because Dave will tell Carol his r_D, the two crooks can trivially recover r_A and thence the shared secret r_B.

$$C \to S: \quad \mathrm{E}_{K_S}^{\mathrm{RSA}}(r_A)$$

$$D \to S: \quad \mathrm{E}_{K_S}^{\mathrm{RSA}}(r_D)$$

$$S \to C: \quad r_A \oplus r_D$$

Since the original protocol is almost symmetrical, the attack could equivalently be performed by having Carol send an invented r_C^3 while Dave sends an overheard r_B^3. Then Carol receives $r_C \oplus r_B$, from which she recovers r_B.

The only trouble with this attack is that Sam might notice that Carol's r_A^3 (or Dave's r_B^3) is a value he already decrypted in the past. This is where Simmons's cutest trick comes in. The mathematical identity

$$(xy)^z \equiv x^z \cdot y^z,$$

which holds *a fortiori* in modular arithmetic, implies that raw RSA encryption preserves the multiplicative structure of its operand. There is an unintended homomorphism such that the encryption of a product is equal to the product of the encryptions:

$$\forall K, a, b : \mathrm{E}_K^{\mathrm{RSA}}(a \cdot b) \equiv \mathrm{E}_K^{\mathrm{RSA}}(a) \cdot \mathrm{E}_K^{\mathrm{RSA}}(b).$$

Carol can send Sam a *blinded* version of r_A^3, namely $r_A^3 \cdot r_C^3$, which Sam will have never seen before[3]. Sam will then extract the cubic root of the blinded value, yielding $r_A \cdot r_C$, and combine it with Dave's value. From that combination, Carol and Dave will easily recover r_A by XORing out Dave's r_D and dividing out Carol's blinding factor r_C. From r_A and the overheard $r_A \oplus r_B$ they can then recover the shared secret r_B as before.

$$C \rightarrow S : \quad r_A^3 \cdot r_C^3 \quad \mathrm{mod}\, N = \mathrm{E}_{K_S}^{\mathrm{RSA}}(r_A \cdot r_C)$$

$$D \rightarrow S : \quad \mathrm{E}_{K_S}^{\mathrm{RSA}}(r_D)$$

$$S \rightarrow C : \quad (r_A \cdot r_C) \oplus r_D$$

We were discussing this problem during a supervision[4] and my brilliant undergraduate student Bruno Bowden suggested breaking the homomorphism by adding hashes. After a couple of attempts we sketched the following modification to the protocol, which appears to be resistant to Simmons's attack.

$$A \rightarrow S : \quad \mathrm{E}_{K_S}^{\mathrm{RSA}}(r_A)$$

$$B \rightarrow S : \quad \mathrm{E}_{K_S}^{\mathrm{RSA}}(r_B)$$

$$S \rightarrow A : \quad \mathrm{h}(r_A) \oplus \mathrm{h}(r_B)$$

The only change from the original TMN protocol is that, in the last message, Sam hashes each of the secrets supplied by Alice and Bob before XORing them. The shared secret between the two peanuts at the end of the protocol is now $\mathrm{h}(r_B)$ instead of r_B.

Even if Carol sends $r_A^3 \cdot r_C^3$ in her first message, which Sam will decrypt to $r_A \cdot r_C$, what she receives from Sam is $\mathrm{h}(r_A \cdot r_C) \oplus r_D$, from which the crooks can obtain $\mathrm{h}(r_A \cdot r_C)$. But it is impossible for them to disentangle $\mathrm{h}(r_A)$ out of it, even with knowledge of $\mathrm{h}(r_C)$ and r_C.

---

[3]The subtle point here is that Carol can generate $\mathrm{E}_{K_S}^{\mathrm{RSA}}(r_A \cdot r_C)$, for any r_C she wishes, without knowing r_A.

[4]Held on Wednesday 2000-03-01.

5.1.2   Maximum rate vs. maximum number of cycles

Even when the acrobatics just described do not introduce security holes, they still only allow decryption and verification (not encryption and signature) for the peanut processors. Thus, many public key protocols continue to be out of reach. But moving to symmetric key protocols will not necessarily solve all the performance problems. If the processor is fast enough to keep up with the cryptography then the bottleneck, especially in ad hoc networks, may move to the latency of transmission. This is especially true in designs like PEN (see section 2.5.5) where sender and receiver are asleep most of the time and need to set up a rendezvous to communicate. In such cases the duration of one run of a cryptographic protocol will probably be dominated not by the encryption time but by the communications time, which will in turn depend on the number of messages exchanged much more than on their length or complexity.

Examining another aspect of the performance problem, is bulk traffic encryption feasible for peanut devices? Here the answer appears to be affirmative. Gladman [116], who wrote optimized implementations of all the 15 AES candidates, reports that his Rijndael takes 361 Pentium III cycles to encrypt or decrypt a 128 bit block (in steady state condition, not counting the initial key setup). A qualitative scaling to a hypothetical 5 MHz peanut processor still gives a respectable 1.8 Mb/s raw encryption throughput which, even allowing for the fact that not all of the available computational power can be devoted to encryption, is still generous compared to, say, Bluetooth's data rate of 0.7 Mb/s.

There are other subtleties, though. We have so far reasoned in terms of peanut processors and emphasized the constraint of a limited maximum rate of computation (small devices cannot compute very quickly). However, in practice the hard limit on a small device is not so much the complexity of the CPU (silicon is cheap) but the size of the battery, whose weight and volume cannot exceed certain thresholds if the device is to be portable, unobtrusive and ubiquitous.

The amount of available energy is therefore finite and small and it must be conserved as much as possible in order to lengthen the interval between battery replacements (or recharges). The constraint amounts to a limited maximum quantity of computation.

In a mains powered system, the rate of computation is the only limit, and any CPU cycle that goes idle is wasted forever—so there is merit in putting your screen saver to good use, calculating its share of the current RSA challenge rather than wastefully displaying kaleidoscopic patterns of bouncing lines. But, in a battery-powered system, the available energy is limited and any CPU cycle that goes idle is a good opportunity to put the device to sleep[5]. We shall come back to this in section 7.2.1.

So, even if peanut devices are capable of encrypting all of their traffic, it may not always be desirable for them to do so unconditionally if this shortens their battery life. If the wireless link is between a MIDI saxophone and a synthesizer module, do I really care that the neighbour can electronically eavesdrop on my note-on and note-off events? He can probably hear the music directly anyway, and is more likely to complain about the noise than to steal my intellectual property! The crypto diehard will never run out of scenarios where encryption is absolutely necessary (e.g. "if he gets the MIDI events, the neighbour will be able to make slight modifications and sell my improvised solos to the record company as his own") but the commercial reality is that in many cases the average consumer will prefer, *ceteris paribus*, the MIDI saxophone whose battery lasts twice as long to the one that encrypts its traffic.

It is therefore important to take into account the interaction between security and power management. The bits-per-joule performance figure of the chosen ciphering system may be much more significant than the bits-per-second one. Maybe this will prompt a comeback of dedicated hardware, against the current tide of doing everything in software on a general purpose microprocessor, and we may see a standard cell for encryption in a corner of some Bluetooth chips. Presumably it is in recognition of this that the Bluetooth encryption algorithm E_0 is a stream cipher based on shift registers: such a design can be implemented in hardware within a small gate budget.

5.2 Personal privacy

5.2.1 The "only dishonest people have things to hide" fallacy

Until now, relatively few members of the general public have taken as a serious concern the protection of the confidentiality of the data stored on the computing devices they own. While this may seem foolish given the inherent insecurity of the typical computer, this attitude is not entirely unjustified: in most cases, the

---

[5]Most conventional systems actually incur too much overhead to be able to do this on a cycle by cycle basis: restarting the crystal oscillator and waiting until its output stabilizes enough to be used as a system clock may take thousands of cycles. With the components used in AT&T's PEN node, the recommended waiting time is 16,384 cycles which, at 14.7 MHz, is over 1 ms. This means that any idle period shorter than 1 ms is wasted as a deep sleep opportunity: you may gate out the clock signal, but you cannot stop the oscillator, which will continue to draw power. But asynchronous designs work without clocks and are particularly well suited to power conscious environments. Leask [169] designed and demonstrated a variation of the PEN node based on the Amulet asynchronous processor rather than on the conventional microcontroller used in the standard design. This clockless node could, while receiving data over its radio interface, go to sleep between one byte and the next!

information held on personal computing devices not used for business has little economic value—both for the owner, who doesn't really care that much if she loses it, and even more so for the potential thief, who can't really be bothered to steal it.

In fact the terminology I just used is inappropriate, linked as it is to a physical metaphor of theft as an activity that takes the loot away from the victim, and to the mental image of a pickpocket stealing a PDA full of addresses. Stealing information is more akin to photocopying than to snatching: it does not imply theft of the medium and therefore does not make the information unavailable to the original owner. So, even if the owner *were* concerned about data loss, she could always make backups but still be blissfully indifferent about the possibility that others might read her information, thereby addressing availability and ignoring confidentiality. This blithe nonchalance about confidentiality makes sense for as long as the user's computers do not hold any great deal of sensitive private information, which has so far been a common occurrence.

This is about to change.

- First, if ubiquitous computing brings computing devices everywhere, then many more activities that used to be conducted in other ways will be mediated by computers. Witness how many ordinary nontechnical people nowadays already write more e-mail messages than paper letters—something that until the first half of the 1990s was only conceivable for utter geeks. Witness how many neophiliacs buy books, food, DVDs and cinema tickets on the Internet; how many of them run their bank account, fill in their tax return and invest on the stock market through the Internet—the most trendy ones via their WAP phone. Imagine how long it will take for the general public to follow suit, especially if the providers bribe their customers to go online[6]. Imagine how many more activities will be mediated by computers of one form or another if wirelessly connected processing nodes are going to be embedded in all the everyday objects that surround us, including tools, appliances, vehicles and clothes.

- Second, if ubiquitous computing makes our environment sentient and personalized, it will be the explicit goal of all these devices to find out as much as possible about us and our preferences. In order to serve us best, our digital servants will learn and remember all our quirks and idiosyncrasies.

- Third, ubiquity brings along a problem of scale. Pieces of information that may appear almost worthless on their own become suddenly much more

---

[6]I recently found out that First Direct, a business without high-street branches that introduced telephone banking in the UK, now offers an Internet-controlled account with better interest rates than their own phone account. For such accounts, the bank no longer sends out statements by snail mail and, most importantly, no longer pays a human operator to answer the customer's calls.

sensitive when many of them are taken together. For an intelligence agency, declassifying any single spy satellite photograph to release it to the press is not a big deal; but declassifying the whole collection would also reveal the surveillance capabilities and the choice of targets of the agency. In an almost exact parallel, for the 21st century gadget freak such as myself who walks around with a digital camera strapped to his belt and takes pictures every day, releasing any single photograph is not a problem, but doing so with the entire timestamped collection would amount to publishing a diary, which has quite different privacy implications. Beyond a certain threshold, a difference in size becomes qualitative as well as quantitative, as appropriately noted by Dijkstra [77] in a delightful classic about the craft of programming:

> one of my central themes will be that any two things that differ in some respect by a factor of already a hundred or more, are utterly incomparable.
>
> History has shown that this truth is very hard to believe. Apparently we are too much trained to disregard differences in scale, to treat them as "gradual differences that are not essential". We tell ourselves that what we can do once, we can also do twice and by induction we fool ourselves into believing that we can do it as many times as needed, but this is just not true! A factor of a thousand is already far beyond our powers of imagination!

- Fourth, it is not at all uncommon for technology originally deployed for some useful and acceptable purpose to be misused for a substantially different purpose. Some of the first hotel door card locks originally worked with credit cards[7]—until VISA sued. In fact, both credit cards, originally introduced as a safer and more convenient payment system, and electronic door locks, originally introduced as flexible access control systems for buildings with a dynamic population of authorized users, are two examples of technologies that have subsequently been exploited for surveillance.

Confidentiality failures of ubiquitous computers will therefore reveal much more about their owners than the isolated personal computing systems of the end of the 20th century ever could.

For those inclined to dismiss this prediction as an instance of exaggerated alarmism, an eye-opening read is Garfinkel's insightful and influential book *Database Nation* [110]. His disquieting inquiry examines in great detail the ways in which businesses, governments and other organizations collect, share and collate information about our private activities. In his opening chapter, he writes:

---

[7]Mark Lomas remarked to me that, to this day, many hotels use credit cards as keys for a room safe, and then added: "I keep an invalid card in my wallet for this very reason".

you may well ask, "Why should I worry about my privacy? I have nothing to hide."

The problem with this word "privacy" is that it falls short of conveying the really big picture. Privacy isn't just about hiding things. It's about self-possession, autonomy, and integrity. As we move into the computerized world of the twenty-first century, privacy will be one of our most important civil rights. [...] To understand privacy in the next century, we need to rethink what privacy really means today:

- It's not about the man who wants to watch pornography in complete anonymity over the Internet. It's about the woman who's afraid to use the Internet to organize her community against the proposed toxic dump—afraid because the dump's investors are sure to dig through her past if she becomes too much of a nuisance.

  [...]

- It's not about the special prosecutors who leave no stone unturned in their search for corruption or political misdeeds. It's about good, upstanding citizens who are now refusing to enter public service because they don't want a bloodthirsty press rummaging through their old school reports, computerized medical records, and email.

Note also that the picture depicted by Garfinkel is based primarily on existing technology and infrastructure—medical records, customer loyalty cards, genealogical databases, car number plate readers, DNA fingerprinting, surveillance cameras, wiretapping and so on. In the case of ubiquitous computing, the threat is amplified by some of the circumstances I mentioned above, such as the fact that learning our preferences will be part of the official mission of these gadgets.

I have heard too many times the insinuating comment that anyone with anything to hide must be a criminal and that honest people have nothing to be ashamed of. This is an arrogant attempt to criminalize our fundamental right to privacy. (Perry Metzger [188] wrote a delightful short novel on the subject.) Why should anyone be surprised or offended that some of us want to keep some things private? There certainly is nothing to be ashamed of in having good sex with your loved one, but isn't it natural to want to draw the curtains?

5.2.2   Leaving traces on shared devices

Ubiquitous computing will introduce many personal gadgets, but at the same time many shared ones as well. The whiteboard will become a large wall mounted display on which I will be able not only to write with the appropriate electronic pens but also to project images and movies held in my key ring; and of course all the people present will be able to download a copy of the contents of the whiteboard

There is nothing particularly novel about this example. Typewriter tapes and carbon copy paper have been a source of intelligence for industrial (if not diplomatic and military) spies ever since they were introduced. I like to mention this case as a physical representation of something that goes on all the time[9] inside computer systems. A few examples follow.

- Ever since its first Windows version in the late 1980s, Microsoft Word offered a list of recently visited documents as entries in its "File" menu[10]. This feature was later adopted by other applications and eventually became a de facto standard. From Windows 95 onwards, the facility is even present in the operating system itself ("Start / Documents"). There is no easily accessible way for users to clear these lists in individual applications—much less on a global system-wide basis.

- Most web browsers keep a history list of recently visited URLs, as well as a cache containing the actual pages. There exist application commands for clearing these, but they are typically well hidden.

- Microsoft's Internet Explorer 5 remembers the values you previously typed in web forms and offers them back to you as automatic completion when you fill in similar pages again. It also offers a similar service for passwords, though thankfully you may say no.

- This behaviour is by no means limited to GUI applications. Most UNIX shells offer a "history" facility that lists the commands previously issued in that session[11]. Some shells, including zsh and bash, even dump this information to a hidden file in the user's home directory so as to make it persistent between sessions.

- The GNU Emacs editor records in its elisp-accessible internal structures every keystroke (or, more generally, input event) it receives. One of the reasons for this behaviour is support for infinite undo. But this practice may have interesting interactions with, for example, any elisp packages that ask the user

---

[9]Often this happens unintentionally, simply because leftovers are not cleaned up. At other times, though, this is done intentionally so as to save users from retyping frequently used strings over and over. The consequences in terms of the disclosure threat are rarely anticipated.

[10]The facility is not mentioned in the 1989 SAA/CUA interface design guide [136]: it was not a standard feature of compliant Windows or OS/2 applications at the time.

[11]This application-level type of leak, like several others in this list, can easily compromise the security of carefully constructed system-level protections. McDonald and Kuhn [186], for example, designed and implemented a steganographic file system for Linux that hides the presence of protected files and directories, but the hints from a history facility would give the game away regardless of the strength of the steganographic protection.

to type a password. Not to mention, of course, that the entire user activity
during that session can be reconstructed and examined. At least this history
is not persistent across sessions.

- Most operating systems that use virtual memory do not wipe the swap file at
  shutdown. Anyone with physical access to the disk may be able to inspect
  fragments of memory snapshots. Not a job for the faint hearted, but potentially a rewarding one, since it will reveal in-memory state, which might
  include cleartext passwords.

- Very few if any file systems actually erase the space previously occupied by
  a file that has been deleted: they just mark it as free and expect a new file
  to overwrite it soon. This means that files that were thought to be deleted
  may in fact be recoverable by someone who knows where to look (or by
  someone who wouldn't know but bought the right utility). Windows 95 in-
  corporated such a utility in the operating system by introducing the "recycle
  bin": "deleted" files are never overwritten unless the system actually runs
  out of unused disk space, and any files that have not yet been overwritten can
  be simply pulled out of the recycle bin and dropped back into the directory
  tree. There is also an "Empty recycle bin" command, which removes all the
  undelete information and marks the data blocks as free; but of course, for
  efficiency reasons, it does not actually wipe them out by active overwriting.

The list above is far from exhaustive. If we move to the realm of servers rather
than staying with the client systems, we find even more ways in which every transaction we perform (phoning home, buying a bar of soap, boarding a plane, ...)
leaves behind what Garfinkel [110], quoting Alan Westin, calls our "data shadow".

Ubiquitous computing will introduce a disturbing crispness to the edge of this
shadow, since every wireless handshake of a wearable device with the devices that
surround it may be timestamped and logged by the Orwellian system as evidence
of our location at a given time. This issue is not unrelated to anonymity, to which
we shall return in chapter 8.

5.2.3   Secure disposal vs. encrypted storage

What we wish to point out now is another aspect of the question, namely the per-
sistence of the disclosure threat even after the devices cease to be in active service.
The tape of the label maker can be inspected by pulling it out of the machine, but
also by recovering it from the garbage. To those who innocently believe that dumpster diving is an urban legend and only happens in movies about teenage crackers
who bring down the US defence network with a 300 b/s modem, I'd like to offer my

photographs (figure 5.3) of a skip[12] full of computer junk including several boxed and labelled backup tapes, presumably dumped because of the obsolescence of the format.

Figure 5.3. A skip full of unloved hardware in Cambridge including—under a full-size photocopier—some neatly boxed and labelled backup tapes.

It is easy to object that a careful operator should have destroyed the media before disposing of them. To put things in perspective, I shall relate the rest of my little adventure with the ink tape from the Dymo machine.

After discovering that the "ink" tape was full of readable information, I tried to imagine what the proper disposal procedure for it might be. Smashing the cartridge with a hammer would not affect the readability of the tape, and neither would cutting the tape with scissors, unless the person doing this were very meticulous indeed. The bundle of unwound tape looked like it stood a good chance of jamming a standard office paper shredder, so I did not attempt that. My best effort was to wrap the bundle of tape in scrap paper and then set fire to it. The operation, not to be recommended as standard practice owing to its unpleasant olfactory consequences and to the mess produced by the droplets of molten plastic, yielded the charred blob visible in the first half of figure 5.4. My initial satisfaction with this result faded away once I noticed that, under the top shell of hard molten plastic, the core of the blob was still a plastic tape that could be pulled out and unwound. Much of the unused "ink" had detached from the film, but the remaining trace was still sufficient to make out the text, as can be seen in the second half of figure 5.4.

The moral of the story is that securely disposing of media that used to contain sensitive information is not as trivial as it may sound. This is a well-known result for magnetic disks: Gutmann [125] explains why writing zeros all over the data is not sufficient to prevent recovery (the memory of the previous bit value can be recognized from the different analogue shapes of these new zeros, so several

---

[12]Or "dumpster" for the benefit of my American readers.

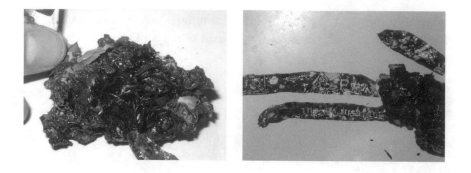

Figure 5.4. What remained of the "ink" tape after trying to burn it.

overwriting passes are necessary, using different bit patterns). Security utilities such as the commercial edition of PGP offer a "file wiping" function that does just that. But Gutmann also explains that slight misalignments of the drive heads over time may leave a trace of an ancient data pattern on the disk even if the same sector is repeatedly overwritten. Intelligence agencies, therefore, for whom the paranoia knob is set to maximum, don't just wipe obsolete hard disks: they also physically destroy them [87].

How does this translate to consumer-grade security for ubiquitous computing? Does your company shred everything it throws away? Observe that an office shredder is typically several times more expensive than an upmarket label maker—and is still incapable of dealing with a spent "ink ribbon" cartridge. Shredders that can crush floppies and videotapes (and presumably Dymo cartridges) are available, but at yet higher prices. More to the point, even those businesses that can afford them will typically only use them for a selection of their waste singled out as being sensitive, such as contracts and personnel records; but the rest of the discarded media and equipment will probably make its way to the normal rubbish bin.

Secure data destruction before disposal of the hardware is probably never going to be economically viable for consumer equipment. Even if it were, though, its major failure is that it would still not protect the user's data in case of loss or theft of the device, or in the case where an attacker takes apart an unattended "public server" device. Data needs to be actively destroyed before the attacker tries to extract it, but the timing of the attack is unpredictable. Sammes and Jenkinson [224] give an interesting description of how police experts should proceed in order to extract information from a suspect's PDA—and of course seizure will occur at no notice.

Encrypting all the data before writing it to secondary storage is a much better solution than sophisticated disposal techniques. First, assuming the cipher is chosen and used properly, it is much, much harder for an attacker to recover information from a physically readable but encrypted hard disk than from one which used to hold plaintext and was later wiped. Second, and more important, if information on the disk is always encrypted, disaster may strike at any time but we will always be protected[13]. As a result the user is free to dispose of the hardware as carelessly as ever, without being subject to the risk of accidental disclosure[14].

This is not a complete solution, though, because data needs to be in plaintext to be used. So there will be parts of the system (for example the RAM) that hold unencrypted data and these will be vulnerable to attack. Probing the memory of a live system is far from impossible: Anderson and Kuhn [14] show elaborate exploits directed at systems designed to resist physical penetration. The most serious concern for ubiquitous consumer-grade electronics comes probably from non-invasive low-cost attacks—the same authors list some in another paper [15]. I found one almost by accident during daily use of my PDA.

My palmtop, an "old faithful" HP 200 LX of 1994 vintage, is essentially a miniature MS-DOS 5.0 machine with a battery-backed RAM disk, plus a ROM disk holding the operating system. The machine boots like a regular PC-XT, using `config.sys`, `autoexec.bat` and associated ancillaries, and runs any ordinary DOS program that fits in its memory. The PDA-specific productivity applications such as calendar, phone book and personal finance are implemented as TSR (Terminate and Stay Resident) modules that can be woken up by special keys. The "Off" button places the machine in low-power standby rather than actually switching it off, and another DOS program can be instructed to hide the display contents with a random pattern, and request a password, whenever the machine wakes up from standby.

One might think that bypassing the password protection might require opening the case and dropping some probes on appropriate pins of appropriate chips in order to read out the memory. This is far from rocket science, since the machine has no physical safeguards against tampering. But it turns out to be overkill. Because all these essential PDA functions such as task switching, suspend, password-based access control and clock-based wake-up are implemented as applications rather than as part of the operating system, there are unexpected interactions and failures.

The one I encountered was that, under very low battery conditions, any additional power drain would abruptly switch the machine off. So, if a programmed reminder turned the machine on (triggering the "password request" function) and made it beep, the power drain from the beeper would switch it off immediately in the middle of that activity. But, on restarting the palmtop using an external power supply, the interrupted program might resume in a slightly inconsistent state. In

---

[13]Clearly, encryption protects the *confidentiality* of our data in the face of unexpected disasters, but it is essential also to take other precautions, such as off-site backup of the encrypted data, so as to protect its *availability*.

[14]We assume that key management has been dealt with appropriately. If not, we might encounter loopholes such as the tamperproof smartcard holding the keys ending up in the same skip as the storage media with all the encrypted data.

some cases, the "XOR with random noise" that was supposed to hide the currently active application screen underneath was performed a second time, with the effect that (say) your balance sheet was visible even if you had not yet typed the password. In others, the system was so messed up that cancelling the request for a password by hitting ESC got you in anyway, instead of switching the machine off as it normally does. The lesson here is that the security of a system may be compromised when the system is operated outside its specifications, even if it is completely bullet-proof under normal circumstances. If you want robustness, you must plan for the unexpected.

Earlier, we suggested protecting the data on secondary storage using cryptography—the assumption being that a secondary storage medium can easily be physically extracted and read in a different machine. The other implied assumption, shown to be false in the case of the HP 200, was that the primary storage was protected by other mechanisms, such as the physical construction of the device. Where this assumption is not realistic it is possible to encrypt even the main memory, as is done in bus-encrypting cryptographic processors such as the Dallas DS5002[15] [80, 79].

The trouble with encrypting everything is that we have to pay the corresponding penalty; and while this may be affordable for most systems in terms of time, for peanut devices it may be beyond budget in terms of energy, as we highlighted in section 5.1.2. So do we want to do it? We probably want the *option* of doing it, but without being obliged to pay the penalty if it is not worth it.

The serious problem then becomes that of offering this flexibility without opening a big hole. If security can be turned off, this may be a benefit for the user in some circumstances, but if the attacker can turn it off as well, then this becomes a liability. The solution I favour uses the Resurrecting Duckling security policy model introduced in chapter 4. In the imprintable state, the owner of the device can decide whether all storage should be encrypted or not, trading off confidentiality for battery life depending on the requirements of the application. If circumstances change, the owner can still reverse her decision, but to do that she must first order the duckling to commit suicide (something that the attacker cannot do) and lose its current state.

The next subtlety in this scenario is the user interface (sections 2.6.1 and 2.6.7): dramatic failures can occur if it is unclear whether the device is in the state where everything is encrypted or in the one where everything is stored as plaintext.

Finally, the key management strategy for the system should be sufficiently compartmentalized: breaking into one device should reveal the secrets of that device, but not those of any other, even if of the same model.

---

[15]This too, however, was broken by Kuhn [164] without the need to open the chip or cryptanalyse the cipher, using a cunning protocol-level attack.

Chapter 6

Integrity

The traditional view of integrity, like that of confidentiality, concerns threats to messages in transit across an unfriendly network. From our point of view, though, we are equally interested in integrity threats to the devices themselves. So, as we did for confidentiality in chapter 5, we shall initially examine the problem of guaranteeing the integrity of messages, but we shall then devote our attention to what happens at the endpoints.

6.1 Message integrity

Message integrity is an essential prerequisite in most application scenarios.

When data is corrupted to garbage, it often becomes immediately worthless. Think of the digital photographs in wireless transit between the news reporter's camera and the multi-gigabyte storage pack inside his rucksack, or of the music tracks that the teenager downloads to her in-ear player by slotting a few coins (e-coins?) into the 21st century juke-box.

Even worse, when data is corrupted to something else that looks plausibly like the original—something more likely to be caused by malice rather than accident—the loss caused by the corruption may be greater than the original value of the data. Think of a customer at a trade fair receiving a beamed business card from an interesting-looking supplier, and imagine the phone number on the card being manipulated by the competitor in the next stall so that, when the customer is ready to buy from the first supplier, he will unwittingly call the second one[1]. Think

---

[1] A similar scam was pulled off (although in a perfectly legal way) against AT&T when it registered the freephone number 1-800-OPERATOR for its operator-assisted long distance calls. With a stroke of genius, its competitor MCI realized that the poor spelling abilities of the general public could be exploited by registering 1-800-OPERATER, thereby diverting a substantial fraction of the traffic meant for AT&T [190]. Appropriation of misspelt names has happened on the web as

of zeros being added to or removed from fields that are prefixed[2] by a currency symbol.

6.1.1 Integrity for point-to-multipoint

Just as we said for confidentiality in the previous chapter, providing message integrity between two endpoints is easy once the problem of authentication has been solved. Once a shared secret is in place, it[3] can be used as a MAC key to validate any messages that the two principals exchange. The more interesting problem is instead that of point-to-multipoint[4] communications, where a simple-minded MAC would not work for the reasons exposed in section 3.2.6.

The point-to-multipoint scenario is actually fairly topical for ubiquitous computing. Among other examples, it is what happens whenever fixed sensors are deployed in the field to give information to mobile devices that might wander nearby.

Imagine, for the sake of argument, miniaturized solar-powered weather stations on top of every lamp post; they would relay their readings of the local temperature, pressure, wind speed etc. to any nearby clients—for example your wristwatch as you go past. Naturally, you want to be reassured that you are getting these weather measurements from a genuine and properly calibrated weather station, not from the bogus repeater of some local prankster.

Let there be a reputable institution that calibrates and certifies those stations. The weather station node could then, on request, exhibit a certificate signed by this institution that said

> I certify that the weather station with public key <*key*> was inspected and recalibrated by me on <*date*> and found to be genuine and accurate.

The weather station could sign each of its readings. Your watch (and any other client receiving those same readings) could verify the signature using the public key in the certificate, and it could verify the certificate itself using the public key of the reputable institution, which it would know axiomatically in the same way as your web browser knows the public key of Verisign.

---

well (see for example http://www.altavitsa.com/, an online lottery site banking on the popularity of the well-known search engine) and I even witnessed the reverse situation. In 1997 I needed to look up the tariffs of our company's cellular connectivity provider; I "guessed" a URL of http://www.vodaphone.co.uk/ and found that it looked distinctly unfamiliar. Explanation: the major cellular operator that I was trying to contact actually uses the cutely incorrect spelling of "Vodafone", and I had landed on the site of a small-fry competitor who thought of exploiting this quirk.

[2]Sigh...(See page 7.)

[3]Or, in actual practice, a session-specific derivative of it.

[4]A.k.a. multicast, a.k.a. broadcast—the subtle and somewhat artificial distinctions are of little practical relevance here.

The main problem with this scheme is the cost of the public key operations: as we said in section 5.1.2, signing is probably going to be too computationally and energetically expensive for a peanut processor to be able to afford it for every reading it sends out.

6.1.2 Guy Fawkes

Several researchers have studied ways to substitute digital signatures with less expensive integrity primitives such as chains of hashes or MACs. The discussion in section 3.2.6 about the transferability of beliefs supported by the three types of integrity primitives has particular relevance, and among the important features of these chained constructions is the extent to which they offer the properties of a signature (in particular non-repudiation) without using one.

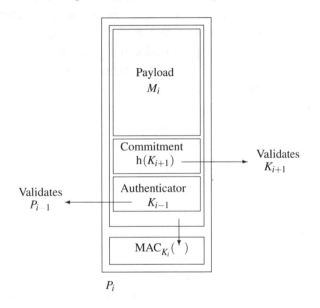

Figure 6.1. The generic packet P_i in the Guy Fawkes protocol.

The Guy Fawkes protocol, due to Anderson *et al.* [13], protects messages with a chain of hashes where each message announces the hash of the key that will validate the next message (the actual key comes later). The core idea is roughly[5] as follows (see figure 6.1): each message M_i is encapsulated in a packet P_i. The

---

[5]The original paper uses a slightly different notation and uses only hashes instead of MACs, but the two presentations are isomorphic in so far as $h(K,M)$ is conceptually (if not cryptologically—see [162]) equivalent to $\text{MAC}_K(M)$. The notation adopted here smooths the transition to the TESLA protocol that follows.

previous packet in the chain, P_{i-1}, which we inductively assume to have already been authenticated, contains a commitment to (i.e. a hash of) a random key K_i. P_i also contains a MAC, calculated with K_i over the rest of the contents of P_i. The key K_i that is necessary to verify this MAC is appended to P_{i+1}.

When P_{i+1} is received, the K_i it contains allows the recipient to verify P_i, while the $h(K_i)$ from P_{i-1} allows the recipient to check that the K_i is indeed the one to which the sender previously committed—otherwise a man-in-the-middle attacker could substitute P_i with his own, including a matching MAC calculated with a new key to be disclosed in a bogus P_{i+1}.

The drawbacks include latency (the sender must be sure that the recipient obtained P_i before sending the P_{i+1} which reveals the MAC key K_i, otherwise an attacker could produce a bogus P_i by altering M_i at will and recomputing a MAC with the revealed key) and the need for the client to catch all messages (as soon as the client misses one message, say P_{j-1}, she misses the commitment to K_j; the chain is interrupted and subsequent messages can no longer be validated).

There is also the bootstrapping problem of having to establish a base for the chain. This could be done with a once-off digital signature if the chain were sufficiently long to amortize its cost.

The combination of those constraints makes Guy Fawkes more suitable for, say, the protection of the frames of a video transmission (where the client is expected to "stay tuned" to the same source for a relatively long time) than for the validation of the readings from our weather station.

6.1.3 TESLA

Other researchers have tried to overcome some of the above limitations. Perrig *et al.* [205] propose a scheme called TESLA (Timed Efficient Stream Loss-tolerant Authentication) which introduces several interesting innovations. The core mechanism is a chain of MACs very similar to Guy Fawkes's. Packet P_i, containing message M_i, is validated by $MAC_{K_i}(M_i)$, also contained in P_i, but can only be verified using K_i, which is revealed in a later packet M_{i+d}. As in Guy Fawkes, there is also a previous commitment to K_i.

Timing is crucial: so long as you receive M_i before M_{i+d} has been sent you can be sure that, if the MAC checks, then you received a genuine packet. There is a trade-off between freshness (you want d to be small, to minimize the delay before a packet can be authenticated) and resistance to network delays (you want d to be large so that you don't have to reject a packet because its authenticator arrived after the deadline), but at least this scheme allows you the freedom to choose the value of d that is most appropriate for your application and network setup. Having $d > 1$ increases throughput compared to the Guy Fawkes case, because it allows you to have more packets in transit. The penalty is the increased delay between reception and authentication of a packet.

Perrig *et al.* go further and equip each packet with several distinct authenticators, released after different delays. So packet M_i will be validated by several different MACs, say three, whose keys will be revealed at $i + d_1$, $i + d_2$ and $i + d_3$ respectively. If you receive M_i promptly, you can authenticate it as soon as the first key reaches you. But if you are experiencing delays, and receive M_i after the first key has been sent, you may still authenticate it as long as it arrives before the *last* key was sent. This redundant scheme provides at the same time fast validation, whenever possible, and tolerance for large network delays. It's no longer a trade-off, it's a trade-up.

As we saw, packet loss was fatal to Guy Fawkes because it broke the chain of commitments. A further improvement allows TESLA to survive this. MAC keys are no longer chosen at random: instead, they come from a reverse hash chain like the one introduced by Lamport [167] and discussed in section 3.4.2. So we have

$$K_i = h(K_{i+1}),$$

with the keys computed in reverse starting from a random value K_n. With this scheme, any key K_j can be validated by any previous known-good key K_i by hashing it $j - i$ times and checking whether the result is K_i. This means that, even if the client loses a packet (or many), the keys found in subsequent packets can still be verified for genuineness.

6.2   Device integrity

6.2.1   The relationship between integrity and authenticity

There is a close relationship between integrity and authenticity. If Alice expects to be talking to Bob, and bad guy Brian tricks Alice into believing that he is Bob, this is a violation of the authenticity of Alice's interlocutor. On the other hand, if bad guy Brian secretly performs brain surgery on Bob (a violation of integrity), Alice will be talking to Bob just as she expects, but this will be a modified Bob who behaves in a different, Brian-induced way. The net result is very similar.

In fact we may imagine a spectrum of brain modifications that Brian could perform on Bob, from a minuscule incision to a complete transplant. At one end of this spectrum Bob would be almost indistinguishable before and after the operation, while at the other he would be a completely different principal. So a violation of the integrity of Bob could, in the most dramatic cases, lead to a change of identity. This gruesome tale makes more sense if we unwind the metaphor and remember that Bob is a computer.

Traditionally, the emphasis is on *network* security (and therefore, as we said, on the confidentiality and integrity *of communications*) rather than on *computer* security, for the good reason that the network is a much weaker link in the chain: it is much easier to attack the network, which is outside your physical control (even more so in the wireless case), than to break into your premises and tamper with the computer on your desk. Still, the computers definitely *are* a link in the chain, and may be attacked. It may be easier to hide in the network cloud and utter messages purporting to be from the computer you know as Bob, but breaking into Bob and altering its software may have the same effect, so much so that the distinction between the two cases becomes somewhat artificial.

6.2.2 Tamper resistance

We said it in section 1.3 and in the introduction to chapter 5 but, the more we explore the issue, the better we can appreciate the subtleties in our own terminology: authentication is a prerequisite for the three security properties of confidentiality (of messages), integrity (of messages) and availability. So is computer security, intended in the narrow sense of ensuring that the Trusted Computing Base behaves as it should. Computer security intended in this narrow sense includes confidentiality (of the secrets inside the device) and integrity (of the device). Armed with this insight we recognize *tamper resistance* as one of the axiomatic bases of security in general: without it, there can be no TCB.

This is relevant in general, but particularly for ubiquitous computing, where nodes (think of the weather stations, or even better of the smart dust mentioned in section 4.3.2) will be left unattended for long periods of time. Unlike the computer on your desk, many ubiquitous computing devices will be very easy for an attacker to pick up, dismantle, subvert and replace in the environment as if nothing had happened. A legitimate node may then end up unknowingly transacting with a maliciously altered one.

It would be nice to be able to invoke the silver bullet of tamper resistance in order to defeat such attacks, but it is much easier to talk about this property than to implement it in practice, especially within the cost and form factor constraints of an embedded processor. Anderson and Kuhn [14] and Kömmerling and Kuhn [161] demonstrate a variety of practical attacks that the typical ubiquitous computing device will probably not be able to withstand unless it adopts an armoured core such as the Dallas iButton [78]—but this may not always be suitable owing to architectural problems such as the limited throughput on the serial link between the iButton and its host.

As we observed in section 3.2, it is impossible to guarantee the integrity of messages that will have to travel over a network under physical control of an adversary. We can protect the messages with codes that will *reveal* whether tampering took

Figure 6.2. The IBM 4758 secure coprocessor.

place, but we cannot prevent tampering from happening. The situation is similar with physical tamper resistance. For a start, it is impossible to stop an adversary from tampering with the device at all: even if we enclose it in a reinforced steel can, it will still be possible for the attacker to flatten it with a sledgehammer. So, when we say that a device is **tamper-proof**, we do not mean that it is impossible to tamper with it, but rather that it is impossible (for an attacker whose resources do not exceed a well-defined threshold) to do so *and thereby* steal its secrets or alter its data. But then, in a parallel with message integrity, we should not underestimate the usefulness of the much cheaper option of making the device merely **tamper-evident**. If the device is made tamper-evident, for example using special seals, the attacker will be able to violate its integrity, but not without leaving a trace of this activity. An analysis of costs and benefits may show this to be, in many cases, a better match for ubiquitous computing than tamper-proofing. (The foodstuff packaging industry reached the same conclusions when, in the late 1980s, Britain's supermarkets were threatened by blackmailers who demanded money in exchange for not dropping poison, or broken glass, in baby food jars. Heitkemper *et al.* [132] report on similar cases in the USA. Most food items now come in tamper-evident, but not tamper-proof, packages.)

It must also be realized that the tampering may not be limited to the onboard code and keys: a very effective attack on the unattended thermometer is simply to replace its analogue sensing element with a bad one. This attack highlights that even enclosing the entire processor, memory and backup battery in a

high-grade tamper resistant enclosure such as that of the IBM 4758 secure coprocessor[6] [233, 137], with only a ribbon connector to interface with the outside world
(figure 6.2), would still leave us vulnerable to direct attacks on its "peripherals".
Bringing the sensor itself within the tamper resistant enclosure may make manufacturing too expensive (the computing and communication core will no longer be a
modular building block) and may in some cases interfere with the proper working
of the sensor. So the transducer may be an Achilles' heel, and it may not be worth
spending large sums on tamper-proofing the core if the sensor cannot economically
be protected[7].

On the other hand, if the sensor and its connection to the core can be protected
with a tamper-evident seal, this inexpensive safeguard has the potential to be more
effective than its expensive cousin. The caveat here is that the integrity of the seal
must be checked manually by human inspection, which is a major liability in the
desired context of "do-nothing technology" where things just happen automatically
as soon as devices are within communications range of each other.

Even if a device is made tamper-evident, one must still watch out for non-
intrusive attacks. Kocher introduced some timing attacks [159] and, with Jaffe
and Jun [158], the technique known as "differential power analysis". Anderson
and Kuhn [15] described various protocol failure and glitch attacks. Anderson and
Bond [18, 45, 46] opened up a new research field by attacking the API complexity
of cryptoprocessor transaction sets (complexity, bugs and security holes often go
hand in hand). Bond, teaming up with Clayton [47], demonstrated the practical
power of such attacks by extracting secret keys out of a 4758 (see section 3.1.3).

In the case of tamper evidence, it is also necessary to take into account the time
that might pass before a broken seal is noticed, and the likelihood of successful
attacks on the sealing mechanism, for which see Johnston and Garcia [145].

We said above that there is no great difference between tampering with Bob's
brain and just pretending to be Bob. In many domains, masquerading attacks can
be effective low tech alternatives to trying to mess with a tamper-proof device. An
ATM is physically as tamper-proof as a safe, but criminals have been known to

---

[6]From the IBM research web site [204]:

> In November 1998, the IBM 4758 became the first device ever to earn a FIPS 140-1 Level 4
> validation—the highest possible rating. This meant:
>
> - The device withstood any physical attack the independent evaluation lab tried.
> - The security of the internal software was validated by mechanical verification of a formal
>   mathematical model.

The device (figure 6.2) costs around 4 k$ and is of similar size to a 3.5″ disk drive.

[7]Having said that, Dallas Semiconductors have just started selling a version of their iButton [78]
which includes a temperature sensor [85, 84]. Whenever it is technically and economically possible
to enclose the sensor inside the tamper-resistant barrier without impairing its operation, this is clearly
the most secure solution.

set up fake cash dispenser machines in order to harvest PINs [8]. This is a "social engineering" instance of masquerading, where the similarity between the copy and the original need only be sufficient to fool the casual user. But protocol-level masquerading is also possible: any device that is not tamper-proof, and whose secrets can therefore be read out in their entirety, is subject to cloning, which brings us back to the unsolved problem of guaranteeing integrity in a "do-nothing technology" context.

The same tamper-evidence technology that makes tampering detectable can be used to guard against cloning. The seal must be impossible to reproduce[8], or one could destructively remove the original seal, tamper with the device and then stick on a new identical seal as a replacement; but if the seal cannot be reproduced, then this also prevents the manufacturing of identical clones. However one can detect that the clone is bogus only by inspecting the seal, which is a physical world operation that cannot be performed automatically at the level of the communications protocol.

6.2.3 Trusted path

Another closely related issue is usually referred to as **trusted path**. When your computer displays a login prompt, there is always a chance of it being the output of a malicious application attempting to steal your password. A "trusted path" between the user and the operating system is needed, such as Windows NT's CTRL-ALT-DEL key chord, to reassure the user that she is talking to a dialog box produced by the OS. As long as one can believe the integrity of the hardware and software foundation upon which the trusted path facility is built, the trusted path ensures that one is invoking the intended function and not a simulation of it.

It is of course possible to defeat such a mechanism by acting at a sufficiently low level: no NT application could, because CTRL-ALT-DEL would bypass it; but an application written for another operating system, for example DOS, could. This is why the "secure attention" key chord was chosen to be CTRL-ALT-DEL: because in DOS this key combination reboots the machine. With any other choice, say CTRL-F1, it would have been trivial to write an NT password harvester in DOS by displaying an NT-like screen whenever the user pressed CTRL-F1; but with CTRL-ALT-DEL, the application doesn't get the keystroke at all because DOS reboots first. It is still possible to capture the appropriate interrupt and trap CTRL-ALT-DEL, but the number of mischievous teenagers skilled in the art probably goes down by an order of magnitude or two[9].

---

[8]Within the resources of the attacker against which we are trying to guard.

[9]Meagre consolation, though: as soon as one of them proudly posts an executable demonstrating his exploit to the appropriate underground web site, all the less capable "script kiddies" will be able to apply it without even having to understand how it works.

The moral of the story is that CTRL-ALT-DEL is the trusted path only if you can be sure that NT is running on that machine: if people can reinstall the OS (because they can boot from floppy or CD, or because they can take out the hard disk and substitute it with another, or whatever) then all bets are off. So you can't have a trusted path if the physical integrity of the device is not guaranteed to some extent. Note however that the Resurrecting Duckling policy of section 4.2 includes an element of tamper resistance in its Assassination principle, so if your computer is Duckling-compliant then it will not be feasible for your[10] attacker to reinstall the OS. In that case you can safely assume that CTRL-ALT-DEL takes you to a login prompt produced by NT.

A trusted path for output (as opposed to input) is also equally important: if your screen displays a request to sign a document, you want to be sure that you are signing what is being displayed and not a statement such as "I hereby pay lots of money to the attacker" surreptitiously substituted by some malicious software after the genuine application displayed the innocent plaintext.

---

[10]Usual caveat: this means "the kind of attacker against which you have chosen to defend yourself", which defines the strength of the tamper-resistance implied by the Assassination principle.

Chapter 7

Availability

Traditionally, availability has been the security property that received the least attention from the scientific and academic community, which focused primarily on confidentiality and the associated cryptographic detail. In the commercial context, though, it is often the one of greatest relevance. This is reflected in the amount of money that businesses are willing to spend on the various facets of their IT operation: substantially more goes into backups, redundant servers, uninterruptible power supplies and on-site maintenance contracts than in line encryptors, tamper resistant key modules or secure coprocessors.

In ubiquitous computing, too, availability is likely to be of primary importance. Computers are notorious for being unreliable compared to almost any other household or office appliance. Ubiquitous computing only stands a chance of taking off if these widely deployed computing gadgets are, and are perceived to be, as dependable as doorknobs, light switches and television sets.

This chapter develops two main themes. Firstly, we examine the denial of service threat faced by a server that can be queried by unknown clients. Along with the classical attacks on the availability of the channel, a novel threat for ubiquitous computing is the *sleep deprivation torture*, where the server is kept awake until its battery dies. The discussion of denial of service attacks on the communications channel and related safeguards owes much to an interesting dinner-time discussion with Pekka Nikander, Tim Kindberg and Kan Zhang at HUC2k[1].

The second theme of this chapter is the development of a simple hardware primitive, the Grenade Timer, which protects a system from service denial attacks staged by malicious mobile code. The grenade timer is unnecessary for processors with a protected mode, but it is a cost-effective protection for the simple microcontrollers that are common in embedded systems.

---

[1]The second international workshop on Handheld and Ubiquitous Computing, Bristol, UK, 2000-09-25 to 2000-09-27.

7.1 Threats to the communications channel

For any system that relies on wireless communications, there is always the risk of a denial of service attack in which the communications channel is made unusable by an attacker who transmits noise on purpose.

7.1.1 Redefining "denial of service"

It is interesting to note that this case does not quite match the definition of denial of service that appears in Gligor's seminal paper [118, 119]. In Gligor's characterization, denial of service is a threat whose perpetrator, whether malicious or accidental, is necessarily an insider, that is to say a user who is authorized to access the system. The reasoning behind this is that outsiders are stopped by the standard access control mechanisms of the system and therefore have no opportunity to deny service to legitimate users. In his model, denial of service is the outcome of a competition among legitimate users for a scarce resource offered by the system, and is a consequence of inadequate insulation between users ("interuser dependency"). In our case, instead, the principal who jams the channel is not a legitimate user of the system; yet there is little doubt that she is denying service to the other users.

One may view the situation in a slightly different light by taking the entire radio spectrum (instead of one specific wireless network of communicating computers) to be "the system"; then, the users of "the system" are all the entities within range that have a radio interface, and we almost fall back into Gligor's model: one user of the system denies service to some of the others. But there is still one remaining subtlety to do with the definition of "authorized" users, which we might logically assume to mean users whose radio equipment has been approved by the FCC or some equivalent organization. In this case we are once again outside Gligor's model, because the attacker who jams the channel may well operate an illegally powerful radio set, or even an EMP (electro-magnetic pulse), to do so.

It appears reasonable to extend the definition of denial of service to include this more general case. The justification is that Gligor was speaking of denial of service *in operating systems* where, unless the access control subsystem is defective, unauthorized users do not have access to the system. Here, instead, there is no access control subsystem that can stop unauthorized users from accessing the physical channel. If we take the view that "authorized" means "with an FCC licence", then the authorization system can only work *a posteriori*, taking offenders to court, but not *a priori*, preventing them from misbehaving in the first place.

We shall now examine what sort of safeguards can be adopted as protection against this type of denial of service. The problem is not specific to ad hoc networking: in fact it manifests itself in any context where wireless communications are employed, and has been studied extensively in the context of electronic warfare, as reported by Schleher [226].

7.1.2 Covert communication techniques

We have no hope of surviving jamming when the adversary is all-powerful and can make the entire spectrum unusable over the spatio-temporal range of interest to us. What we may be able to do is to drive up the cost of jamming, making it much more costly for the attacker to impede communication than for legitimate nodes to conduct it.

Two widely used techniques are *frequency hopping* and *direct sequence spread spectrum*. In frequency hopping, the raw physical transmission occupies a bandwidth ΔW; the system, however, uses n such slots, for a total bandwidth occupation of $n\Delta W$. At regular time intervals of Δt, the transmitter switches to another bandwidth slot, chosen among the n available ones by means of an unguessable pseudorandom sequence produced by a keystream generator of the type used in stream ciphers (see section 3.1.5). The receiver must follow the same sequence of hops in synchrony in order to listen to the transmitter. There are arrangements for moving to the next slot when the designated one is already occupied (or too noisy, which amounts to the same thing in practice). An attacker wishing to jam the channel must either discover the hopping sequence or jam a sufficient number of slots, therefore employing much more power than the transmitter. The ratio between the power required for transmitting and that required for jamming is called the *process gain*.

Spread spectrum works in a more complicated way (the signal is multiplied by a high frequency pseudorandom sequence and is recovered by correlation with that same sequence) but the precise details of the technique are in fact irrelevant to our discussion. All that counts is that, as in frequency hopping, you will only know where the signal is if you know the pseudorandom sequence used by the transmitter. If you don't know the sequence, you will be forced to jam a much wider bandwidth in order to make the signal unintelligible.

It should be clear that this protection is conditional on transmitter and receiver having previously established some shared key material to be used to seed the keystream generator. If communication occurs between principals that know each other and is preceded by authentication, then a shared key will generally be established during that step, in which case the problem is solved.

7.1.3 Speaking to unknowns

In many cases of interest, however, it is necessary to speak to unknown principals, the typical case being that of public access servers. It is easy to imagine a protocol whereby an unknown client contacts the server, securely establishes a shared key with it (for example using Diffie-Hellman [90]) and proceeds to communicate with it under the protection of frequency hopping or spread spectrum, safe from jamming attacks by third parties.

But does this buy us very much? The bad guy is still free to run the above protocol with the server an arbitrary number of times, always pretending to be a new unknown client. He will not be able to jam any communications that previous clients have already established with the server, but he may make it impossible for any new clients to join—as well as tying up valuable resources on the server.

This particular problem is not limited to wireless communications: it occurs whenever a publicly accessible server is made available to unknown clients. In such cases, some may suggest identifying the source of the time-wasting connections and blacklist it. But this solution has several problems. First, it may not be trivial to decide whether a frequent user of the system should be seen as a friendly enthusiast or a malicious attacker (but then an anti-congestion policy might not care to differentiate). Second, to establish that any principal is a frequent user, the server is forced to devote storage to logging information and this itself may give rise to other service denial attacks. Third, a determined and resourceful attacker will mount her denial of service attack through multiple paths—as happened in early 2000 with distributed denial of service attacks to popular web sites [60].

7.1.4   Plutocratic access control

A much better solution is what I like to call **plutocratic access control**: users must pay to get in. This has the double advantage of dissuading overenthusiastic clients *and* compensating the server for any extra work. A notable case of adoption of this strategy occurred in the 1990s, when a charge of 70 $ per 2 years was introduced for the registration of an Internet domain name—a service that used to be free[2]. By introducing a non-uniform charge structure, where using the service costs more the busier the service is, a feedback mechanism can be established to keep usage at an optimal level (microeconomics, systems theory and control theory provide the mathematical tools to tune the parameters of the system in order to achieve stability). This is what is commonly done in such diverse systems as telephone networks, cinema theatres and airlines—more statically for phones, more dynamically for airlines.

MojoNation [28] plans on doing something similar on the net: users would earn "Mojo" (the system's currency) by offering resources to the system, such as

---

[2]The charge is sufficiently small to be well within the range of private individuals, but also sufficiently non-negligible to work as a deterrent against abuse. It wasn't, however, enough to stop the eccentric entrepreneur/speculator Nichi Grauso from registering half a million domain names corresponding to dictionary words and surnames (including mine) in a grandiose cybersquatting operation costing around 30 M$ [194]. By the way, cybersquatting is of course a form of denial of service.

the spare CPU cycles of their computers; and they would be charged Mojo for using resources made available by others.

An interesting observation is that "*pecunia non olet*" ("money has no smell", the famously cynical reply by Roman emperor Vespasian, who introduced public urinals, to his subordinates' comment about the stinginess and indignity of charging for their use). As long as they all pay, the profit-minded server has no reason whatsoever to care who the clients are. Even if they access the server as part of an attack on its availability, the server receives the same money whether it is from the attackers or from the innocent clients; and if they saturate its capacity, it only means that the server has just made as much money as it possibly could. One could develop this argument to point out that e-commerce outlets can be successful without insisting on tracking their customers using loyalty cards, cookies and other related identifiers. But let's not stray off course.

Where collecting payment from the clients is too costly or cumbersome, the same feedback mechanism can still be established by making users "pay to charity". The advantage of remuneration is lost, but that of congestion control is maintained. Perhaps the metaphor should be "sacrificially burning banknotes" rather than "paying to charity", since the server doesn't actually care whether the money goes to a good cause or not; the only thing of interest to the server is that the client pay a penalty of some sort for accessing the service. This discourages the indiscriminate and greedy behaviour observed in the clients when a resource is available for free. In our case the pricing structure will be set so as to make it uneconomical for an attacker to deny access to other clients by buying all the available slots. (This will still be ineffective against an infinitely rich and/or foolhardy attacker like Grauso.)

Mark Lomas suggested[3] a fairer variant of plutocratic access control: instead of forcing all clients to pay or burn money, the server asks them to send cheques as guarantees, with the understanding that they will be cashed if the client misbehaves, but destroyed if the client was honest. A similar concept is presented by Reichenbach *et al.* [216] in the context of what they call "multilateral security" (balancing the different security requirements of the parties involved in a transaction). To avoid, for example, the nuisance of spam, your system will automatically refuse email from unknown parties unless it comes with a payment, with the semantics of "If you think this mail was a waste of your time, you may keep this money".

7.1.5 Cryptographic puzzles

One way to force the users to pay a penalty was introduced by Juels and Brainard [147] and further refined in the context of authentication by Aura, Nikander and

---

[3] At a meeting of the Cambridge security group held on 2000-10-06.

Leiwo [27]. The technique is known as the cryptographic puzzle. The server thinks of a random nonce[4] N, generates its image y through a hash h, as in $y = h(N)$, hands out y to the client and refuses to speak to the client again until she can produce the preimage N by brute force. Of course the client should not be able to do this at all if h is a proper one-way function; to account for this, the server actually sends a hint together with y, consisting for example of the first k bits of N. The choice of k will be tuned to the computational capabilities of the typical client.

The server should be careful to guard against the situation in which the malicious client does not even try to compute the correct preimage of y and simply bombards the server with random guesses whose only purpose is to consume time and computing cycles on the server for the verification. A neat solution is to use N as the key to the keystream generator that will produce the appropriate pseudo-random sequence for frequency hopping or spread spectrum. This way, if the client does not have the correct N, she cannot even speak to the server, who therefore will waste no time verifying bogus answers.

The weak point of this solution is the bootstrapping phase. The server needs to be able to broadcast its challenges to potential clients. For clients to have a chance to pick them up before having established any secret with the server, these challenges must be available in a "well-known" place in the radio spectrum, which is to say transmitted in a static frequency slot or spread using a published sequence. An attacker may then deny service at low cost by jamming this necessarily overt and unprotected channel, without which none of the covert channels may be used.

We have not yet found an elegant safeguard against this. In engineering terms, what the server can do is to devote substantial power to the transmission of the challenges compared to that employed for the covert communications protected by secret sequences. This way, the bootstrapping phase is protected using brute force, while the actual communications are protected by the process gain of the hiding technique. Since a chain is always as weak as its weakest link, it will probably make sense to tune the system parameters so that the power required for jamming is approximately the same in both cases.

7.2   Threats to the battery energy

7.2.1   Peanut devices have limited energy

Quantitative decisions should take into account not only power (which accounts for the size and rating of the transmitter) but also its integral, i.e. energy (which accounts for the attacker's electricity bill). Otherwise, if the transmission of the

---

[4]See footnote 3 on page 176.

challenge takes milliseconds while the protected communication that derives from it goes on for several minutes, there is again an asymmetry that the attacker will exploit in order to deny service at the lowest possible cost.

This observation leads us neatly to another service denial threat which is novel and specific to ubiquitous computing: battery exhaustion, first mentioned in a paper I wrote with Ross Anderson [240].

Often, speaking of "server" conjures up an image of a large and powerful computer. In computer manufacturers' catalogues, the servers are usually the machines with the largest case, the fastest processor, the biggest disk and the highest price tag, while the clients are the tiny and inexpensive desktop machines[5]. In the context of ubiquitous computing, however, devices are often handheld, embedded, wireless, miniaturized and, by implication, battery powered[6]. Size and weight constraints on the device translate directly into constraints on the battery (which often ends up consuming a substantial portion of the total weight budget) which in turn severely limit the total amount of energy available to the device. In 2000, realistic figures for the energy consumption of a CPU + memory + transceiver multichip circuit and for the energy capacity of a typical cell imply a lifetime of the order of only a few days (if that) if the circuit were operated continuously. This is clearly unacceptable to the user, especially if we take into account the ubiquity, meaning that every week hundreds of devices around the home and office would require a battery replacement or a recharge.

We encountered this problem early on at ORL in the late 1980s, in the context of our Active Badge project (see section 2.5.1). Hundreds of badges are deployed at our site, each powered by two coin cells, and great pains were taken by the designers to manage power consumption so as to make those batteries last for as long as possible—the penalty being the maintenance workload of periodically having to unscrew the case, throw away the old batteries, put in the new ones, screw the case back together and test the gadget, for every single one of them. Having to do this every six months is a chore, but not as much as it would be if the interval

---

[5]It is ironic to note that, etymologically, the server is the "servant", the "assistant", the one "who serves or ministers to the requirements of another" (*OED* [203]); and therefore the client, or customer (who "is king"), or master, should logically be the more important of the two.

[6]For those who do not believe the validity of the implication: I once suggested to my AT&T colleague Alan Jones that we investigate powering small gadgets using kinetic generators such as those that automatically recharge the batteries of electronic wristwatches as their owners move about. His insightful reply was that the minuscule power output of the kinetic generator is insufficient for anything more complex than a wristwatch, and if we could reduce the power consumption of our devices to wristwatch levels, then battery exhaustion would no longer be a concern, given that regular wristwatches now run for years on a single cell. (Indeed, at the cheap end of the spectrum, the lifetime of the cell nowadays often exceeds that of the watch—in particular that of the plastic strap, whose replacement tends to cost as much as a new watch.)

were one week. The badge spends most of its time asleep, waking up only to beacon its identity every 15 seconds. A light sensor lengthens this period if it detects
darkness, with the effect that the badge is automatically switched off if left in a
drawer or face down on a desk. (With an on-off switch, it would have been easy to
forget to switch the badge back on when picking it up again the next day.)

We since had to deal with the same problem again with the Active Bat (section
2.5.3) that replaced the badge, and with PEN (section 2.5.5), our experimental platform for ubiquitous ad hoc wireless networking. Power saving is a prime concern
in PEN: the nodes are designed so that inactive subsystems (for example the radio)
can be switched off whenever possible and the communications protocols introduce
a rendezvous concept to allow nodes to get in touch with each other despite being
asleep most of the time [114]. As we said (see footnote 5 on page 111), using an
asynchronous design Leask [169] even managed to stop the processor during the
idle time between the individual bytes of a received packet.

At any rate, independently of any of the AT&T Laboratories projects with
which I am especially familiar, any design for battery powered devices will have
among its primary goals that of keeping the unit in deep sleep for the greatest possible proportion of its duty cycle.

All this is to say that, in the ubiquitous computing environment, a server may
actually be, contrary to popular iconography, a tiny machine with very limited resources. It may often consist of little more than a sensor with minimal processing
and communication facilities—think for example of the Berkeley Smart Dust [150]
we mentioned in section 4.3.2.

In this environment, energy exhaustion threats are a serious danger, and are
much more damaging than better known denial of service threats such as CPU
exhaustion or channel jamming; once the battery runs out the attacker can stop and
walk away, leaving the victim disabled. I call this new attack the **sleep deprivation
torture**. Like the ill-fated prisoners of war on whom this cruel treatment was first
inflicted, our gadgets can't survive for long without sleep.

7.2.2   Resource reservation

A very general safeguard against denial of service is resource reservation. Some
share of the server's resource is reserved for known legitimate users, who get a certain guarantee of availability; the rest is allocated to serve unknown users, without
making any promises. With this strategy, unknown users cannot deny service to
known ones. Going back to Gligor's original model, it is still possible for one legitimate user to deny service to another, but the same strategy applied to a finer grain
(reserve a fixed share of the resource for each of the legitimate users) can once
again come to the rescue. The price to pay is the inefficient use of the resource:

for each user who does not consume his entire allocation, there is a slack that is unconditionally wasted. As a consequence, the resource is underutilized and needs to be overdimensioned. This is almost always too expensive. It would amount to building a telephone system capable of handling the situation where all subscribers use their phone at the same time, despite the fact that in a steady state condition the network typically carries a few orders of magnitude less traffic.

What is usually done instead is to dimension the system to handle the steady state traffic of requests plus a little margin, accepting the possibility of congestion in exceptional circumstances whose relative incidence is part of the specification of the system. Airlines, for example, are notorious for their practice of "overbooking" (selling more seats than are available on the aeroplane in order not to waste the spare capacity left over by customers who decide at the last moment not to turn up), which shows that filling the plane is worth more to them than the bad publicity and compensation claims from the unlucky passengers who are occasionally denied boarding.

A useful way to regulate this practice is a quota facility, such as that present in the UNIX file system. Each legitimate user is allocated a fixed fraction of the shared resource (this fraction need not be the same for all users), but the sum of all the fractions merrily exceeds 100%[7]. This means that, if every user were to claim the portion of resource to which she is entitled, congestion and service denial would occur; at the same time, though, under average load no single user will be able to deny service to others if the parameters are chosen so that no individual quota approaches the safety margin (i.e. the difference between maximum capacity and average load). I used a similar arrangement in my SMS server [241].

Hard resource reservation (i.e. without overbooking) at coarse granularity can be used as a safeguard against the sleep deprivation torture in the following way. If the server has a primary function (such as sending the outside temperature to the meteorological office every hour) and a distinct auxiliary function (such as sending the current temperature to anyone who requests it) then these functions can be prioritized. The reservation mechanism can ensure that the higher priority use receives a guaranteed share of the battery energy regardless of the number of requests generated by the lower priority uses. Even just turning on the receiver to listen to unexpected messages may become a rationed activity.

The highest priority use of all may be battery management: if one can accurately estimate the amount of usable energy remaining, then the service can be monitored and managed—provided that the process does not itself consume too much of the resource it is intended to conserve.

---

[7]We may distinguish between hard and soft resource reservation according to whether the sum of the allocated shares is below or above unity. Only hard resource reservation gives absolute guarantees against denial of service.

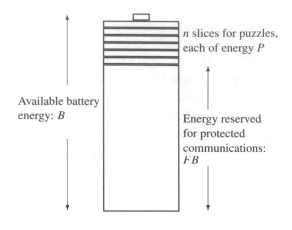

Figure 7.1. The energy budget.

This strategy may be combined with the one previously developed for the protection of the communications channel in the following way[8] (see figure 7.1). The server places a hard reservation on a fraction $F < 100\%$ of its available[9] battery energy B and devotes that to communication protected by a secret keystream (using frequency hopping, spread spectrum or whatever). The remaining $(100\% - F)B$ energy is divided by P, the energy required to broadcast one puzzle, to yield n, the number of puzzles that can be issued:

$$n = \left\lfloor \frac{(100\% - F)B}{P} \right\rfloor .$$

The server may now evenly space its puzzle broadcasts over its desired lifetime L: the time slot for each puzzle will have a duration of $S \triangleq \frac{L}{n}$ (see figure 7.2). The energy available for protected communications, $F \cdot B$, may be managed using a soft resource reservation mechanism, such as the quota system mentioned above, perhaps with an additional adaptive element, to share it fairly but efficiently among the clients who might solve some of the proposed puzzles. This system ensures that the server will always be contactable at regular intervals over its planned lifetime, independently of the amount of activity of its clients.

There are a number of implementation details that require attention. For example we implicitly assumed that the server can listen on several different

---

[8]The discussion that follows is very qualitative, and the simple formulæ presented here are meant as a clarification of the explanation rather than as an aid to computing numerical values. However, on second reading it felt as though the abundance of new symbols introduced more confusion than clarity. A legend is provided in table 7.1 on page 144.

[9]We assume either that the processing and resource management costs are negligible, or that they have already been estimated and deducted from the available energy budget.

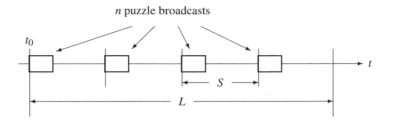

Figure 7.2. Time line for puzzle broadcasts.

"subchannels" (as defined by their respective keystream sequences) at once, but this is typically not possible for the cheaper receivers. We may accommodate this problem by dividing the time available for protected communication into slots, for example at puzzle broadcast boundaries, and by ruling that solving one puzzle grants the right to communicate to the server in the kth slot after the current one.

Note that setting $k = 0$, meaning that solving puzzle i gives a client the right to speak to the server from the moment in which challenge i is issued until the moment in which challenge $i + 1$ is issued, may be wasteful of bandwidth: since solving the puzzle is meant to take a nontrivial amount of computation (and therefore time), it will be impossible for any client to make use of the initial portion of the allocated time interval. In fact, depending on the parameters of the system, if the time T taken by a standard client to solve the puzzle is typically longer than the duration S of one time slot, it will be impossible to communicate at all. Obviously, k must be chosen to satisfy the constraint $k \cdot S \geq T$. Greater values of k will correspond to lesser demands on the computational capabilities of the clients, but also to greater communications latency.

In practice there are good reasons for setting k to a high value despite the latency this introduces. Given that the purpose of the puzzle is to make denial of service more expensive, it may be *desirable* to make the time to solve the puzzle several times (say, w times) longer than the duration of the slot for protected communications: $T = w \cdot S$. This will mean that, even if the attacker solves puzzles continuously and jams every subchannel it discovers, it will only be able to affect $1/w$ of them, assuming its computational power is comparable to that of the standard client[10].

Another detail is that, even in the case of a sophisticated server capable of listening on several subchannels at once, it will be desirable to reintroduce time slots anyway to limit the validity of the solution to any given puzzle. The contract

---

[10]Alternatively, we may view the situation as requiring the attacker to be w times more computationally powerful than the standard client in order to be able to jam all subchannels.

	Type	Description
B	energy	Amount of battery energy available to the server for communications (i.e. net of any other activities such as computation or power management).
F	dimensionless	Fraction of the available battery energy reserved for *protected* communications.
k	dimensionless	Number of protected transmission time slots to be skipped before finding the one corresponding to the current puzzle.
K	crypto key	What you get by solving the puzzle. Can be used to generate a pseudo-random scrambling sequence that will define a subchannel.
L	time	Lifetime. We wish the battery to last for at least as long as this.
n	dimensionless	Number of puzzles that the server will issue given the available energy.
P	energy	Amount of server energy required to broadcast one puzzle.
S	time	Slot duration, i.e. time between broadcasts of new puzzles.
T	time	Average time required for a "standard client" to solve one puzzle.
t_0	time	Instant at which the server broadcasts the first puzzle (or, to put it another way, starts using its battery).
t_1	time	Instant from which the server will start listening on the subchannel defined by the solution to the current puzzle.
t_2	time	Instant until which the server will listen on the subchannel defined by the solution to the current puzzle.
w	dimensionless	Workload factor. Ratio between the time it takes to solve a puzzle and the time between two successive broadcasts of puzzle challenges.

Table 7.1. Cheat sheet.

implied by the puzzle will not be

> solving this puzzle will give you a key K from which you may derive a sequence that defines a channel on which I will be listening for you indefinitely

but rather

> solving this puzzle will give you a key K from which you may derive a sequence that defines a channel on which I will be listening for you from time t_1 to time t_2; if you have not contacted me by t_2, tough.

Without doing this, the server should be prepared to commit sufficient resources to each subchannel to be able to listen on it from the time of the broadcast of the corresponding puzzle to time $+\infty$ (which in practical terms means $t_0 + L$, i.e. the time when its battery is meant to run down).

Yet another practical detail concerns the arbitration of collisions between clients who have solved the same puzzle and are trying to contact the server on the same subchannel. At first sight, this is perfectly analogous to the case of collisions on a computer network using a shared physical medium, such as Ethernet, and might be addressed with similar mechanisms involving collision detection and randomized backoff from an exponential distribution. The difference here is that at each new attempt the client needs to pay the penalty of solving a new puzzle; moreover, with the overheads mentioned above, the total latency may become unacceptable.

But these are the wrong concerns. The classical collision resolution algorithms adopted in computer networks assume *cooperating users* who will back off for the prescribed time in order to avoid a new collision; while here, where by hypothesis we are dealing with malicious clients whose purpose is to deny service to their peers, we must assume that those clients will purposefully behave in the most disruptive way possible. The rule for exponential backoff becomes futile, since it will be ignored precisely by those principals most likely to be involved in collisions.

Our only safeguard here is the puzzle itself. An attacker will solve all the puzzles it can and transmit on the corresponding subchannels to generate collisions that impede others from communicating with the server. We cannot stop this. All we can do is to make this activity expensive in terms of both time and energy.

7.3   Threats from mobile code

Mobile code is now an established development in distributed systems, and is already part of the deployed Internet infrastructure in so far as most desktop browsers run Java. Cellular telephones have already become miniature web browsers and it will not take long for vendors to want to push new functionality into their customers' phones or even SIM cards, much like web sites nowadays do with Java applets and ActiveX controls. More advanced uses of mobile code have been envisaged in the form of itinerant agents [67].

It seems plausible to expect that ubiquitous computing and mobile code will eventually intersect, with small pieces of code roaming around from one device to another in our environment. There will be many uses for such an arrangement, of which automatic firmware updates, configuration management, resource discovery and personalization will probably be seen as the least imaginative. However useful the application, though, mobile code will ultimately be unacceptable in the marketplace without proper system-level safeguards; otherwise its introduction will dramatically decrease reliability and, ultimately, personal safety. Interesting though it may be to have a fridge capable of reordering food over the Internet when it finds itself empty, the conventional fridge may still be preferable if the computationally endowed one is vulnerable to viruses that randomly defrost it or turn it off, spoiling its contents in the process[11].

To protect the host system from untrusted mobile code, one should first explicitly identify the security properties to be safeguarded. Farmer *et al.* [105] offer an excellent taxonomy of the security issues for mobile agents, but place the emphasis on the more difficult problems of protecting the agent, compared to which the protection of the host is easy. So does Ordille [202], who examines trust as the agent roams along a path not determined in advance. In our case, though, the most pressing concern is simply to avoid denial of service attacks. In particular, we wish to be able to limit the amount of processor time that the guest program will consume.

This is especially important for devices that integrate several functions. Anderson and Bezuidenhoudt's practical experience with frauds against digital prepaid electricity meters [19] suggests the following insight. If you imagine a multifunction meter containing not only the system software from the electricity company but also some code from the user's bank which takes care of reloading the meter with money when necessary, you will see that the electricity company needs to be sure that the banking program cannot take over control of the processor. Otherwise, if a poorly (or maliciously) written banking application got stuck in an endless loop, the meter would no longer be able to turn off the power once the available credit balance were exhausted.

7.3.1   The watchdog timer

The most general mechanism for limiting the resources consumed by mobile code is probably a processor with a protected mode facility, on which the operating system can implement pre-emptive multitasking. The guest program is run in real mode and, when its allotted time expires, it is stopped by the operating system running in protected mode. Address protection also prevents the guest program from reading or writing memory outside its allotted segment, thereby addressing first-order confidentiality and integrity concerns[12].

Where the hardware does not provide a protected mode facility, running mobile code safely is more difficult. Emulating protected mode in software is not a viable option, since checking the legitimacy of every instruction being run leads to unacceptable performance. Static verification before execution, as in Java, requires that the language in which the program is expressed be suitably restricted (but this is not unreasonable for mobile code, if only for portability reasons); however, since the

---

[11]Let us not forget that viruses were the earliest and arguably still the most widespread instances of mobile code.

[12]Second-order problems are still possible, such as violations of confidentiality through the exploitation of covert channels, but we won't go into details here.

halting problem is undecidable, static verification cannot in the general case establish whether a given program might exceed an assigned running time. Accepting only object code that was previously checked and signed by some trusted authority, as happens in the ActiveX architecture, may be appropriate in some circumstances but gives fewer guarantees on the actual behaviour of the code, while at the same time imposing more serious centralized restrictions and/or vulnerabilities[13].

Practically all modern microprocessors offer a protected mode, so the discussion about alternatives may at first appear to have only historical interest. However we should not underestimate the fact that, at the scale of deployment envisaged for the ubiquitous computing scenario, one of the primary operational directives will be "low cost", and that a sub-dollar difference in the cost of the processor may make the difference between success and failure in the marketplace. Besides, embedded applications tend to use single chip microcontrollers, for which the availability of a protected mode (with the associated complications in the memory management architecture) is still much less common than for microprocessors for desktop systems.

Another observation is that a server based on the latest microprocessor and preemptive multitasking OS is such a complex system that people are now forced to look with suspicion at claims of availability guarantees based on the properties of its kernel. It is not uncommon for builders of mission critical systems that must run 24×7 to adopt a "belt and braces" attitude and supplement those kernel guarantees with a hardware *watchdog timer*.

The concept of a watchdog timer is powerful yet deceptively simple. The timer is basically a counter that is decremented at every clock tick and that will reset the processor when it reaches zero. It is used to ensure that a software crash will not hang an unattended machine. The software must periodically prove to be working by reloading the counter; if it fails to do that for too long, the watchdog will eventually reboot the system[14].

The watchdog timer was originally developed for high reliability embedded systems such as those used for industrial process control. The rationale was that EMI and electrical surges in a noisy environment could flip bits of the memory at random and therefore cause the execution of meaningless code. Commercial implementations are available either as an external chip or as integrated in the microcontroller [81, 82, 83]. But watchdog timers are now also used in PC-based servers; they are available as PC expansion cards [32, 138] (sometimes they are even included on the motherboard) and are supported by several BIOS manufacturers [142, 212].

---

[13]Not to mention that all bets are off if the user, who can't stand all the silly and incomprehensible security questions, chooses to run the guest code anyway despite the absence of a valid signature.

[14]Sadly, though, cases have been witnessed where crashed code is stuck in an endless loop from which it keeps reloading the timer. You can't beat Murphy.

7.3.2   The grenade timer

The watchdog timer, however, despite its usefulness for controlling a program that might accidentally run astray, cannot protect the system against a malicious program that purposefully tries to keep the processor to itself. The operating system could tell the guest program "I am about to execute you, and I will grant you up to 20 million clock cycles; if you have not returned control to me by then, you will be terminated". But if by hypothesis we use a processor where all code runs in real mode, the above is pointless: without the distinction between real mode and protected mode, if the operating system can load the counter with the value "20 million cycles", then so can the guest program, which is therefore free to extend its own lifetime indefinitely.

Ross Anderson and I were thinking about this problem in the context of providing a restricted execution facility for mobile code that might run on the PEN hardware node developed at AT&T Laboratories Cambridge [146]; this portable short-range wireless system uses the TMP93PS40 16-bit microcontroller from Toshiba (based on the TLCS-900/L processor) which, like most other microcontrollers, does not offer a protected mode.

Inspired by the watchdog timer concept, we came up with a construction that solves the above problem. We call it the *grenade timer*. It allows a system without protected mode to limit the execution time of a guest program.

The novel idea is to build a counter that cannot be reloaded once it is running. An egg-timer set to count downwards for five minutes can easily be stopped or wound back at any time during its countdown; however, a hand grenade whose fuse has been lit will definitely explode after the set number of seconds, even if you put the pin back in. We want our counter to be like a grenade: once the operating system has pulled out the pin and tossed the fizzing grenade to the guest process, no authority in the world (not even the operating system itself) must be able to postpone the scheduled explosion.

We may however provide an escape mechanism that makes the explosion happen immediately: this is equivalent to firing a bullet into the fizzing grenade to make it blow up prematurely. This is a useful thing to do when a well-behaved guest program wants to return control to the operating system before having consumed its entire quota of allocated cycles.

We complete the metaphor by explicitly saying that the operating system wears thick armour that protects it from explosions: when the grenade goes off (which corresponds to the processor being reset), the guest process dies, but the operating system is unharmed.

This simple construction adds a "poor man's protected mode" to the processor: as long as the grenade is fizzing, the system is in real mode and the executing process can't escape the fact that it will have to relinquish control when the grenade goes off[15]. When the grenade is not fizzing, the running process is by definition in protected mode, because it has the power to set the delay and pull the pin to start the countdown if and when it wishes.

It may be instructive to compare the relationship between the watchdog timer and the grenade timer with that, examined in section 3.2.2, between the CRC (cyclic redundancy check) and the cryptographically strong one-way hash: the CRC only resists random errors, while the hash (which is more expensive to compute) also resists malicious attacks. The CRC is designed to detect random bit errors such as those due to telecommunication noise; but an attacker may flip unimportant bits in a forged message until it yields the desired CRC, therefore making the forgery undetectable. The hash, however, is designed to stop just that, and makes it computationally infeasible to generate a message with a given hash output. The situation is somewhat similar with our timers. The watchdog timer is designed to interrupt programs that might accidentally lock up, but is insufficient to stop programs that actively try to circumvent it. The grenade timer, instead, explicitly addresses the case of malicious attacks. Mathematically-inclined readers might informally summarize this state of affairs with a proportion—the grenade is to the watchdog what the hash is to the CRC:

$$\text{grenade} : \text{watchdog} = \text{hash} : \text{CRC}.$$

At the circuit diagram level, the external interface of the grenade coprocessor as described so far (which contains little more than a counter) is as follows, and is illustrated in figure 7.3.

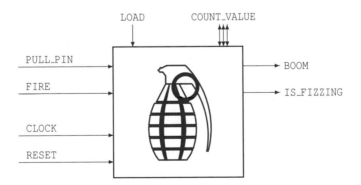

Figure 7.3. External interface of the grenade timer.

---

[15]The position to which the processor jumps on reset will always run in protected mode and therefore needs to be safeguarded from unauthorized changes, otherwise the guest program could substitute itself to the operating system code and bypass any protection. See section 7.3.3.

The RESET input brings the device in a known initial state: it is a necessary system-level facility outside the control of the main processor and we shall not consider it any further here.

The device[16] is in real mode when IS_FIZZING is 1 and in protected mode otherwise. The LOAD input and the COUNT_VALUE data bus may be used to load a new counter value, but only in protected mode, i.e. when IS_FIZZING = 0.

The PULL_PIN input only works from protected mode. When raised, it causes the device to start counting down from the currently loaded count value; IS_FIZZING goes to 1 as the count starts.

When the counter reaches 0, the BOOM output (to be connected to the main processor's RESET line) goes to 1 for one clock cycle and IS_FIZZING comes back to 0.

The FIRE input only works[17] while IS_FIZZING is 1; it forces the explosion to happen (BOOM will go to 1 for one cycle) and the fizzing to stop, but it does not reset the counter to 0, so that the operating system can read the current COUNT_VALUE to see how many ticks remained when the grenade exploded.

7.3.3   Limiting the addressable range

The mechanism so far described only protects against the guest program not relinquishing control, but not against integrity or confidentiality violations. This is serious: if the guest can overwrite the OS code, any protection can be circumvented. Placing the OS in ROM, as is frequently done in embedded systems, makes it safe from modifications; but the working area would still be subject to corruption. Besides, in an environment supporting dynamic updates to the system, the OS could be held in Flash or RAM.

This issue may be addressed by augmenting the grenade timer with some extra lines that intercept the processor's address bus (see figure 7.4). The grenade timer, while fizzing, masks out the top bits of the address bus (even only one bit is sufficient in principle if one wishes to save on pin count) and replaces them with a fixed page address defined by the operating system before pulling the pin. This prevents the guest program from reading or writing memory or I/O addresses outside the authorized page.

There are however some subtleties to do with passing control from the OS to the guest and with calling OS services from the guest. We have thought of mechanisms to deal with those issues, which we shall briefly sketch below, but we don't find them particularly elegant. The quest for better solutions goes on.

---

[16]Or, more precisely, the system that incorporates it.

[17]Since FIRE is unresponsive when PULL_PIN works and vice versa, an attempt to minimize pin count might combine PULL_PIN and FIRE into a single input line whose function would depend on the state of IS_FIZZING. Here, for clarity, we prefer to keep the two signals distinct.

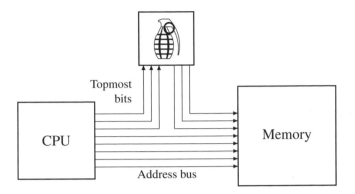

Figure 7.4. Restricting the range of accessible addresses.

To call the OS from the guest, the program pokes a system call request into a well-known memory location designated as a mailbox, protects it with a CRC for integrity, and raises FIRE. This resets the processor, which jumps into the OS. The start-up code of the OS checks the mailbox and, if the CRC matches, proceeds with the evaluation of the request (other criteria will decide whether to honour the request, including sanity checks on the parameters and the amount of ticks left over in the grenade timer when it was shot). The CRC is then deleted by the OS, so that the presence of a valid one can be taken as a guarantee of freshness; this allows the OS to distinguish a system call from a genuine reset due to external causes. Finally, the grenade timer is restarted and the guest code is reentered, as described below.

To pass control from OS to guest we envisage a special section of code spanning the page boundary. The code starts in protected mode, raises PULL_PIN as it crosses the boundary and then finds itself in real mode with the grenade fizzing. The obvious limitation of the fixed entry point may be overcome by using another mailbox in a similar way.

Chapter 8

Anonymity

As we have seen in chapter 5, the more our gadgets become ubiquitous, sentient and personalized, the more they are likely to hold information about us that we may wish to keep secret. We have examined ways to protect the confidentiality of information held in the devices, and of information exchanged between devices.

Sometimes, though, even if the contents of the communication are protected, the identities of the principals taking part in the communication constitute equally sensitive information. In extreme cases, the fact that a communication is taking place may be something that ought to be kept secret. Peter Wright [266], former Assistant Director of Britain's secret service MI5, wrote the following about the communications of his "Watchers" (agents conducting covert surveillance operations):

> Later, MI5 brought in a complicated system of enciphering Watcher communications. I pointed out that this made no difference, since their signals would now stand out even more against the Police, Fire and Ambulance Service communications, all of which were en clair (uncoded). They did not seem to understand that the Russians were getting most of the intelligence from the traffic itself, rather than from the contents of the messages. Traffic analysis would tell them when and where a following operation was being conducted, and by cross-checking that with their own records they would learn all they needed to know.

Despite appearances, this translates fairly directly to civilian contexts and personal privacy. In societies where cash has been all but replaced by plastic and cheques, a bank or credit card statement is almost like a diary. At every purchase it tells you in which city the account holder was, at what time, and in what shop.

Part of the trouble is that there are powerful commercial interests in keeping things traceable, as shown by Garfinkel [110]; the honest citizen is no longer just up against the intelligence agencies, but against the large corporations too. Chaum, privacy advocate [62, 64] and inventor of many fundamental anonymity-related cryptographic primitives, from mixes [61] to blind signatures [66], created a company (Digicash) around his invention of untraceable digital cash [65], but saw it fail in the marketplace.

Attempting to cover the subject of anonymity with any pretence of completeness would bring us well outside the scope of this book. Relevant work for ubiquitous computing includes not only anonymity of communications and payments, but also for example confidentiality of location, as investigated by Jackson [143] in the context of the ORL Active Badges (see section 2.5.1). Even though few people wear Active Badges outside research laboratories, the problems of disclosure of location information are now relevant to the general public because of the ubiquity of mobile phones, which can be easily misused as locating devices by whoever has access to the network information. (The network must know the cell in which any given mobile terminal is, or it could not route incoming calls to it—and there has been work on correlating the signals of several base stations to locate terminals with higher resolution than the cell size.) All this could take a book by itself. We shall instead concentrate on a specific topic to which I brought an original contribution, namely anonymous auctions.

This chapter consists of two main parts. Firstly we develop the "cocaine auction protocol" as a way to conduct an anonymous auction in the absence of a trusted arbitrator. This also includes an examination of the subtle trust issues in regular auctions. Then we examine the anonymity layer on which the auction protocol is built. I propose an implementation technique that does not use any cryptography, and show that this novel approach offers substantial performance gains. Interestingly its security, while using mechanisms that were once considered dubious, turns out to be essentially equivalent to that of a cryptographically strong alternative, so long as we use realistic threat models. Furthermore the anonymous broadcast primitive is also interesting from the protocol modelling point of view in that, for many cases, it gives a more faithful representation of what actually happens.

8.1 The Cocaine Auction Protocol

8.1.1 Why a cocaine auction?

Several extremely rich and ruthless men[1] are gathered around a table. An auction is about to be held in which one of them will offer his next shipment of cocaine to the

---

[1] To prevent grammatical rules from becoming sexist statements, we normally split the roles of the principals between male and female personæ; but the drug dealers of this dramatization look so much more plausible as ugly, cruel cigar-smoking men that I felt it would be more offensive than flattering to include any ladies. Of course some may now perversely call this an even more sexist statement...

highest bidder. The seller describes the merchandise and proposes a starting price. The others then bid increasing amounts until there are no bids for 30 consecutive seconds. At that point the seller declares the auction closed and arranges a secret appointment with the winner to deliver the goods.

Why are we interested in this scenario? One reason is that although electronic auctions are a very hot topic (witness the pioneering online auction house eBay [93], whose stock grew 1300% in the first seven months after their 1998 IPO), their privacy and trust implications have yet to be adequately discussed.

In the eBay model, for example, the auction house's profit is a fixed percentage of the final sale, but at the same time bidders are asked to reveal to the auction house in confidence the maximum amount they are prepared to bid, so that the house can run the bidding process on their behalf without their having to be online for several days. This is putting the fox in charge of the hen house. The auction house could easily and undetectably exploit its knowledge of the bidders' limits to drive up the sale price—possibly introducing a fake bidder—in order to pocket the maximum commission. Users simply have to hope that the auction house will behave properly. EBay addresses some of the other trust concerns, such as whether users should trust other users: there is an interesting "peer review" system in which everyone gets a reliability rating from the principals with whom they interact. But while this mechanism may be valuable, it still cannot be used to justify the trustworthiness of the auction house itself.

We introduce the cocaine auction scenario as an exaggerated case that makes the trust issues unambiguous. We may assume that, in a game with such high stakes and shady players, nobody is going to trust anybody else any more than strictly necessary. We may also assume that the people who take part in the auction all know each other (otherwise one of them might be a police agent), but that no-one who places a bid wants to be identified to the other bidders or to the seller. Nobody except buyer and seller should know who won the auction; and even the seller should not be able to find out the identity of the highest bidder before committing to the sale. But none of the participants should have to trust any other: the protocol cannot rely on a judge or policeman to act as arbitrator and must instead be self-enforcing.

Data protection issues are a further reason for wanting an anonymous auction protocol. In the eBay model, each user has all her transactions logged, together with her personal data, and is at the mercy of abuses by the auction house and other participants, such as the resale of personal information to marketers, insurers or even thieves with a plausible tale ("May I please buy the list of all those who recently bought gold jewellery? I sell a really good polish."). Serious political difficulties may arise from the US practice of storing and reselling such information as this violates the data protection laws of several other jurisdictions, including the

European Union. If an auction site were to adopt protocols that prevented it from finding out the identity of bidders (or at least of unsuccessful bidders), then it would be in a much better position to claim that it had taken all reasonable steps to comply with data protection principles.

Finally, there were at least two amusing cases of life imitating art. The week before this research was presented at the Information Hiding Workshop 1999, some Internet-savvy scoundrels *did actually offer a shipment of drugs on eBay*, with bids reaching 10 M\$ before the auction was noticed and shut down [225]. A few months later, a well known soft drink producer launched a promotional campaign whose home page was `http://www.cokeauction.com/`.

8.1.2   The protocol

We shall now build our anonymous auction protocol assuming the availability of a mechanism for broadcasting messages to all the participants without revealing the identity of the sender ("anonymous broadcast"). The implementation of the anonymity layer will be discussed in section 8.2.

The other communication primitive we shall use is plain non-anonymous broadcast, where an identifiable principal delivers a message to all the others. Since in our scheme the identity of the seller is known to the buyers, the buyers' messages are anonymous, but the seller's are not.

The basic protocol is fairly simple and is organized as a succession of "rounds" of bidding. Round i starts with the seller announcing the bid price b_i for that round. Buyers have up to Δt seconds to make an offer (i.e. to say "yes", meaning "I'm willing to buy at the current bid price b_i"). As soon as one buyer anonymously says "yes", he becomes the winner w_i of that round and a new round begins. If nobody says anything for Δt seconds, round i is concluded by timeout and the auction is won by the winner w_{i-1} of the previous round, if one exists. If the timeout occurs during round 0, this means that nobody made any offers at the initial price b_0, so there is no sale.

A couple of details need fixing before this protocol will work satisfactorily. Firstly, the seller needs a mechanism to identify the winner: if all the buyers ever say is just "yes", then anybody can go to the seller, offer him the final sale price and obtain the goods instead of the real winner—which is highly undesirable. This problem can be solved by ensuring that each "yes" message also contain a one-way function of a nonce[2]: before completing the sale, the seller will then ask the winner to exhibit the original nonce, which nobody else could produce.

Secondly, once the auction is over, the seller might prefer to give a *secret* appointment to the winner ("see you on Tuesday at 06:30 in the car park of Heathrow

---

[2]See footnote 3 on page 176.

terminal 2") rather than exchanging suitcases of cocaine for cash under the noses of all the losing bidders. On the other hand, the identity of the winner should not be revealed to the seller until the latter commits to the sale. This is to protect the winner from the situation in which the seller says "So who won the auction? Oh, it was you? Well, anyone else would have been fine, but you're from the wrong family, so I won't sell to you after all, even if you've won". To enable the seller to send an appointment to the winner only, but before knowing the winner's identity, we make the previously mentioned one-way function g^x (mod n), where x is the nonce chosen by the bidder and g and n are public system-wide parameters. So each anonymous "yes" message will be of the form g^{x_i}, with x_i chosen arbitrarily by the winner w_i of round i. When the auction finishes, say at round f, with principal w_f committing to buy at price b_f with a "yes" message of g^{x_f}, the seller chooses a nonce y and performs a Diffie-Hellman key exchange with the winner w_f (who is still anonymous) by broadcasting g^y and then the appointment encrypted under the session key $g^{x_f y}$. The winner is the only buyer who can compute this key.

A number of minor variants to the protocol are possible. For example, before the first round the seller could specify, either algorithmically or by enumeration, the succession of bid prices $\{b_i\}$; then he would no longer have to broadcast b_i at the beginning of each round, because each winner w_i would implicitly refer to the corresponding b_i in the "well known" succession.

A variant at the opposite end of the conciseness v. robustness trade-off [1] is to have the seller broadcast, at the beginning of round i, not only b_i but also the "yes" message ($g^{x_{i-1}}$) of the winner of the previous round. This may help arbitrate races between bidders who both said "yes" to the same b_i. The bidders themselves could include in the "yes" message the value b_i to which they are responding.

We shall not, however, discuss this type of implementation detail any further. Let us instead examine some of the ways in which the principals could misbehave, and whether the protocol is (or can be made) robust against them.

8.1.3 Attacks

There are limits to what can be achieved at the protocol level. It is always possible, for example, to subvert an auction when an appropriate combination of participants colludes against the others. For example, if all the bidders conspire against the seller, one of them can buy the shipment cheaply and divide it with the others later (a practice known as "ringing"), either in equal parts or perhaps even running a separate private auction and splitting the money that didn't go to the seller. Similarly, if the seller plants an ally among the bidders, he can push the final selling price as high as the other bidders will bear (though at the risk of not being able to actually complete the sale). We do not believe that all such attacks can be detected, let alone stopped, by any particular auction protocol: the culprits can plausibly deny their involvement, since the "trace" of externally observable messages of an auction involving a collusion could always have been generated by an "honest" auction as well. Some specific conspiracies may be detectable by protocol level mechanisms, as we shall see; but we will not attempt to guard against the others.

Seller not selling to highest bidder

Does the protocol force the seller to sell to the highest bidder? No, since the seller can always generate the session key starting with the g^x produced by whichever bidder he prefers, and nobody will be able to tell that this happened just by looking at the commitment message. One might object that, so long as the price is strictly increasing from one bid to the next, the seller is guaranteed to lose money if he does not sell to the highest bidder—but the real world is more complicated than that, with all sorts of possible scams and double-crosses. We will differentiate two cases.

In the first, the seller sends an encrypted appointment message to the winning bidder but attempts some treachery in it. For example, he might have a sweetheart deal with one of the participants allowing him to match the best openly bid price, and might send the winner an appointment he has no intention to keep. In such a case, the winner's recourse is to blacken the seller's "good name" by complaining about the disappointment afterwards around the cocaine dealing community. We will consider this case no further.

In the second, the seller encrypts the appointment message using the g^x supplied by someone other than the winner. In this case, the cheated winner can broadcast an accusation and prove that the seller is dishonest, simply by publishing his last x. Anybody can then verify firstly that that x really corresponds to the g^x from the highest bidder and secondly that the message from the seller does not decrypt to anything meaningful using that x. At that point all the bidders take out their sub-machine-guns and the seller greatly regrets his dishonesty. Note that the cheated highest bidder manages to accuse the dishonest seller without exposing his identity, since he still sends out x anonymously. So this protocol ensures that most misbehaviour of this sort can be publicly exposed without loss of anonymity for the cheated accuser.

Seller bidding at his own auction

The exception is of course where the seller bids at his own auction in order to raise the price, overshoots, and finds himself the winner. He is unlikely to accuse himself by broadcasting x; but might he offer the shipment to anyone else?

Let us assume that he selects a g^x sent by one of the next-highest bidders, whom we will call Mr. N, and broadcasts an appointment message encrypted under g^{xy}, in the hope that Mr. N (whose identity is unknown to him) will keep quiet in exchange for a chance to buy the goods. When Mr. N sees that he can decrypt the secret appointment using his own g^x, he knows that the seller is cheating, since that message should have been sent to the highest bidder instead. So he can either expose the scam by exhibiting his own x as before and cause the barrels of all the Uzis in the room to converge on the seller; or he can accept the appointment and buy the shipment he would otherwise lose. (He might perhaps haggle over the price when he meets the seller there, but by then he will have lost his ability to cause immediate bodily harm to the seller from the comfort of anonymity.)

So, when the seller tries to deal with someone other than the apparent winner, there seems always to be one principal who could expose him as a cheater, although in some sub-cases it is possible that the potential accuser might prefer to stay silent. A seller "with wife and kids", noticing that this situation carries a life risk greater than ε, might never attempt such a scam; but the more adventurous Scarface type on the fast track to the top might occasionally be prepared to run the risk.

Thus in practice the other principals still have no way of knowing for sure that an auction they lost was run "legitimately". So they might want a way for all the participants to verify that the seller did encrypt the secret appointment to the highest bidder, although they should not be able to decrypt the message themselves. They might also want some reassurance that the appointment message decrypts to something meaningful. Both these assurances can be given by a cut-and-choose protocol. The seller broadcasts not one g^y but twenty (perhaps at the beginning of the auction) and once the auction concludes, he then offers a choice of twenty different encrypted appointment messages, such as "06:30 Tuesday in the car park of Heathrow terminal 2", "23:20 Monday behind the George and Dragon", ..., and will reveal up to nineteen of the y values in response to challenges.

It may well be that our drug dealers do not care to pay for the extra complexity of such a protocol. If the main risk is felt to be the seller bidding at his own auction, then even if he overbids and is forced to sell to himself under penalty of being discovered, there is nothing to stop him from running a new auction some time later, pretending to have received a new shipment from his suppliers. (This applies to commodities like cocaine or memory chips, but not to unique and recognizable items such as stolen Rembrandts, where a cut-and-choose protocol might be preferred.)

Deadbeat bidders

A general consequence of anonymity is that it is hard to hold anonymous principals responsible for anything. In particular, it is hard to guard against "deadbeat bidders", i.e. participants who win an auction and then do not turn up with the cash to buy the goods. With the protocol described so far, they would get the encrypted appointment but not show up, and the seller would not know who to blame. While deadbeat bidders would not gain much (and would certainly not get any free cocaine), their behaviour will certainly annoy the other participants. If repeated undetectably over a series of auctions, deadbeat bidding could amount to a denial of service. One might argue that nonpayment lies outside the scope of the auction protocol, which should only designate a winner and a sale price; but it is still reasonable to seek ways in we might at least identify persistent deadbeats.

The approach used by "respectable" online auctioneers such as eBay is to enable clients to build up a reputation for honest dealing. One might try to transplant this to the cocaine auction by giving each principal a pseudonym; but as soon as the winner turns up to collect his cocaine, the link between his name and pseudonym becomes obvious, unless the actual delivery of goods is also conducted anonymously. In fact, even in the "respectable" case, service denial attacks can be mounted by any principals who can repeatedly acquire new identities.

This problem raises complex issues related to identity certification, which in itself might be a concept that our mistrustful drug dealers unconditionally reject *a priori*. Here we will merely point out a major practical pitfall. Suppose that some acceptable technical mechanism has been devised to create a certification authority. For example, one might set up a k-out-of-n identity escrow scheme with a very high k, say $3n/4$: after a certain level of missed appointments, or deadbeat bids, were detected by the audience, everybody could cooperate to unmask the disruptor, in a way reminiscent of Blaze's "angry mob cryptanalysis" [36]. Mechanisms for setting up the underlying threshold signature schemes without a trusted party are known [73]. But the real problems are likely to come from the application detail, such as the plausibility of the excuse that the subject might put forward to justify his absence (was he arrested "honestly", or did he pay the police to arrest him?).

Do auction houses have a future?

One of the questions asked by many businesses is whether the convergence of computers and communications could destroy their niche. Even banks worry about "disintermediation" as their corporate customers raise loan capital on the markets directly. What does the future hold for auctioneers?

A traditional auction house adds value in a number of ways. Some of these, such as marketing, may be easier to do on the net; others, such as providing assurance that the goods on offer are as described and are the lawful property of the seller, may be harder. But comparing the cocaine auction with existing ones does tell us something about transaction costs. In conventional auctions, bidders must identify themselves to the auctioneer, who can exclude any known deadbeats; and although there is no formal mechanism to detect when a friend of the seller is bidding secretly for him, there is a deterrent in that a seller who buys his own merchandise ends up out of pocket by the auctioneer's commission.

In many sectors of the economy, from securities trading to the provision of airport taxi services, it has been found that regulated markets build confidence and attract custom. The question for regulators is precisely how much to regulate. We hope that comparing conventional auctioneers (and the new online firms such as eBay) with the fully disintermediated environment of the cocaine auction protocol may provide some useful insight.

8.2   The anonymity layer

To make the cocaine protocol usable, we must also supply a mechanism that allows the bidders to anonymously broadcast their "yes" message.

8.2.1   The dining cryptographers

The "dining cryptographers" construction introduced by Chaum [63] addresses precisely this problem. In his now classic story, several cryptographers are gathered around a table for dinner, and the waiter informs them that the meal has already been paid for by an anonymous benefactor, who could be one of the participants or the NSA. The cryptographers would like to know whether they are indebted to one of their own number or to the agency. So Chaum incrementally constructs a protocol through which, after the sharing of what are effectively one time pads between selected pairs of principals, each principal outputs a function of her "I paid/I didn't pay" bit and everyone can later work out the total parity of all such bits. As long as not more than one of the cryptographers says "I paid", even parity means that the NSA paid, while odd parity means that one of the diners paid, even if nobody can figure out who.

Various extensions are then proposed, including one in which the principals are arranged in a token ring and transmit integrity-checked blocks rather than single bits, so that collisions[3] can be detected.

For the system to work, collisions must be controlled by ensuring that the round trip period of the token is much smaller than the typical time between the seller announcing a new price and a bidder responding "I'll buy". Furthermore, the procedure for dealing with collisions must take into account the nature and aims of the principals: it might be inappropriate for us to simply invite colliders to retransmit

---

[3]Only one cryptographer at a time can say "1" and be heard. Since the resulting anonymous bit is the XOR of those transmitted by the individual principals, if at most one principal transmits a "1" and all others transmit a "0", we can infer as appropriate that nobody said "1" or that one anonymous principal said "1". But if more than one principal sends a "1", the protocol no longer works—it can only tell whether an even or an odd number of principals transmitted a "1".

after random intervals, as Chaum does, since two principals might both retransmit as soon and as often as possible in an attempt to secure the bid, thereby causing collisions ad infinitum.

Pfitzmann proposes an ingenious optimization [209] that guarantees to resolve a collision between n participants in at most n rounds—while the probabilistic approach suggested by Chaum cannot guarantee an upper bound.

Despite this, the cocaine auction protocol implemented using "token ring dining cryptographers" is fairly expensive in terms of communications. Even ignoring the initial cost of setting up the pairwise one time pads and of any retransmissions caused by collisions, each participant must send at least one message to his neighbour for each round in which one untraceable bid may be sent by one of the parties, plus another one for the second trip round the loop which is needed to communicate the result to all participants. Calling n the number of participants, r the number of rounds of bidding needed before the auction results in a sale and K the "dilution factor" introduced to spread out transmissions over several rounds so as to minimize collisions, the protocol so far described requires $2 \cdot n \cdot r \cdot K$ such messages to be sent. (Pfitzmann's cited construction allows K to be much smaller than in Chaum's case by lowering the retransmission costs on collisions.)

We shall now show how a simple assumption about the nature and properties of the physical transport layer, directly inspired by a specific implementation technology, dramatically reduces these costly transmission requirements.

8.2.2 Anonymous broadcast based on physics

The original idea for the cocaine auction protocol arose in the context of the discussion about possible applications for a short-range radio networking facility such as that provided by Bluetooth (or Piconet for us at the time). We envisage that the drug dealers of our story might hold in their pockets little radio transmitters similar in shape and size to car key fobs, and that unobtrusively pressing the button on the device would cause the transmission of the relevant "yes" message (a transmitter with a slow processor, unable to do modular arithmetic quickly, might rely on a precomputed list of g^x for various x).

By using radio, each message sent is automatically broadcast to all principals; and it can be anonymous, as long as we simply omit to mention the sender in the link-layer header. Only one such message is needed per auction round, so in terms of transmissions the entire auction only costs r messages, as opposed to $2 \cdot n \cdot r \cdot K$ (plus the extras we hinted at) for the dining cryptographers implementation.

The savings are dramatic and worth investigating in greater detail. As it turns out, they come from having questioned a basic assumption in protocol modelling, namely that communication is point-to-point. This trick can be exploited in a variety of interesting cases that have nothing to do with auctions.

8.2.3   A fundamental protocol building block

Traditionally, cryptographic protocols are described as a sequence of steps of the form

$$A \rightarrow B : M$$

indicating that principal A sends message M to principal B. In the general case it is proper to assume a primitive that sends a message from a specific sender to a specific recipient; indeed in most cases this is what the communications API offers. Other constructions are typically derived from this one: for example, broadcasting the same message M to all the members of a domain $\mathcal{D}$ can be represented by a trivial, if inefficient, iteration. Anonymous sending can be achieved by more elaborate constructions which rely on building an untraceable tortuous path across a multiply connected network, in which intermediate relay nodes hide the route that the message is going to take next [61, 122], or on diluting the payload in a cloud of messages sent by a community of principals, each of which might have been the actual sender [63], or on broadcasting a message which only some subset can decipher [36].

Let us now reverse the perspective and take "anonymous broadcast" as the fundamental primitive. The following notation

$$A \; ? \overset{\nearrow}{\underset{\searrow}{\longleftrightarrow}} \mathcal{D} : M$$

shall signify that principal A broadcasts message M anonymously into the domain $\mathcal{D}$. This means that all principals in $\mathcal{D}$ receive M, and given any two messages M_1 and M_2 that have been anonymously broadcast at different times into $\mathcal{D}$, no principal in $\mathcal{D}$ (except the originators) is able to tell whether they came from the same principal or not.

From here we can derive non-anonymous broadcast by naming the sender in the message, as in

$$A \overset{\nearrow}{\underset{\searrow}{\longleftrightarrow}} \mathcal{D} : M \;\; \equiv \;\; A \; ? \overset{\nearrow}{\underset{\searrow}{\longleftrightarrow}} \mathcal{D} : (A,M)$$

and point-to-point send by naming both the sender and the recipient, as in

$$A \rightarrow B : M \;\; \equiv \;\; A \; ? \overset{\nearrow}{\underset{\searrow}{\longleftrightarrow}} \mathcal{D} : (A,B,M).$$

Many security papers are concerned with the strength of the mechanisms used to bind names such as A and B to M: but we are not concerned with non-repudiation, only with its dual, namely plausible deniability. We simply note that a basically anonymous broadcast primitive, coupled with weak mechanisms to name the claimed sender and the supposedly intended receiver, is what *really* happens in practice in many common cases, including radio and Ethernet. (Human speech is also a form of local broadcast, anonymous only in crowds, and yet there are many places—not just Japanese paper houses—where it's conventional to ignore messages addressed to others.)

At the physical level, whether in the one-bit bus of Ethernet or in the "ether" of radio waves, it is actually the point-to-point messaging facility that is obtained as a composite construction built on top of anonymous broadcast. The practice of prefixing each outgoing message with the globally unique ID that Ethernet adapters receive during manufacture is a convention which a malicious node can easily ignore.

Physical anonymous broadcast as a genuine networking primitive requires a shared communication medium and thus is only practical in local networks. In the wide area, its usefulness is limited by issues of transmission power, propagation delay and bandwidth: if only one principal can transmit at a time without collision, larger domains mean that more principals are forced to stay silent while one of them is transmitting. Above a certain domain size, routing becomes the preferred option in order to reduce the transmission power and increase the aggregate bandwidth. So basing a cryptographic protocol on the anonymity properties of the physical broadcast primitive limits it to the local area. The drug barons can hold the efficient version of the auction around a table, with key fobs in their pockets or with an Ethernet connecting their laptops, but to hold an auction over the Internet from their swimming pools it appears that they would have to implement the anonymity layer using the more tedious classical techniques. This problem is also faced by Jackson [143], who finds he cannot use the otherwise desirable physical broadcast technique in an Active Badge application because of power and scalability limitations.

In summary, the anonymous broadcast primitive has two main advantages. The first is efficiency: even before taking anonymity into consideration, in a shared transmission medium sending one message from A to B or sending one message from A to anyone else in the domain has exactly the same cost. It is foolish to use a formalism that hides this, and end up being forced to send $\#\mathcal{D} - 1$ messages rather than one when broadcast is really intended. Moreover, under some assumptions that we shall examine in greater detail next, a shared medium can give anonymity practically for free, thus saving the many redundant messages otherwise needed to hide the real traffic. It is thus convenient to be able to leverage off these valuable properties when designing a higher-level protocol.

The second reason is clarity: by more closely modelling what goes on during the transmission of a message, we are in a better position to evaluate the actual security properties of our system. Bluetooth is always broadcasting to anyone in range, even when the application invokes an API primitive with the advertised semantics of "send this message from A to B".

8.2.4   The strength (or weakness) of broadcast anonymity

Although the network addresses sent out by most nodes in conventional computer
and communications systems can be forged easily, it would be naïve to conclude
that every transmission on a shared physical medium provides strong anonymity.
Pfitzmann, who extensively analysed techniques to reduce user observability in
communication networks [206, 207, 208, 211, 209], mentioned broadcast over a
shared medium as a possible low-level anonymity layer, but then dismissed it in
favour of more elaborate solutions based on cryptography as it could not provide
unconditional security. This is a valid objection: an opponent who can observe
the transmissions at a low enough level will generally be able to distinguish the
participants.

For example, in cable and radio transmissions, at the physical level the distance
between transmitter and receiver affects both the received power and the transmission delay. Several conspiring nodes who could observe these parameters might
well be able to identify the senders of most of the messages. We are not interested
in the trivial case in which all nodes but one conspire against the last, but in more
serious cases where three or four nodes can, between them, tell whether the last
message came from here or from there.

A transmitter might randomly vary its power output to prevent direction finding
using signal strength measurements; but the relative amplitude will still be visible,
and precise timing information will anyway be what tells most to a well equipped
attacker. The game could include directional receiving and transmitting antennas;
a "defensive" environment such as a naked Faraday cage that maximizes reflections and echoes; or a "hostile" environment with unseen receivers in every ceiling
tile and surveillance cameras in every pot plant. Bidders might even use extreme
electronic warfare techniques (see Schleher [226]) to try to frame each other by
causing certain messages to be received by only some subset of participants. Radio-
frequency ID systems can identify individual transmitters by their analogue characteristics (as reported by Goldberg [121]); to block this, the principals might have
several buttons in their pockets which they use once each as they wander around.

However, many of the attacks open to a resourceful opponent are independent of the strength of cryptography in use. Equipment can be abused. In 2001,
the press took notice when the FBI used some kind of key logger to obtain the
PGP passphrase of an alleged mobster [96]; but, as a matter of fact, hardware
keystroke recorders are nowadays sold as commercial products [6]. Software keyboard sniffers can be installed in laptops, possibly remotely via virus or trojan infection, and signal back using the user's net connection; to get extra points for style,
the sniffer programs might even use a soft tempest transmitter [165] as the back

channel. If the above is impossible, casino-style hidden cameras and microphones can be used to observe user input. There may be infrared lasers to measure bidders' blood oxygen levels and special toilets to collect biological samples to measure stress. One should bear all this in mind when dismissing anonymous broadcast as insecure compared with the "mathematically provable" untraceability of the dining drug dealers' scheme. An opponent who forces us to think about unconditionally secure cryptography may also fly below the mathematics and steal the plaintext at the level of electronics, physics or biology. In such cases, the strength of cryptographic mechanisms is only one factor of many. It is probably fair to say that the attacker equipped to break the anonymity of our physical broadcast will have little trouble in bypassing strong cryptography (wherever it is employed) by simply observing the keys or plaintext directly.

At less exalted levels, we have to consider the economics of the attacker and the defender. It is significant that defence (making broadcast anonymous by blanking out the "from" header) may require only a small change in the firmware of a standard node, and might even be performed in software depending on how "shallow" the network adapter is; but attack (sensing the signal strength, timing, phase, polarization or analogue transmitter characteristics of received messages) is a lower level and thus more expensive operation.

Chapter 9

Conclusions

Ubiquitous networked computing has the potential to change our lifestyles and to cause a technological revolution of similar impact to the advent of the Internet. It will open up a fantastic range of new ways for technology to interact with us. The networked gadgets of the new generation will no longer look like computers and will blend invisibly in our daily lives. They will evolve from a few large, multipurpose, unreliable techno-monoliths to a multitude of small, dedicated, simple and non-threatening appliances.

Most of the benefits of ubicomp emerge from *synergy* between those simple and specialized devices: what makes the difference is not that your appliances are now clever, but that they are talkative, sociable and cooperative, making use of each other's services as appropriate. *Communication* is at the core of the ubicomp vision. For this vision to become reality, a substantial infrastructural deployment will be needed—not so much at the physical level, but rather in terms of protocols and standards: what will be absolutely necessary is a harmonization of the way in which those devices are meant to interact. The failure to enforce compatibility at the application layer is the principal reason for the practical failure of IrDA, and the reason why Bluetooth's profiles [42] are of paramount importance.

A portion of this "soft infrastructure" will be devoted to security. In this context, I see the potential for at least three types of expensive security mistakes. The most obvious is insufficient security: weak or nonexistent protection leading to direct losses through successful attacks. The second is the waste of large amounts of money in costly solutions to the wrong problems—such as building a global top-down public key infrastructure when most principals are peanuts that can't do public key operations anyway. The third, and most ominous, is the unwitting—or, much worse, intentional—deployment of an Orwellian system that will turn ubiquitous computing into ubiquitous surveillance.

The scientists and engineers who design the technologies of tomorrow's world have a responsibility to oppose the development and deployment of any that are too easy to misuse. Phil Zimmermann [271], who was harassed for years by the US Government for having written and released the strong encryption program PGP, was speaking to policymakers rather than technologists when he said the following, but the core of the message is the same:

> The Clinton Administration seems to be attempting to deploy and entrench a communications infrastructure that would deny the citizenry the ability to protect its privacy. This is unsettling because in a democracy, it is possible for bad people to occasionally get elected—sometimes very bad people. Normally, a well-functioning democracy has ways to remove these people from power. But the wrong technology infrastructure could allow such a future government to watch every move anyone makes to oppose it. It could very well be the last government we ever elect.

> When making public policy decisions about new technologies for the government, I think one should ask oneself which technologies would best strengthen the hand of a police state. Then, do not allow the government to deploy those technologies. This is simply a matter of good civic hygiene.

To rely on the law to prevent the abuses that an insecure technology infrastructure makes possible, he warns, is unwise:

> while technology infrastructures tend to persist for generations, laws and policies can change overnight. Once a communications infrastructure optimized for surveillance becomes entrenched, a shift in political conditions may lead to abuse of this new-found power. Political conditions may shift with the election of a new government, or perhaps more abruptly from the bombing of a Federal building.

The last sentence is an accurate prediction of the dramatic shift in policies triggered by the World Trade Center attack of 2001-09-11. The day after the tragedy, a heartbroken but lucid Matt Blaze [37] issued his own warning against this kind of reaction:

> I fear that we will be seduced into accepting what seem at first blush as nothing more than reasonable inconveniences, small prices to pay for reducing the risk that terrorism happens on our soil again, without assessing fully the hidden costs to our values and to the robustness of our society. Worse, I fear that we may allow these things to simply happen, without the debate and exposure that an informed open society would and must demand.

If ubiquitous computing takes off as anticipated, then the extent to which ubicomp systems are made secure (under all the various aspects that we discuss in this volume) is going to have an economic and social impact of dramatic proportions.

It is my hope that this book, by exploring some of the novel technical aspects, will contribute to a greater awareness of these important security issues, and that the systems we eventually deploy will be designed to be at the same time useful to us and hard to misuse against us.

Appendix A

A short primer on functions

I like to explain cryptographic primitives using some elementary concepts from set theory, such as functions and bijections. I find that this approach helps me describe those primitives in a simple yet rigorous way. Some readers, however, may not be familiar with the mathematical-sounding terminology, so to them I provide this brief appendix as an introduction (or as a review for those who only saw this at school too many years ago).

This is not a mathematics book and, while I personally like maths, I am aware of the famous advice about equations that Stephen Hawking received when writing *A Brief History of Time*. To the initiated, a well-written formula can be at the same time more compact, more accurate and more readable than the natural language prose it replaces; to everyone else, however, it just looks like scary gobbledygook. Since this appendix is written primarily for the reader who does *not* already know the code, the main description shall always be in plain English; I shall however also add the corresponding formulæ as parenthetical remarks or footnotes, for the benefit of those who consult these pages just to check that we agree on terminology and notation and also for the laudably curious who want to learn the code eventually. While we are at it, I shall also give you a brief cheat sheet (table A.1 below) listing the meaning of the mathematical hieroglyphs used in these formulæ.

A.1 Sets

A set is an unordered collection of elements. The set B of the suits of a deck of cards, for example, has four elements: $B = \{\clubsuit, \diamondsuit, \heartsuit, \spadesuit\}$.

A subset K of a set B is itself a set, and it may contain only elements that already belong to B. For example, the set $K = \{\spadesuit, \clubsuit\}$ of black suits is a subset of the set B

169

Symbol	Reading
$\subseteq$	*subset* is included in *set*
$\in$	*element* belongs to *set*
$\times$	cartesian product
$\forall$	for all
$\exists$	there exists
!	one and only one (NB: not universally recognized)
$\vert$	such that
#	cardinality (number of elements in a set)

Table A.1. Symbols commonly used in set-theoretical formulæ.

of all suits[1].

Given two sets A and B, their cartesian product $A \times B$ is the set of all possible pairs (a, b) such that a belongs to A (written $a \in A$) and b belongs to B. For example, if A is the set of Jack, Queen and King[2] and B is the set of suits introduced above, then their cartesian product is a set of twelve pairs, each representing a card:

$$
\begin{aligned}
A \times B = \quad & \{(J,\clubsuit), (J,\diamondsuit), (J,\heartsuit), (J,\spadesuit), \\
& (Q,\clubsuit), (Q,\diamondsuit), (Q,\heartsuit), (Q,\spadesuit), \\
& (K,\clubsuit), (K,\diamondsuit), (K,\heartsuit), (K,\spadesuit)\}.
\end{aligned}
$$

With another example, if A is a set of 6 children and B a set of 7 movie genres, the cartesian product $A \times B$ contains $6 \times 7 = 42$ pairs:

$$
\begin{aligned}
A &= \{Anna, Miyuki, Mathilda, George, Carl, Douglas\}; \\
B &= \{animation, comedy, romance, action, horror, western, musical\}; \\
A \times B &= \{(Anna, animation), (Anna, comedy), \ldots, (Douglas, musical)\}.
\end{aligned}
$$

A.2   Relations

Any subset R of $A \times B$ defines[3] a **relation** R from A to B, written

$$R : A \to B.$$

---

[1]This is written $K \subseteq B$, and is also read "K is included in B".

[2]This is written $B = \{J, Q, K\}$.

[3]To be rigorous we ought to distinguish between the set of pairs $R \subseteq A \times B$ and the relation $\mathcal{R} = (R, A, B)$ defined not only by that set of pairs but also by the domain and range. This is because two relations with the same pairs but with a different domain or range are in fact distinct, as will be apparent in the discussion below on the transformation from an injection to a bijection. In practice, however, this additional precision is rarely necessary; so, for the sake of notational simplicity, we shall use the same name for both the relation and the set of pairs, identifying the domain and range explicitly wherever required, as in $R : A \to B$.

We call A the **domain** and B the **range** (sometimes *codomain*) of R.

With A and B being the sets of children and genres introduced above, one possible subset R_1 could be the relation "likes": the pair (a, b) is in R_1 if and only if child a likes genre b. Another possible subset R_2 might be the relation "has seen"; and your fertile imagination might come up with much more complicated ones, such as "has an unmarried female relative who starred in a movie of the following genre between 1970 and 1982"[4].

It is common to represent graphically each element (a, b) of the relation as an arrow from a to b, as in figure A.1. We also say that b is a's **image** and that a is b's **preimage**, but note that a may have several (or no) images and similarly for b's preimages.

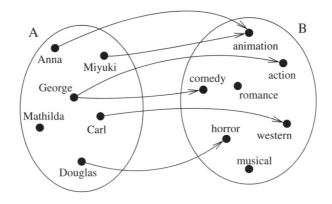

Figure A.1. The relation R_1 (likes) between two sets A (children) and B (movie genres).

A.3 Functions

Any relation $f : A \rightarrow B$ such that every element of the domain A is the origin of exactly one arrow[5] is called a **function** (sometimes *application*) from A to B. In other words, we have a function whenever each element a of the domain has one and only one image. The relation "likes" of figure A.1 is not a function because Mathilda does not like any of the listed genres and because George likes two of them.

---

[4]Note that some of these relations might consist of the empty set, for example if none of these children has an unmarried female relative who... etc. This is fine: the empty set, written $\emptyset$, is a subset of any set.

[5]This is written $\forall a \in A : \exists ! b \in B \mid (a, b) \in f$, where the little-known exclamation mark means "one and only one".

When we do have a function, the fact that each element is the origin of exactly one arrow allows us[6] to use the notation $f(a) = b$ to denote the (unique) image of an element of the domain.

We can classify functions (figure A.2) according to the number of arrows that land on each element of the range B. If each element of B receives at least one arrow, the function is **surjective**. If each element of B receives at most one arrow, the function is **injective**. If each element of B receives exactly one arrow, the function is **bijective**.

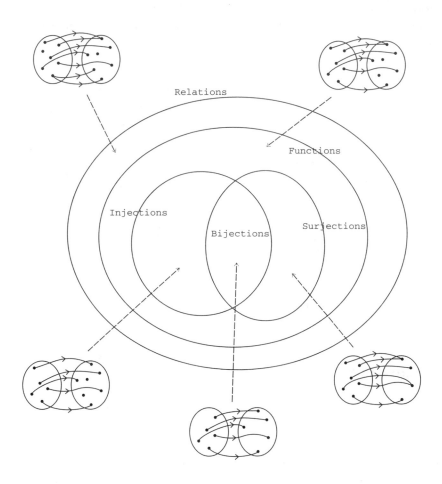

Figure A.2. A taxonomy of relations, with examples.

Clearly a bijection (another way to say "a bijective function") is at the same

---

[6]Some authors are happy to speak of "multi-valued functions", but with our definitions this is an oxymoron. If it's multi-valued, it's a generic relation, not a function.

time an injection and a surjection. It defines a one-to-one correspondence between the sets A and B. Note that any injection $f : A \to B$ yields a bijection if we remove from its range the elements that don't receive any arrows. The bijection obtained from f is $\tilde{f} : A \to \tilde{B}$ where $\tilde{B} \subseteq B$ is defined as the subset of B whose elements have a preimage[7].

Any bijection can be inverted, because every element of the range has a unique preimage. In other words, given a bijection $f : A \to B$ there always exists an inverse bijection $f^{-1} : B \to A$ such that, if you follow the f arrow and then the f^{-1} arrow, you get back where you started[8].

If there exists an injection from A to B, then the number of elements of A cannot exceed that of B: for each element in A there is one in B (just follow the arrow to find it), plus there might be some elements of B which don't get any arrow[9]. Therefore, if there is a bijection from A to B, then the two sets have the same number of elements, because any bijection has an inverse and both are also injections.

Using a "counting" argument it is also easy to go in the reverse direction and prove that, if A and B have the same number of elements and there exists an injection $f : A \to B$, then f must be a bijection.

A.4 Functions of many arguments

So far we have only discussed functions $f : A \to B$ of one argument. But if the domain is composite, as in $A = C \times D \times E$, then the argument of the function $f : C \times D \times E \to B$ is really a triple[10]: $f(a) = f((c,d,e)) = b$. With a trivial extension of the notation we may describe functions of many arguments by dropping the inner parentheses: for each function of a single composite argument there is a corresponding function of many arguments, as in $f((c,d,e)) = \hat{f}(c,d,e)$, and unless we are in pedantic mode we shall consider them the same and not insist on the distinction.

Given a function of n arguments

$$f : A_1 \times A_2 \times \ldots \times A_n \to B,$$

if we give it n arguments we obtain a value from its range; but if we give it fewer arguments, say $k < n$, we obtain another function (this time of $n - k$ arguments).

---

[7]This is written $\tilde{B} \triangleq \{b \in B \mid \exists a \in A : f(a) = b\}$.

[8]This is written $\forall a \in A : f^{-1}(f(a)) = a$.

[9]This is written $\#A \leq \#B$, where $\leq$ is "less than or equal to" and $\#S$ is the **cardinality** of set S, i.e. the number of its elements.

[10]Or a pair, or a quadruple, or whatever else, depending on the number of elementary sets in the cartesian product. We say "t-uple", or briefly just "tuple", to refer to the generic case without specifying the number of elements between the parentheses.

This process is known as **currying**. Assume for example that $k = 1$: we obtain function g, a curried version of f, by assigning a constant value, say α, to one of the arguments, say the first. The function g of $n-1$ arguments gets its tuples from the corresponding ones of f in the obvious way: you just feed f the constant value α as its first argument, and the arguments of g as the others[11].

For an example, think of the function $f(start, end)$ as giving the price of a subway ticket between two stations. If you fix the *start* station to be the one nearest your home, you obtain the curried function $g(end) = f(\text{home}, end)$, which takes only one argument (the destination station) and returns you the price of a ticket from your home station to the chosen destination.

---

[11]This is written

$$g: \quad A_2 \times \ldots \times A_n \to B$$
$$\triangleq \{(a_2, \ldots, a_n, b) \in A_2 \times \ldots \times A_n \times B \mid (\alpha, a_2, \ldots, a_n, b) \in f\}.$$

Appendix B

Existing network security solutions

Here we review the security solutions adopted in a variety of distributed systems, from the Internet to cellular telephony. This is meant to be a sampler rather than an exhaustive reference. Of course, not all of these solutions can be replicated verbatim in the ubiquitous computing context; however, getting familiar with existing work will teach us a few lessons and remind us not to reinvent the wheel, while at the same time allowing us to appreciate the need for new solutions in the cases where the preconditions are different.

Because this material is a bit more technical than the rest of the book, I have chosen to put it in an appendix rather than in a regular chapter. As Bill Cheswick wisely says in the foreword of Rubin's brilliant book [223], "it's okay to skip the hard parts", and if you choose to skip this appendix you will not miss the main message of this book. On the other hand, if you are curious about the inner workings of some real-world systems whose names sound familiar, I hope you will find a useful introduction in the pages that follow.

If you wish to explore these issues in greater depth, you will probably have to choose different books for different topics. As for background reading on Internet protocols, Stevens [244] is an excellent introduction to TCP/IP, but doesn't have much to say on security. A more up to date but higher level primer is Greenberg [124], which does give a fair share of attention to security: the wide scope of the book makes it impossible for the author to give too much detail, but he offers valuable insights. Among the security textbooks, Gollmann [123] is perhaps the one with the best treatment of network security. Garfinkel and Spafford [111] is good, but somewhat too narrowly focused—it's a Unix sysadmin book, really. The anonymous *Hacker's Guide* [21] is fairly superficial and is not recommended, despite its good supply of references to useful material.

If you only have time to consult one book, pick either Rubin [223] or Anderson [11]. They are both rare combinations of clarity and competence—you can't go wrong with either. Rubin is more practical and business oriented; it goes directly into specific security solutions you can apply today. Anderson has a much broader scope and is an eye-opening awareness builder. If you're still thinking about it, get both anyway—you won't regret it.

B.1   Needham-Schroeder

B.1.1   The original protocol

Needham-Schroeder [196], published in 1978, is one of the earliest and most influential authentication protocols for distributed systems.

It assumes that a principal Alice wishes to authenticate herself across the net to another principal Bob who has never seen her before. Both Alice and Bob know the authentication server Sam[1], who will help in the introduction. Alice contacts Sam and receives from him a "ticket"[2] that she can show to Bob to prove her identity. The actual protocol runs as follows, in five steps.

Firstly, Alice tells Sam her name and that of the principal with whom she wants to talk (i.e. Bob). She is implicitly asking Sam to send her a communications key and a "letter of introduction". She also sends him a nonce[3] N_A, which Sam will have to return to her to prove that his message is a response to Alice's current enquiry rather than a replay by some man-in-the-middle of a previously recorded reply.

$$A \rightarrow S : A, B, N_A. \qquad \text{(Message 1)}$$

Sam replies by sending Alice a secret packet encrypted under the key they share, K_{AS}. This contains, among other things, a ticket that she can show to Bob and a randomly generated session key K_{AB} to encrypt traffic between Alice and Bob.

---

[1]In the sense that Alice and Bob, like all the other principals who "know" Sam, each share a separate secret key with him, which was originally established when they were "introduced" to him.

[2]This is later terminology, introduced by Kerberos, which we'll see next, but we might as well use it for the ancestor too.

[3]The term "nonce" is defined by the *OED* [203] as "In full *nonce-word*. A word coined for one occasion.". In their paper, Needham and Schroeder use it to mean "(number) used only once", and the term is now generally used with these semantics in the context of cryptographic protocols. The nonce is a number invented by Alice just for this run of the protocol. It does not need to be unguessable (one should say so if it does), only different from any other number used in that position in other runs. Lomas later introduced the term "confounder" for a value used *precisely* once in an authentication protocol, after observing that in many circumstances a "nonce" is actually used twice. However, this more accurate term has not yet attained widespread usage.

$$S \rightarrow A : \mathrm{E}_{K_{AS}}(B, N_A, K_{AB}, TICKET_{AB}), \qquad \text{(Message 2)}$$

where

$$TICKET_{AB} \triangleq \mathrm{E}_{K_{BS}}(A, K_{AB}).$$

Note that the ticket also contains K_{AB}—that's how Bob will get to know about that key—but is encrypted under K_{BS}. Because K_{BS} is unknown to Alice, she cannot read the contents of the ticket, which is why Sam has to tell her K_{AB} separately. An eavesdropper, meanwhile, not knowing either K_{AS} or K_{BS}, will not be able to read the session key K_{AB} from Sam's message. Sam mentions B in his reply to Alice so that she can check that no man-in-the-middle altered her request in message 1.

Alice now sends Bob the ticket made for her by Sam.

$$A \rightarrow B : TICKET_{AB}. \qquad \text{(Message 3)}$$

Bob observes that the ticket could have only been produced by Sam because of the K_{BS} encryption, and therefore accepts that Sam is vouching for Alice. This is a subtle point: Needham and Schroeder effectively use conventional cryptography to implement a poor man's digital signature—except that it isn't quite a signature in the sense that it could not convince a third party (this is similar to what we said about the MAC: see section 3.2.6). From the ticket, Bob learns K_{AB}. At this point Alice and Bob share a key that they could use to secure their further communications. Bob, however, unless he kept a track of all the keys previously sent to him by Alice, cannot be sure that message 3 isn't a replay of a similar message he received in the past; and if it were, the attacker would be tricking him into reusing an existing key. To guard against this, he challenges Alice with a nonce.

$$B \rightarrow A : \mathrm{E}_{K_{AB}}(N_B). \qquad \text{(Message 4)}$$

Alice decrements Bob's nonce before returning it, thereby proving that she could read it in plaintext, and therefore also proving that she knows K_{AB} herself.

$$A \rightarrow B : \mathrm{E}_{K_{AB}}(N_B - 1). \qquad \text{(Message 5)}$$

After this, both parties are happy to use K_{AB} to encrypt the rest of their communications.

B.1.2 Denning-Sacco

In 1981, Denning and Sacco [86] discovered a problem with this protocol. In their paper they remark that

> If communication keys and private keys are never compromised (as Needham and Schroeder assume), the protocol is secure

but they hypothesize that a communication key[4] might be compromised

> due to negligence or a design flaw in the system, i.e. an intruder may be able to break into the AS or into A's or B's computer and steal a key.

Under this assumption, they highlight the following attack. The enemy Charlie, who controls the network, records messages 3, 4 and 5 exchanged by Alice and Bob, steals the session key K_{AB} by some unspecified means, and from then on can impersonate Alice when talking to Bob. Firstly, he replays message 3 to him:

$$C \rightarrow B : TICKET_{AB} \equiv E_{K_{BS}}(A, K_{AB}). \qquad \text{(Message 3')}$$

At this point Bob, who doesn't keep track of past session keys and therefore does not notice that this is a replay, challenges this pseudo-Alice with a nonce:

$$B \rightarrow C : E_{K_{AB}}(N_B). \qquad \text{(Message 4')}$$

But Charlie, who has stolen K_{AB}, has no problem in decrypting the message and answering just like Alice would:

$$C \rightarrow B : E_{K_{AB}}(N_B - 1). \qquad \text{(Message 5')}$$

Denning and Sacco fix this problem (and save on the total number of messages) by using timestamps instead of nonces. The basic mechanism is that, instead of having the verifier send the prover a nonce and expect it to be returned, the prover spontaneously sends a timestamp to the verifier who checks whether it is "fresh" (i.e. sufficiently recent). So the exchange between Alice and Sam becomes

$$A \rightarrow S : A, B, \qquad \text{(Message 1'')}$$

where Alice no longer sends Sam a nonce, and

$$S \rightarrow A : E_{K_{AS}}(B, T, K_{AB}, TICKET''_{AB}), \qquad \text{(Message 2'')}$$

where Sam's response has a timestamp T which Alice can use to check the freshness of the message and ensure that it is not a replay. The ticket also contains the same timestamp:

$$TICKET''_{AB} \triangleq E_{K_{BS}}(A, K_{AB}, T),$$

---

[4]This is what we call a session key, i.e. the K_{AB} above.

which allows Bob to check its freshness once it receives it from Alice in the third, and now last, step of the amended protocol:

$$A \rightarrow B : TICKET''_{AB}.$$ (Message 3'')

At this point there is no further need for a handshake between Alice and Bob because, if the messages are fresh, then they are not replays.

There are two main objections to this line of reasoning. The first is that, if we accept that session keys like K_{AB} may be compromised, it is only a small step from that to accept that the "private" keys like K_{AS} and K_{BS} might be compromised by the same mechanism (especially since they are longer-lived and therefore have a larger window of exposure); if this happens, the addition of timestamps does not cure the problem. The second is that the use of timestamps requires synchronized clocks across the system (to within a certain tolerance), and this requirement might not be trivial to fulfil in a secure way[5].

Despite this, these observations are not without merit: the most famous of Needham-Schroeder's derivatives, Kerberos, which we shall examine next in section B.2, does indeed make use of timestamps instead of nonces.

Before closing the discussion on Needham-Schroeder, it is worth noting the difficulty of assessing whether all possible attacks on a given protocol have been taken into consideration and whether the protocol actually does what its designers intended, even for a protocol consisting only of a few messages. As the conclusion of the original article [196] highlighted,

> protocols such as those developed here are prone to extremely subtle errors that are unlikely to be detected in normal operation. The need for techniques to verify the correctness of such protocols is great, and we encourage those interested in such problems to consider this area.

Needham himself gave a significant contribution towards this goal two decades later, when he created the BAN logic of authentication with Burrows and Abadi [56, 57].

B.2   Kerberos

Kerberos [160] is a network authentication protocol based on Needham-Schroeder, originally developed at MIT for the Athena project in the mid-eighties. It adopts the Denning-Sacco fix (section B.1.2) of using timestamps instead of nonces (tickets have a limited lifetime). This has its benefits, but means that the system depends on secure clock distribution.

---

[5]We effectively end up widening the perimeter of the Trusted Computing Base (see section 3.5.2) to include the whole clock distribution subsystem.

Kerberos is a fully engineered authentication and key management system rather than just an abstract sequence of messages with some well defined properties, as reflected in the fact that reference [160] above is a 100-page Internet RFC rather than a 10-page journal paper. Variants of Kerberos have been adopted by many flavours of Unix; nowadays even Windows 2000 follows suit.

In Kerberos, the Sam of the previous section is split into two[6]: an Authentication Server (sometimes called Key Distribution Centre), which "recognizes" Alice at login, and a Ticket Granting Server, which gives her a ticket to talk to her chosen server Bob. The AS, too, gives Alice a ticket (a slightly different one, called a "ticket-granting ticket"), just so that she can talk to the TGS. Whereas in Needham-Schroeder (with the Denning-Sacco fix) Alice got a ticket from Sam and then talked immediately to Bob, here Alice must first talk to the first half of Sam, get from it a ticket to talk to the second half of Sam, and get from that a ticket to talk to Bob.

This split between the two functions of Sam is for performance and scalability. The AS needs to share secret keys with all the possible Alices (clients, such as workstations), while the TGS needs to share secret keys with all the possible Bobs (resource servers that the Alices wish to access, such as printers); if these two subsystems are separate, it is easier to dimension them appropriately.

Tickets have a limited lifetime (a few hours is typical), but may be reused many times before expiration, so this scheme allows Alice to interact with the AS once and then use the same ticket-granting ticket many times with the TGS to talk to several Bobs.

In terms of usability, this arrangement has the significant advantage of providing users with a "single sign-on" facility. The human user of the client computer we indicated as Alice only has to enter her password once at the beginning of her session (login) and she can then communicate with all the resource servers that she is authorized to access[7]. This works as follows: the secret key $K_{A,AS}$ that Alice shares

---

[6]For us, this has the unfortunate notational side effect of generating a principal AS, who might conceivably have a public key K_{AS}. This looks confusingly similar (in fact identical) to our notation for the secret key shared between A and S, which we just used in the previous section. In the interest of clarity (?) we shall refer to the two halves of Sam using their official Kerberos names of AS and TGS, rather than inventing one-letter homebrew names for them. The confusion may be mitigated by the knowledge that we make no use of public keys in this section.

[7]Subtlety: this narrative exposes the weakness of the practice of referring to principals with anthropomorphic names such as Alice. Now that we have to make a distinction, is Alice the computer or its human user? The answer in this case is that what identifies the principal "Alice" at the server end is ultimately the (hash of the) user's login password, so the essence of Alice is carried by the user, not by the computer. We may still (improperly but plausibly) call "Alice" the computer onto which user Alice is logged, given that it acts as her digital representative in the protocol, as long as we realize that another computer will be "Alice" as soon as the user logs in elsewhere. This terminological impropriety becomes less and less pretty when we realize that user Alice might log into several computers at the same time and therefore have several simultaneous digital representatives, which by the above argument we should all call Alice. Hmmm.

with the AS is the hash of the user's login password. During login, Alice asks the AS for a ticket-granting ticket, which she gets in a packet encrypted under $K_{A,AS}$. As part of the login procedure, the user types her password into her Kerberos client software, which hashes it and uses the result to decrypt the AS's packet. The user password is then wiped from the client software, so that it will not be compromised by an attack on the client machine. For the rest of the session, Alice simply uses the ticket-granting ticket several times to contact the TGS in order to get tickets for the individual resource servers.

The user password is never transmitted over the network and is never stored anywhere. This is a significant improvement over, say, Telnet. As pointed out by Bellovin and Merritt [30] and readily admitted in the official document [160], though, the scheme is still vulnerable to password guessing attacks as described in section 3.4.1: the attacker just eavesdrops on the replies returned by the AS to the various Alices and tries to decrypt them using candidate $K_{A,AS}$ keys obtained by hashing guesses from his dictionary.

In terms of management, this scheme offers the benefit of centralized security policy management. By suitable configuration of the AS and TGS, an administrator can define who is authorized to access what for the whole "authentication realm", which is the set of clients and servers with which the AS and TGS share secret keys.

A realm typically corresponds to an administrative domain: each organization, or perhaps each site of an organization, will establish its own. Kerberos provides for cross-realm authentication by allowing the TGS of realm X to be a principal in another realm Y. This allows a client in realm X to obtain a ticket for a server in realm Y. Realms are usually arranged hierarchically and an authentication may follow a complex path along the tree. It is however necessary for all the servers involved to be online before the requested ticket can be issued.

B.3   Public key infrastructures

For a public key system to work on a large scale, a way to manage and distribute public keys must be deployed. In particular, one must avoid the man-in-the-middle attacks (section 3.4.3) that become possible if malicious principals can convince their unsuspecting victims to accept forged public keys as those of their intended correspondents.

The CCITT X.509 recommendation [59], published in 1988, was the first serious attempt at such an infrastructure. It was part of the grander plan of X.500, a global distributed directory intended to assign a unique name to every principal (person, computer, peripheral, ...) in the world—so called *Distinguished Names*. In this context, X.509 used *certificates* (i.e. signed statements) that bound unique names to public keys. Originally this was meant to control which principals had the right to modify which subtrees of X.500, but soon its use as an identity instrument became prevalent and it is used today to certify the public keys used with SSL/TLS, the protocol used for secure access to web sites which we'll discuss in section B.5. Web sites wishing to accept credit card transactions typically have an encryption key certified by a company such as Verisign whose public key is well known; customers entering credit card numbers or other sensitive data can check the certificate to ensure that the public key with which the data will be encrypted is certified by Verisign to belong to the intended recipient. X.509 is thus an example of a hierarchical public key infrastructure with a comparatively small number of master certification authorities on which all name certificates ultimately depend.

However, the software that did most to bring public key cryptography into the mainstream was Zimmermann's PGP, which we already mentioned in section 3.4.3. One of PGP's conceptual innovations, apart from the practical one of actually existing, was the rejection of this hierarchical infrastructure of certification authorities in favour of a decentralized "web of trust" in which all the users, as peers, mutually certify the validity of the keys of their interlocutors. Users may thus obtain unreliably certified keys over insecure channels, as long as they can build "chains of trust" starting from people they know and leading to those keys.

There have been at least two attempts to get the best of both worlds. SPKI (Simple Public Key Infrastructure) by Ellison [100, 101] and SDSI (Simple Distributed Security Infrastructure) by Rivest and Lampson [220], two related initiatives that eventually joined forces, also reject the concept of a single global certification authority. They bind keys directly to capabilities rather than via names. One of the core concepts is that of *local names*—identifiers that do not have to be globally unique as long as they are unique in the context in which they are used. Global names can be reintroduced as needed by placing a local name in the relevant context. So "Microsoft's public key" becomes "DNS's .com's Microsoft's public key", with DNS being a privileged context.

Without a single root, a user of the system must repeatedly make decisions on the validity of arbitrary keys and may at times be requested to express a formal opinion on the validity of the key of another principal (by "signing" it). For consistency it is desirable that these actions be governed by a policy. Let us examine a couple of examples—we shall refer to PGP for concreteness, since this is probably the most widely deployed system among end users.

As we saw in section 3.4.3, PGP lets you assign various "trust levels" to introducers of keys and it lets you define a threshold that the rating of an unknown public key must reach. Such a rule amounts to a policy stating which keys to accept as valid. However, the interesting aspects, as usual, come up in the details. A fundamental but easily neglected element of this policy would be a precise operational definition of when to classify an introducer as untrusted, marginally trusted or fully trusted.

The dual problem, equally interesting and probably just as neglected by individual users of PGP, is that of establishing a policy to govern one's signing of other people's keys. This is important if one wishes to be considered as a trustworthy introducer by others. One possible such policy might say:

1. I shall only certify a key if I have received or checked it in a face-to-face meeting with its owner.

2. Moreover, I shall only certify a key if I have personally verified the passport of its owner.

3. Whenever I sign a key, I shall record date, key id and fingerprint in a signed log that I keep on my web page.

Such a policy is known as a *certification practice statement*, and can offer some procedural guarantees about the quality of the certifications that one has performed. It gives an independent observer a chance to assess the relative quality of the certification offered by different introducers (assuming that their claims about compliance can be believed).

An observer could for example remark that the policy above, while apparently very strict, does not actually ascertain whether the named principal controls the private key corresponding to the public key being signed. Alice might follow the above policy and still sign a public key that Bob presents as his, but which he instead just copied off Charlie's web page. This would not allow Bob to read Alice's (or anybody's) correspondence to Charlie, but it would enable him to damage Alice's reputation as a trustworthy introducer ("Look, she signed that this key belongs to Bob, but it's not true! She's too gullible to be an introducer!"). We might try to fix this hole by adding a challenge-response step to the policy: Alice shall only sign Bob's key if Bob is able to sign a random number chosen by Alice[8].

One lesson from all this is that policies, like ideas, tend to become clear only after we write them down in detail. It will be much harder to spot a methodological flaw if the de facto policy has never been explicitly stated. This even applies to the above "fix": without a more explicit description of how to perform the challenge-response, it is impossible to say whether the proposed exchange is safe or still vulnerable to a man-in-the-middle attack. For example, Bob might offer to certify Charlie's key and simultaneously present it to Alice as his own for her to certify.

---

[8]Subtlety: Bob should take appropriate precautions to avoid being framed by Alice, who might make him sign something unfavourable pretending it's just a random number—this would be a "chosen protocol attack" like the one discussed in section 3.2.5.

She gives him a random challenge, he passes it to Charlie and Charlie provides the required signature. Bob now sends this signature to Alice who mistakenly certifies the key as Bob's.

Certification practice statements are even more important when we are dealing with a commercial or government certification authority rather than with private individuals using PGP. Such statements typically also set out the precise circumstances in which certificates will be revoked (cf. section 4.1.1), and what liability (if any) will be borne for errors.

B.4   IPSEC

IPSEC [154], or IP-level security, provides authentication and encryption at the IP level. It properly pertains to IP version 6 (all IPv6-capable hosts must implement it), but it may be retrofitted to IPv4 (systems may optionally implement some of the features).

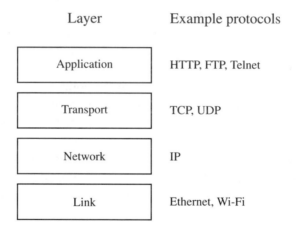

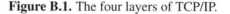

Figure B.1. The four layers of TCP/IP.

The TCP/IP architecture [244] defines four layers, as shown in figure B.1. At the bottom is the **Link**, or "interface", layer, which specifies the physical, electrical and media access details, and anything else that is controlled by the device driver for the particular network interface of the host. Ethernet, Wi-Fi and so on belong here. Next is the **Network**, or "internet", layer, which specifies how to send individual datagrams from one node to another; this is where IP belongs. On top of this is the **Transport** layer, which specifies how to provide a channel between two hosts. TCP (reliable) and UDP (unreliable) belong here. Finally there is the

Application layer, home of protocols such as Telnet, FTP and HTTP. Each layer uses the services of the layer below and offers its services to the layer above.

IP is connectionless and stateless: datagrams are sent from one host to another independently of each other and with no guarantees about delivery. Since IPSEC works at this level, it can only guarantee the integrity and confidentiality of individual datagrams, not of connections. There is however some shared security state between the endpoints: session keys, their validity intervals, the cryptographic algorithms to be used and other ancillary values such as serial numbers. This state is held in data structures called "security associations". Each datagram must be sent or received within the context of a specific security association.

The mechanism that provides integrity is the "IP authentication header" or AH [152], while the one providing confidentiality (plus some integrity) is the "IP Encapsulating Security Payload" or ESP [153]. These fit into the layering scheme in the way that we shall now describe.

The general pattern is that the entire packet (header plus payload) from the higher level becomes the payload of the lower level packet. So, the lower in the protocol stack you go, the more overhead you find[9]. This is what happens, for example, when a TCP segment is transported by an IP datagram (figure B.2).

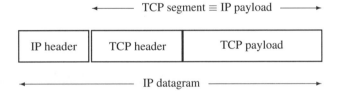

Figure B.2. A TCP segment inside an IP datagram.

Integrity, authentication and non-repudiation, depending on the choice of options, are provided by the Authentication Header (AH), which is a supplementary optional header of an IP datagram. It is essentially a MAC calculated over the rest of the packet, header included, but excluding any of the fields that need to change

---

[9]Some people find this counter-intuitive; they feel it's the *higher* layers that provide extra overhead compared to the Zen-like purity of sending bits on the wire. But this depends on the point of view. Ultimately, data is generated at the application level. When, say, Telnet sends an A, at the top level this is only one byte; but as it goes down the stack, each layer adds its own header overhead in order to be able to deliver this keystroke to its destination. It is certainly true that the lowest-level packet contains plenty of overhead generated by the upper layers: in fact, ignoring fragmentation, it *includes* all the higher level packets. Precisely for this reason, then, there is more overhead in packets at the bottom than in those at the top—despite the fact that much of this overhead was generated in the upper layers.

in transit (e.g. "time to live"). The AH can be used in transport mode (where the IP header of the original datagram is used as the header of the new one) or in tunnel mode (where the whole of the original datagram is protected by the AH, and a new IP header is prepended to that). The obvious costs introduced by the AH are latency and processing load on the nodes that generate and check the header.

Confidentiality, integrity and authentication, depending on the choice of options, are offered by the Encapsulating Security Payload (ESP), which "encapsulates" the IP datagram in optional layers of encryption and signature. Here, too, there are two distinct modes, depending on whether the original IP header goes outside or inside the ESP. In transport mode (figure B.3), the segment from the upper layer goes into the Encapsulating Security Payload and is optionally encrypted, but the IP header doesn't, and stays outside in cleartext to direct the packet to its destination. If encryption is turned on, eavesdroppers will not be able to read the contents, but they will know the source and destination of the packet.

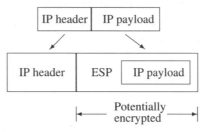

Figure B.3. IPSEC encryption: transport mode.

In tunnel mode (figure B.4), the entire IP packet (header and payload) is encapsulated in the ESP. Because the IP header is in the section of the packet that might be encrypted, it cannot be used for routing, so the entire ESP must become the payload of an enclosing IP datagram whose header is left in clear. This mode can be used to implement a VPN (virtual private network), for example to join the gateways of two geographically separated LANs over the public Internet. Eavesdroppers will know that packets are flowing between the two gateways, but they will not know which hosts from one LAN are talking to which other hosts on the other one.

Both the AH and the ESP mechanisms depend on source and destination sharing a secret to be used to key the relevant cryptographic algorithm. The question of how to distribute such a shared secret is, as always, a delicate issue. As a baseline, the standard requires conforming implementations to support "manual configuration", that is to say having a human configure each system with the appropriate keys. Apart from that, a modular architecture is defined which will support multiple key distribution and management strategies. This makes it possible to abandon

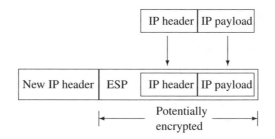

Figure B.4. IPSEC encryption: tunnel mode.

an old key management method if it proves to be flawed.

Because IPSEC operates at the IP level, it is transparent to applications: legacy applications will not require any modification in order to have their traffic protected. However, for the same reason, IPSEC cannot provide application-level security services (such as authenticating and protecting the session between the bank's web server and the customer's home computer) and will therefore have to be complemented by other solutions, such as SSL/TLS which we are going to examine next.

There is significant overlap between the functionality offered by the AH and ESP mechanisms. Ferguson and Schneier [106] offer an extensive review of IPSEC and highlight many other redundancies, arguing that the architecture needs to be drastically simplified, or its own complexity will prevent it from ever being secure. They document a number of security flaws caused by a baroque abundance of redundant features and suggest radical simplifications such as "eliminate transport mode", given that tunnel mode can emulate it by making the outside header a copy of the inside one, and "eliminate the AH protocol" since all the necessary authentication can still be performed within the ESP. Apart from specific protocol errors, the pervasive problems they identify are unnecessary complexity, unnecessary flexibility, lack of clarity in the documentation, and lack of explicitness about the goals that individual mechanisms are meant to achieve. They ascribe these problems to the fact that IPSEC was designed by a committee rather than by a small focused group. Anyone who has attempted to understand IPSEC solely from reading the RFCs will find it hard to disagree with these criticisms. On the other hand, what IPSEC provides is still an improvement over the status quo. Ferguson and Schneier conclude with the following assessment:

> We strongly discourage the use of IPsec in its current form for protection of any kind of valuable information, and hope that future iterations of the design will be improved. However, we even more strongly discourage any current alternatives, and recommend IPsec when the alternative is an insecure network. Such are the realities of the world.

B.5 SSL/TLS

SSL, which stands for "Secure Sockets Layer", was originally conceived and developed by Netscape as a security protocol for web-based e-commerce. Most of the bugs were shaken out by the time development reached version 3, at which point SSL was deemed sufficiently mature to be adopted by the IETF, which renamed it TLS ("Transport Layer Security") version 1.0 [89]. Unless one is making a point about specific subtleties, SSL and TLS are for practical purposes the same thing; however the subtleties are sufficiently significant that the two incarnations do not interoperate. In what follows we shall call the protocol simply TLS for brevity, since we refer to the RFC, but most of the technical comments also apply to SSL v3.

TLS is now widely deployed and is implemented by the major browsers and web servers. It is the protocol behind the `https://` URLs and the golden padlock or key that graces your browser when you visit such secure sites and the authentication succeeds. It provides session-oriented authentication, integrity and confidentiality over the Internet. Unlike IPSEC, it is not specific to IP: it lives at a higher level in the protocol stack, between the transport layer and the application layer, and it runs on any reliable transport protocol.

TLS actually consists of several sub-protocols: the bottom one is the TLS Record Protocol, which provides confidentiality (via a symmetric block or stream cipher) and integrity (via a MAC). Several other protocols may run on top of it, and in particular the TLS Handshake Protocol, which allows the server and the client at the two ends of the connection to authenticate each other and to negotiate encryption algorithms and session keys. Other TLS sub-protocols that run on top of the record protocol include the "change cipher spec protocol" and the "application data protocol".

TLS is stateful. Its "connection state" includes the identifiers for the specific algorithms used for compression, encryption and MAC, plus their parameters (keys and initialization vectors). Within one TLS session there are separate connection states for the "read" and the "write" direction, and there are also separate "current" and "pending" states when a transition is about to happen. The initial state always specifies no encryption, compression or MAC; transitions to other states, and establishment of the appropriate parameters, are governed by the handshake protocol.

The handshake protocol works roughly as follows. The client contacts the server by sending a "ClientHello" message. The server responds by sending a "ServerHello" message. With these greetings, the two parties negotiate various parameters including the algorithms they wish to use, chosen between the suites[10]

---

[10]Algorithms are not chosen individually: each party has a list of prepackaged combinations that

of algorithms that both of them support. Random values are also generated and exchanged.

An optional authentication phase follows. If the client requested it, the server sends its public key certificate. The client, who is expected to know the public key of the issuing certification authority[11], verifies the signature on the certificate. To ensure that the certificate has not been replayed from somewhere else, the client also challenges the server by encrypting a random value with the server's claimed public key. The server will only be able to exhibit the plaintext if it has access to the private key. If all this succeeds, the client has now verified the identity of the server. The server can in turn authenticate the client if it so wishes[12]. After this, the parties exchange a "ChangeCipherSpec" message, which activates the "pending" connection state, committing to the newly negotiated security parameters. From that point onwards, the communication is secured (encrypted etc.) and application data may be exchanged.

In the interest of efficiency, TLS allows caching of the connection state. The client can send a "session ID" in its hello message and, if the server finds a matching one in its cache and does not consider it stale, the previously established state can be reused without having to re-run the handshake protocol with its expensive public key operations. The expiration time for a session is parametric, but will be typically set to a few hours. This statefulness can be exploited even if the application protocol running over TLS is stateless (like HTTP). This means, for example, that a client can visit a secure web site, run the handshake protocol, get the golden padlock, visit several pages (each with its multitude of HTTP downloads for the pages, the frames and the images), go to some other site, come back to the secure site within a reasonable time, and never have to perform the handshake a second time.

While on the subject of efficiency, we note that the use of asymmetric asymmetric ciphers[13] allows the HTTPS exchange to be performed with minimal load on the client, since the expensive operations of decryption and signature are only performed on the server. According to Anderson [11, section 19.5.1] this design choice was a mistake, since desktop web browsers typically have more spare cycles than the servers they visit; this leads to a poorly balanced situation where the clients

---

it supports, but mixing and matching is not allowed. This is a good thing, security-wise.

[11]Web browsers ship with a number of embedded root certificates, such as Verisign's, in order to bootstrap this process.

[12]In HTTPS, the web server is required to have a certificate, but the browsing client is not. At the time of writing, very few individuals (as opposed to companies) hold suitable public key certificates anyway. If the application requires client authentication, it must resort to some other mechanism such as HTTP Basic Authentication.

[13]Sometimes public key ciphers are called "asymmetric" because encryption and decryption use different keys, unlike in conventional ("symmetric") ciphers. I like to call "asymmetric asymmetric" those public key ciphers that have been tuned to make encryption much faster than decryption (see section 5.1.1).

sit idle and the servers struggle even with the help of hardware crypto accelerators. But this asymmetry may still have its benefits after all in the forthcoming scenario of "mobile commerce"[14], where clients may be devices such as WAP or i-Mode cellular phones, endowed with what I refer to in this book as "peanut processors" (small and not very powerful CPUs).

Greenberg [124, section 2.2.2.3] observes an interesting problem in the enterprise context: TLS does such a good job of providing an end-to-end secure communications session that it upsets firewalls, because they cannot look at the traffic to decide whether to allow it through or not. Punching a hole through the firewall to allow TLS traffic in and out is potentially a violation of the security policy that the firewall is meant to enforce, since the traffic carried by TLS could be anything, including dangerous inbound pollutants (e.g. viruses) and sensitive outbound secrets (the formula for Coca-Cola or whatever it is that the company makes). On the other hand, forbidding TLS traffic across the firewall boundary prevents the inside users from accessing outside sites in a secure way, forcing them to use insecure methods. Proxy servers at the firewall boundary have their share of problems too, which the author discusses. In general, this problem appears to be an instance of a conflict between two partly incompatible security policies—the firewall's, which says "the company must be able to check anything that goes in and out", and the accountant's, which says "you are not authorized to type the company's credit card number other than over a secure channel".

The high level comparison with IPSEC highlights complementary advantages and disadvantages: unlike IPSEC, TLS provides application-level end-to-end security, and as such is not transparent to applications, which need to be modified in order to take advantage of it; on the other hand, for this same reason, TLS allows the applications to request the specific level of security that is appropriate for their needs.

B.6 GSM

The GSM digital cellular telephone network[15] is an example of a system in which devices are originally registered with one principal (the home network), but may later need to be authenticated by other principals that the first one does not completely trust (the other networks visited by the mobile user during roaming) and to whom therefore it does not want to reveal all its secrets. It is instructive to observe

---

[14]The latest fashionable buzzword, coined in late 2000 as the successor to "e-commerce", is actually "m-commerce". Yuck.

[15]Given the abundance of special terms and acronyms related to GSM, to facilitate cross-referencing with other documentation, throughout this section we shall consistently use the official GSM terminology and abbreviations, as specified in [104].

how GSM deals with this problem [103, 52]. Note that, to limit the computational costs, no public key primitives are used in this system.

When the user buys a phone, or more precisely when the user sets up a contract with a provider, she receives a smartcard known as the SIM (Subscriber Identity Module) containing a unique 128-bit "individual subscriber authentication key" *Ki*. This key is also stored in a database (at an authentication centre, or *AuC*) at the provider, along with identifying information for the subscriber. This provisioning phase establishes a common secret between the subscriber and the service provider of the home network.

Once this shared secret is in place, it is easy for the home network to authenticate the subscriber whenever she wishes to place a call. The subscriber (shown as *P* for *Prover* in the following protocol listing) sends a call setup request to the network; the network (*V* for *Verifier* in the listing) challenges the subscriber with a random nonce *RAND*; the subscriber must prove ownership of *Ki* by transforming the nonce with the A3 cryptographic algorithm[16] keyed by *Ki*, yielding the subscriber response *SRES*.

$$P \to V : \quad callSetupRequest$$
$$V \to P : \quad RAND$$
$$P \to V : \quad SRES \triangleq \mathrm{MAC}^{A3}_{Ki}(RAND)$$

At this stage, the Verifier cannot distinguish the Prover from a man-in-the-middle attacker who overhears and repeats the Prover's reply *SRES*. But the next step of the protocol makes this impersonation fruitless: both the subscriber and the network compute a confidentiality session key *Kc*

$$Kc \triangleq \mathrm{MAC}^{A8}_{Ki}(RAND)$$

using a different algorithm called A8[17] on the same input data and then use this key to encrypt, under stream cipher A5, all the subsequent traffic for that call.

$$transmitted \triangleq \mathrm{E}^{A5}_{Kc}(voice)$$

The session key *Kc* is never transmitted and is computed using a shared secret to which the man-in-the-middle has no access; therefore the traffic it protects cannot be decrypted by the attacker.

---

[16]In a futile and counterproductive attempt at "security by obscurity", GSM defined a number of cryptographic algorithms but never officially published them. A5 is a stream cipher, while A3 and A8 are MACs. Following Kerckhoffs' prediction [155], there were leaks, and some of the algorithms made their way into textbooks—Schneier [227], for example, contains source code for one version of A5 (there is provision for up to 7 variants of A5 in the standard [103, section 4.8]). A few years later, Biryukov, Shamir and Wagner [35] came up with a real-time cryptanalytic attack on the strong variant known as A5/1, which by that time was fielded in about 130 million units.

[17]To be precise the algorithm is the same, and A3 and A8 just select different portions of its long output. This way, the computation only runs once.

What happens, however, when the subscriber visits a geographical location served by another network operator, in the course of what is known as "roaming"? Security-wise, the above protocol would still work if the visited operator just acted as a man-in-the-middle and relayed messages between the subscriber and her home network. However, even without considering problems of network delay, the outcome would be the establishment of a confidentiality session key between the subscriber and the *home* network, whereas the whole point of efficient roaming is for the subscriber to establish a key with the *visited* network, otherwise the payload (voice and data traffic) would be forced to travel back all the way to the home network. There is therefore a requirement for a mechanism that will allow the roaming subscriber and the visited network to establish a session key, but without disclosing the subscriber key to the visited network—otherwise the latter could impersonate the subscriber, and it would not be desirable from a systems point of view to have to trust unconditionally all the networks that a subscriber might possibly visit.

The approach chosen by GSM is for the home network to precompute a series of "triples", each consisting of the challenge nonce *RAND*, the corresponding response *SRES* and the corresponding session key, and send them to the visited network when the subscriber registers there. This allows the visited network to challenge the visitor for a fixed number of times. The visited network can ask the home network for more triples when necessary. If the visited network misbehaves or leaks and the triples are compromised, it is still not possible for the holder of the triples to impersonate the subscriber on another network.

It is worth observing that A5 only protects the traffic between the subscriber (known as mobile station or *MS*) and the base station system (*BSS*). Such traffic is encrypted to prevent the kind of eavesdropping via radio scanners that used to be popular against analogue (first generation) cell phones. The link between a base station and the rest of the system, however, often still operates in cleartext. As a matter of fact, there is provision in the standard for this link to be encrypted, but operators tend to leave the facility switched off.

When we found out about this, a group of us at Cambridge led by Ross Anderson set out to exploit this hole with an attack [10]. This was in response to a challenge presented by MobilCom, a subsidiary of Deutsche Telekom, who proudly dared anyone, in exchange for a prize of about 45 k$, to communicate at the expense of the SIM card associated with the phone number 0171-3289966. We found it quite hard to get in touch with anyone from that company willing even to acknowledge the existence of the challenge; and when we finally got through to someone who did, the offer had been silently withdrawn. Leaving to the reader any considerations about the credibility and professional integrity of the company, let us briefly review the technical aspects of the attack we planned but never carried out. As we shall demonstrate, the lack of encryption on the link from the base station to the rest of the network compromises not only the confidentiality of the subscriber's calls, but also the integrity of the account, in the sense that an attacker can place calls for which the victim will have to pay.

We start by transmitting a call setup request as in the first step of the authentication protocol described above. We do this from a modified handset so that we can identify ourselves to the base station using (i.e. faking) the *IMSI*[18] of the target phone, which is assumed to be known. We need to be roaming, so we perform this operation in a network that is not the home network for the target SIM. The visited network will then request some triples from the authentication centre of the home network. We intercept the unencrypted back-end microwave link of the local base station (there is one even on the roof of one of our University buildings, so physical access is no problem) and eavesdrop on the triples as they arrive. We load them into our modified handset so that we can respond to the challenges of the base station. The first authentication will fail, unless we go to a more complicated setup that allows us to use the captured triples in real time, but this is no problem: if we harvested n triples, we can still place $n - 1$ calls for free, which will be charged to the account of the target SIM.

B.7 Bluetooth

B.7.1 System overview

Bluetooth is an embedded radio system for short-range communication between small devices, and is the commercial system whose intended usage pattern most closely matches the ubiquitous computing and networking scenario that is the focus of this book. It is the newest among the real world systems that we discuss in this chapter; sadly, it also appears to be one of the least secure (only surpassed by 802.11, see section B.8 next), and the two circumstances are probably not unrelated.

This section was originally written in late 2000, before any Bluetooth products were available commercially, and was based on the published 1.0B specification [41, 42]. Since then a few Bluetooth-enabled products have hit the market, from PCMCIA adapters to cellular telephones, headsets and even data projectors. The specification has been updated to 1.1 [43, 44], but there have been no significant changes in the security section, so these considerations still apply.

The specification [41, chapter 14] acknowledges that

> the system has to provide security measures both at the application layer and the link layer

---

[18]International Mobile Subscriber Identity—a numeric name for the subscriber, stored in the SIM card, presented by Prover to Verifier in the call setup request and required by Verifier to look up the corresponding *Ki* in the database held at the *AuC*.

but then only describes link-layer security features, so we shall concentrate on those.

Before moving to the security aspects, a brief description of Bluetooth is perhaps in order. An early technical overview by some of the system architects is in Haartsen *et al.* [126], while the web site [40] offers many items of introductory material aimed at different kinds of audiences, including of course the cited specification documents [43, 44]. For the many to whom the full spec will be hard to digest, a much more readable alternative is Bray and Sturman [49].

Bluetooth was initially intended as a "serial cable replacement": a short-range (10 m or less) radio link between a laptop and a printer, between a cellphone and its headset, between a digital camera and a desktop computer. The inherent features of the medium have however also opened up other scenarios which would not be practical with a wired solution.

Bluetooth devices communicate in the unlicensed 2.4 GHz radio band known as ISM (the same as microwave ovens) using frequency hopping over 79 channels[19] to combat interference. The hopping frequency is 1600 Hz. The data is transmitted at a symbol rate of 1 MHz and the maximum (net) data rate is 723.2 kb/s.

Two main configurations are available: **point-to-point** between two units, and **point-to-multipoint** where the channel is shared among several units. A **piconet** is a set of Bluetooth devices sharing a channel. One of the members of this set will be the **master** of the piconet, governing channel access, while the others will be **slaves**. Up to 7 active slaves are allowed in a piconet; the others must be dormant, in a **parked** state. Piconets (each with its own hopping sequence, determined by the device address of the master) may overlap, and a single node may in theory take part in several at the same time[20].

B.7.2 Security services

The security services provided by Bluetooth are authentication and encryption. The authentication algorithm, called E_1, is a MAC based on SAFER+ (one of the 15 AES candidates that didn't make it to the finals) with a 128 bit key, while the encryption algorithm, called E_0, is a stream cipher using 4 linear feedback shift registers, with a key whose length can be set between 8 and 128 bits in increments of 8 bits. This variability is to accommodate locales where the use of strong encryption is prohibited. Still, the default "strong" key size is only 64 bits rather than 128, and

---

[19]Except in France where some of the band is unavailable and only 23 channels can be used. The same situation used to exist in Spain, but this was recently remedied. It is hoped that France will follow suit and release the rest of the ISM band by 2003.

[20]In practice, though, this is difficult to achieve, because the node has to keep in sync with two completely unrelated masters. Besides, unless the node has two separate radio receivers, the achievable data rate is going to be small.

the larger size appears to be there only in case it becomes necessary later[21].

There is no provision for the use of alternative algorithms. On the one hand this is a welcome simplification that eliminates an otherwise necessary negotiation phase and the associated risks of chosen cipher attacks; on the other, there might have been better choices for the algorithms. The one based on SAFER+ was an untested gamble at the time (when triple-DES might have been a more prudent choice) and became more of a loser after the AES semifinals. It is natural to wonder why the 1.1 revision of the Bluetooth specification did not replace both algorithms with constructions based on the AES winner Rijndael. This comment gains strength as further weaknesses are highlighted: Jakobsson and Wetzel [144] report on some that were discovered by Bleichenbacher, and new ones have been found by Fluhrer and Lucks [108].

At the highest level, Bluetooth link security may be described as follows. When two devices wish to communicate securely, they establish a shared secret called a *link key* (these come in many flavours, and can be established in a variety of ways). This key may be temporary or semi-permanent. If temporary, it lasts only for one session, i.e. for as long as the device that holds it remains in the current piconet. If semi-permanent, it may be reused in later sessions, so that when the two devices meet again they don't have to regenerate one[22].

Once a link key is (or is assumed to be) in place[23], entity authentication is carried out via a simple challenge-response subprotocol in which the verifier Alice sends out a random challenge AU_RAND_A and the prover Bob (called "claimant" in the Bluetooth spec) returns a MAC of it and its own "Bluetooth device address" BD_ADDR_B, computed using the link key:

$$A \rightarrow B : \quad AU\_RAND_A$$
$$B \rightarrow A : \quad SRES \triangleq \text{MAC}^{E_1}_{Link\_key}(AU\_RAND_A, BD\_ADDR_B).$$

The device addresses are publicly known, so Alice can compute *SRES* herself and see if it matches. If it does, this proves to Alice that Bob knew the link key. If mutual authentication is desired, the challenge-response is performed again in the other direction.

---

[21]This choice is dubious. With most asymmetric ciphers, a longer key implies greater computational effort. But this tradeoff does not apply to symmetric ciphers in the same way. As a matter of fact, several modern symmetric ciphers that accept variable-length keys, for example many of the AES candidates, actually always use full-length keys internally—the shorter keys being simply padded before use. In the absence of external regulations to the contrary, there is no compelling reason not to use the longest possible key length. Besides, qualitatively speaking, 64 bits is not terribly far from the 56 bits of DES which are now commonly recognized as insufficient (see section 3.1.3).

[22]But it can still be revoked if necessary, hence the "semi-".

[23]Observe that we are not necessarily referring to a semi-permanent link key: in fact, the first authentication is performed just after establishing the *initialization* key (see item 4 on page 198), which is a temporary kind of link key.

An additional output of the E_1 algorithm is the so-called "Authenticated Ciphering Offset" (ACO), which is used as one of the inputs to the E_3 algorithm (essentially a hash function) that generates the encryption key. Other inputs include the current link key, the device address of the master and a 128-bit random number[24].

Of course the random number needs to be communicated to the other device, otherwise it would be impossible to generate the same key at both ends. The specification isn't as clear as it could be on this issue, but it appears that this number (indicated as *EN_RAND*) is transmitted in clear from the master to the slave [41, sections 14.2.2.6 and 14.2.2.8]. Since the device addresses are not secret, the secrecy of the generated encryption key K_C ultimately depends only on the secrecy of the link key. So let's look in greater detail at the procedure to establish a link key.

B.7.3   Link keys

The link key, as we said, is a 128-bit number shared between two or more devices. Four different types of link keys are defined [41, section 14.2.1].

1. The combination key K_{AB}.

   The standard type of link key is the combination key K_{AB}, which is specific to the pair of devices A and B. If device A also wants to talk to device C, it will have to establish another combination key K_{AC} with it, and so on. This means that each device using combination keys must store a list of them, one for each device with which it communicates. These keys may be semi-permanent, i.e. they may be persistent across sessions. In other words, if my laptop once talks to the office printer on the first floor and establishes a link key with it, if I come back to that same printer a week later it might still use the same link key for the communication with that printer, without having to re-establish a link key. This makes sense in so far as the establishment of a link key is an "expensive" operation which might force the user to type PINs into devices. (More on this shortly: see the paragraph about the initialization key on page 198.) The drawback of this arrangement is the need for each device to store a list of known devices and corresponding combination keys. Practical implementations will only remember the most recently used ones, which might in turn lead to denial of service attacks aimed at flushing useful link keys out of the cache.

---

[24]To be precise, things are somewhat more complicated than implied by the above description: what E_3 hashes together to produce the encryption key K_C is the current link key, a 128-bit random number and a 96-bit COF (Ciphering Offset), which in turn is obtained from either the master device address or the ACO depending on whether the link key is a master key. See [41, section 14.2.2.5].

There is a straightforward protocol [41, section 14.2.2.4] for the generation of a new combination key from the previous link key. Each of the two devices generates a random number (LK_RAND_A or LK_RAND_B) and sends it to the other device by XORing it with the current link key. Each one of these numbers is stirred up by hashing it via an algorithm called E_{21} with the Bluetooth address of the device that produced it, to yield another number (LK_K_A or LK_K_B), as follows:

$$LK\_K_A \triangleq h^{E_{21}}(LK\_RAND_A, BD\_ADDR_A),$$
$$LK\_K_B \triangleq h^{E_{21}}(LK\_RAND_B, BD\_ADDR_B).$$

The new link key is then obtained as the XOR of the locally and the remotely generated numbers:

$$K \triangleq LK\_K_A \oplus LK\_K_B.$$

After authentication, as described above, to confirm the success of the exchange, the old link key is discarded. (Clearly, eavesdroppers who knew the previous link key and listened to this exchange will know the new one too.)

2. The unit key K_A.

For devices that cannot afford the memory to store many link keys, or which expect to have to connect to a great number of different peers, the simpler and pretty insecure arrangement of a unit key K_A is adopted. The unit key is generated once and for all when the device is first turned on by hashing a random number with the device's address:

$$K_A = h^{E_{21}}(RAND, BD\_ADDR_A).$$

After generation, this key is "stored in non-volatile memory and (almost) never changed" [41, section 14.2.2.3]. Device A then uses this same key as the link key for all its connections. Whenever A needs to give its K_A to another unit B, the two units set up an initialization key (*q.v.*, page 198) and then A sends B her K_A XORed with the initialization key. Therefore the secrecy of the unit key depends on that of the initialization key.

It is obvious that, with this setup, any device that ever speaks to A will learn this long-term K_A. From then on it will be able to eavesdrop on all of A's conversations, to impersonate A to any other device and by implication to mount man-in-the-middle attacks between A and anyone else wishing to speak to A. This is bad.

3. The temporary key K_{master}.

The temporary K_{master} key is used in point-to-multipoint situations where a master node wishes to communicate (broadcast) the same information to several slave nodes. If this were implemented by re-encrypting the same information to each of the slaves (using a separate combination key for each connection) then the bandwidth available to the piconet would be reduced by a factor of n, while at the same time the computational load on the master would increase by n. For greater efficiency, the master may generate a master key and use it as a common link key for all the devices in the desired broadcast domain. This key is only for temporary use: when the master concludes the broadcast, it instructs the slaves to fall back to their previous link keys. The master key is transmitted to each slave individually, "encrypted" under a key whose secret component is ultimately the existing link key between the master and the slave. The details are not terribly relevant and can be found in [41, section 14.2.2.8]. The important point is that the only secret that an eavesdropper must know in order to learn K_{master} from the observed exchange is the existing link key between master and slave.

4. The initialization key K_{init}.

   The initialization key K_{init} is a temporary key established and used whenever two devices that wish to communicate do not yet share a link key. The important detail is that the generation of the initialization key accepts external input from the human user, in the form of a PIN code of variable length. The user enters the PIN manually in both devices, so an eavesdropper does not gain any information about it. The generation of an initialization key is typically followed by authentication and by the exchange of a longer term link key, either a unit key or a combination key.

   The specification makes it clear that the length of the PIN is variable, as far as the link-layer security API is concerned, and that PINs between 0 and 16 octets will be accepted. It is less clear whether this freedom of choice is passed all the way up to the user, or only up to the application, which will then impose a fixed format for the user (the latter option seems more likely). If the chosen PIN is shorter than 16 octets, it is padded with extra octets taken from the *BD_ADDR* of the claimant unit. Apparently, this is to ensure

   > that K_{init} depends on the identity of the unit trying to connect to it (at least when short PIN codes are used)

   [41, section 14.2.2.1], though if this were a worthy goal it is not clear why hashing the whole of the PIN with the whole of the address wouldn't be a better alternative, especially since this padded PIN is about to be hashed with a random number through E_{22} anyway. The spec goes on to warn that

A fraudulent Bluetooth unit may try to test a large number of PINs by each time claiming another *BD_ADDR*. It is the application's responsibility to take countermeasures against this threat. If the device address is kept fixed, the waiting interval until next try is permitted is increased exponentially.

Delegating to the application layer the responsibility to thwart brute force PIN search attacks is a bit of a cop-out, especially just after admitting that the addition of the *BD_ADDR* in the mix isn't much of a safeguard. Since the typical PIN is expected to be only 4 decimal digits [41, section 14.2.1], many PIN search attacks will probably be feasible in real time. A fatal flaw, pointed out by Jakobsson and Wetzel [144], is that the eavesdropping attacker may verify PIN guesses without talking back to the victim devices, simply by performing the verification portion of the protocol. The authors also present an active attack in which the attacker initiates communication with the victim and then, through repeated attempts at PIN guessing, eventually steals the PIN that was entered in the victim device.

In summary, all the security of Bluetooth communications rests on the secrecy of the link key: any eavesdropper who knows the link key between A and B may overhear their conversations, since the encryption key can be derived from the link key and the messages exchanged over the air.

Despite this, there seem to be several circumstances in which the link key could be compromised relatively easily, i.e. without any cryptanalysis or invasive attacks.

When a device uses its unit key as a link key (case 2 above), it effectively reveals the link key to any principal with which it establishes a connection. In this particular case the device exposes itself not only to the threat of disclosure but also to that of impersonation.

In the more secure case where a combination key (case 1) is used instead of a unit key, the procedure by which the key is computed in the two devices ultimately depends on the secrecy of a PIN code that a user must manually enter into both devices (case 4). This has several problems. Firstly, PINs with sufficient entropy to provide adequate security against brute force attacks will be too inconvenient for users to type; this is reflected in the spec's mention of 4-digit PINs as the expected typical case, and has the obvious consequences. Secondly, allowing users to choose PINs is unwise, and opens the door to intelligent dictionary attacks on "easy numbers" that are likely to be substantially more efficient than the already affordable brute force 0000–9999 ones. There seems to be no good reason for asking users to invent their own PIN, especially since this is not a long term secret that they ought to remember but only an ephemeral one used to bootstrap the link between two devices. Thirdly, the alternative suggested in [41, section 14.2.1] is also flawed:

For many applications the PIN code will be a relatively short string of numbers. Typically, it may consist of only four decimal digits. Even though this gives sufficient security in many cases, there exist countless other, more sensitive, situations where this is not reliable enough. Therefore, the PIN code can be chosen to be any length from 1 to 16 octets. For the longer lengths, we envision the units exchanging PIN codes not through mechanical (i.e. human) interaction, but rather through means supported by software at the application layer. For example, this can be a Diffie-Hellman key agreement, where the exchanged key is passed on to the K_{init} generation process in both units, just as in the case of a shorter PIN code.

If such a purely wireless solution were adopted, a device that did Diffie-Hellman over the air could never be sure of having established a bond with the intended partner and not with a malicious node that also happened to be in radio range. As suggested in section 4.2.4, we can do better than this.

Another important observation by Jakobsson and Wetzel [144] is that ensuring communications confidentiality is only part of the story, and that Bluetooth security should cover much more—in particular, confidentiality of location. They present practical attacks that, given an easily deployed network of listener nodes at locations of interest, pinpoint and log the location of users who carry Bluetooth devices. When the victim devices are in *discoverable mode* (i.e. happy to talk to strangers), there is a trivial active attack. When they are not, the authors show how to identify the originating device (i.e. recognize it's the same between different transmissions) just by eavesdropping on the channel.

The fact that many people do not even recognize such location attacks as security leaks is the main reason why the system is weak against them. Mobility is one of the attributes of ubicomp systems that were absent in traditional distributed systems, and it requires not simply new solutions but an awareness of the new problems.

B.8   802.11

The IEEE 802.11 wireless networking standard [139] together with its variations 802.11a and 802.11b, also known as Wi-Fi and used primarily as a convenient Ethernet replacement for laptops within homes and offices, has become rather popular in recent years. In 2001 it came under the spotlight for a succession of papers and working attack programs which unequivocally demonstrated the vulnerability of its security subsystem. To describe the flawed system in great detail now would be akin to beating a dead horse and would produce a section destined to premature obsolescence, since those security problems are thankfully being worked on as I write. (A cynic might say that Bluetooth needs the same kind of treatment in order to become more secure.) I am therefore simply going to refer the interested reader to the attack papers, from which the workings of the (in)security mechanisms of 802.11 as originally designed and deployed, and as they existed at the time this book went to press, can be gathered more easily than from the voluminous standard document.

The Wired Equivalent Privacy (WEP) algorithm is part of the 802.11 standard; its name describes its intended goal. Base station and mobile terminal establish a common secret key (the standard does not specify how this should happen; often a key is obtained by hashing a user-supplied password and loaded into all the devices of the network) and then encrypt all subsequent traffic using that key. This is meant to exclude from the communication any devices that don't know the key.

In February 2001, Borisov, Goldberg and Wagner [48] published on their web site a draft document highlighting several flaws in WEP. They also described a variety of attacks that exploited those flaws: a passive attack (eavesdropping plus statistical analysis) to decrypt traffic; an active variant of the same, primed by injecting known plaintext; an active attack to construct valid encrypted packets; an active attack to flip selected bits in an existing packet; an active attack to reroute traffic elsewhere—unencrypted; and an attack that, after building a 15 GB table using techniques from the previous attacks and a day's worth of traffic, could decrypt every transmitted packet on the fly. All these attacks were devised after discovering mistakes in the published protocols, but were not actually carried out by the authors at the time.

Then Fluhrer, Mantin and Shamir [109] discovered some weaknesses in the key scheduling algorithm of the widely deployed RC4 stream cipher, and in particular found it completely insecure in a certain mode of operation which WEP happened to adopt. Once again this was a scientific paper based on the analysis of the cipher and of the published protocol, and the attack described in it had not been attempted on an actual 802.11 network.

Shortly afterwards, in August 2001, Stubblefield, Ioannidis and Rubin [245] implemented and optimized the attack invented by Fluhrer *et al.*, demonstrating its practicality and effectiveness:

> We believe that we have demonstrated the ultimate break of WEP, which is the recovery of the secret key by observation of traffic.

The only thing they didn't do was to release their attack code to the public.

But even this was quickly remedied: before the end of the month there were not one but *two* groups with working open-source code (AirSnort [53] and WEPCrack [214]) that replicated this exploit and made the software available to anyone on the Internet. As observed by Stubblefield *et al.* [245],

> Once a flawed system is popular enough to become a target, it is usually a short time before the system is defeated in the field.

Anyone with an 802.11 installation could now personally verify its vulnerability. Being able to replicate this completely passive (and therefore undetectable) eavesdropping and cracking attack made for a much more convincing demonstration of the insecurity of WEP than the brilliant cryptanalysis in the Fluhrer *et al.* paper [109].

The lesson from all this is, once again, the one that goes back to Kerckhoffs (see section 3.1.2). The 802.11 working group did not, to its credit, rely on security by obscurity, but at the same time it did not expose the cipher system to competent peer reviewers. In the words of Borisov *et al.* [48]:

> Wired Equivalent Privacy (WEP) isn't. The protocol's problems are a result of misunderstanding of some cryptographic primitives and therefore combining them in insecure ways. These attacks point to the importance of inviting public review from people with expertise in cryptographic protocol design; had this been done, the problems stated here would have surely been avoided.

At the time of writing, the standards group is busy redesigning the protocols to address all the flaws exposed above. This is the mature and sensible attitude to adopt, as opposed to trying to cover the loss of face by ignoring or denying the existence of the vulnerabilities. While WECA (Wireless Ethernet Compatibility Alliance), an industry consortium, is predictably cautious in acknowledging the problem [264], it is to be hoped that anyone working on ubicomp security, and on security in general, will pay attention to the practical lesson taught by these attacks. It is fortunate that the vulnerabilities of this system were first discovered and pointed out by responsible researchers and not by malicious underground villains who would have simply performed the cracking and eavesdropping at leisure while keeping quiet about it. The embarrassing failure of WEP is the best evidence of the usefulness and necessity of hostile peer review and of the value of full disclosure. As noted by Anderson in his comment on the Sklyarov arrest [12],

> Security research at an internationally competitive level is inherently an adversarial business; the field advances through a coevolution of attack and defence. Understanding and documenting the vulnerabilities of existing systems is critical to progress.

A system can only be called secure if it demonstrably withstands the attacks of competent adversaries. System builders should be grateful for the existence of competent attackers who are motivated by academic credit rather than malicious intent. Security by obscurity, i.e. actively hiding one's design, is futile, but so is just keeping quiet about it in the vain hope of not attracting unwelcome attention. For a company, or for a consortium of companies, having one's product cracked early by a small group of researchers is certainly embarrassing; but being broken later, after the product is fielded in hundreds of thousands of instances, is much more embarrassing, not to mention expensive. Trying too hard to avoid the embarrassment of the first kind is often a good way to attract that of the second.

Think how much worse off we would be if those respectable academic and industrial researchers had been prevented from publishing their findings about the insecurity of the system. It is naïve to assume that nobody else could have discovered the same weaknesses: we could paraphrase a popular slogan and say that "if cracking poor security is outlawed, only outlaws will do it". Instead of well-reasoned papers pointing out the flaws of the current system and possible remedies, we would only face[25] raw attack software, widely circulated among underground rings of script kiddies. Wireless installations such as the one in your office would be regularly abused. Meanwhile, in the absence of an open, independent and explicit exposition of the problem, the industry would just deny its existence, assuring users that everything is fine.

Recent legislation, such as the US's Digital Millennium Copyright Act under which Sklyarov was arrested, criminalizes reverse engineering and breaking security systems. It implicitly promotes a grim state of affairs such as the hypothetical one just described—not even "security by obscurity", just "insecurity by cover-up".

A swordsman may remain undefeated for his whole life if he never ventures outside his dōjō—but would you rank him as a strong one? Accepting the challenge of determined adversaries, and learning from the successful attacks of one's opponents, is necessary to build up strength. If we really intend to build secure systems, we must humbly learn the rules of the game.

---

[25]From the muzzle end.

Annotated bibliography

Many authors are wary of including URLs in their bibliographies, given the volatile nature of the web. Some choose to stick to tradition and cite only paper references, preferably only to well-established journals; others apologize in advance that some links might be broken by the time the reader gets to them. The most dedicated ones promise to keep an up-to-date version of the bibliography on their web site. I won't even try: I know all too well that, for me, *it'll never work*™.

Nonetheless, as a scientist, I welcome the web as a fantastic resource and I believe that being able to look up research papers on the web is extremely useful. While I genuinely love paper-based libraries, in particular the many outstanding ones to which I have access at the University of Cambridge, I also entirely agree with Lawrence [168]:

> With the web, scientists now have very convenient access to an increasing amount of literature that previously required trips to the library, inter-library loan delays, or substantial effort in locating the source. Evidence shows that usage increases when access is more convenient [...], and maximizing the usage of the scientific record benefits all of society.

I am therefore providing you with URLs wherever possible. If you find a broken link, just take it to mean that "at some point in time, this paper was available electronically, with this file name". While it's true that stuff moves around a lot on the web, it's also true that almost nothing ever gets deleted. Even if the paper has now disappeared from its former location, a web search on author name and file name is likely to yield other copies of it[1].

I have annotated many of the entries to help you decide whether chasing them up is going to be worth your time. A star (like this one: ⋆) highlights the 5% or so of them that I think you will find most interesting and useful as a reader of this book. I have also provided you with reverse pointers that tell you on which page(s) of this book each bibliographic entry is referenced.

---

[1]In contrast, a search on author name and title is likely to return mostly *citations*, rather than actual copies.

[1] Martín Abadi and Roger Needham. "Prudent Engineering Practice for Cryptographic Protocols". Tech. Rep. 125, Digital Equipment Corporation Systems Research Center, Jun 1994. `ftp://ftp.digital.com/pub/DEC/SRC/research-reports/SRC-125.pdf`. (Ref: p. 156.)

> ★ One of the most important papers on the design of cryptographic protocols, written by two of the authors of the BAN logic [56]. Abadi and Needham distil their considerable experience into a list of plain and sensible principles, and demonstrate their worth by nonchalantly breaking an impressive series of published protocols which violated those principles. An outstanding and very instructive paper.

[2] Gregory D. Abowd and Elizabeth D. Mynatt. "Charting Past, Present, and Future Research in Ubiquitous Computing". *ACM Transactions on Computer-Human Interaction*, **7**(1):29–58, Mar 2000. ISSN 1073-0516. `http://www.acm.org/pubs/citations/journals/tochi/2000-7-1/p29-abowd/`. (Ref: p. 9.)

> An extensive and well-researched survey article that reviews the first ten years of ubicomp through a wide selection of representative projects. The authors weave a coherent story by identifying three research themes and evaluating the progress along those axes, pointing out what has been achieved and what remains to be done.

[3] ACM Sigmobile. "MobiCom—ACM International Conference on Mobile Computing and Networking". `http://www.acm.org/sigmobile/confs/mobicom.html`. (Ref: p. 9.)

> The home page of the Mobicom conference, with links to the pages of the individual editions from 1995 onwards.

[4] Scott Adams. *The Dilbert Principle*. HarperCollins Publishers Inc., Apr 1996. ISBN 0-8873-0787-6. (Ref: p. xvii.)

> The popular Dilbert strips are only interludes in this witty satire of the corporate world. Adams's prose is as effective as his cartoons and his portraits of businessmen, managers, employees and scientists are as accurate as they are hilarious.

[5] Michael D. Addlesee, Alan Jones, Finnbar Livesey and Ferdinando Samaria. "The ORL Active Floor". *IEEE Personal Communications*, **4**(5):35–41, Oct 1997. `ftp://ftp.uk.research.att.com/pub/docs/att/tr.97.11.pdf`. Also available as ORL Technical Report 97.11. (Ref: p. 35, 37.)

> Describes the ORL Active Floor, in which floor tiles are instrumented with high precision strain gauges to measure the time-varying distribution of weights of the contents of the room. A full technical description of the system is complemented by a comparison to existing sensor systems and by a description of experiments attempting to recognize individuals by their footsteps.

[6] Allen Concepts, Inc. "KeyKatcher computer monitoring system", 2001. `http:`
     `//www.keykatcher.com`. Featured in *Wired* 9.10, Oct 2001, p. 172. (Ref: p. 164.)

> A tiny hardware attachment, to be fitted between keyboard and pc, which looks
> like a cable adapter plug and records all the keystrokes it sees. To review them,
> take it out of your victim's computer, install it in your own, and type your secret
> password.

[7] Edward Amoroso. *Fundamentals of Computer Security Technology*. Prentice Hall,
     1994. ISBN 0-13-305541-8. (Ref: p. 3, 60, 83, 222.)

> A rigorous yet very readable textbook covering the foundations of computer se-
> curity (threat trees, access control, security policies etc.) with an emphasis on
> mathematical modelling. Pre-chews the often obfuscated first-hand sources and
> presents their contents in a consistent and understandable framework. Sets each
> topic in its historical context and provides authoritative references. A very valu-
> able tutorial and reference, which also features a well-annotated bibliography.

[8] Ross Anderson. "Why Cryptosystems fail". *Communications of the ACM*,
     37(11):32–40, Nov 1994. `ftp://ftp.cl.cam.uk/users/rja14/wcf.ps.gz`.
     (Ref: p. 3, 82, 131.)

> The landmark paper that first pointed out that actual security problems in fielded
> systems usually have little to do with cryptography, and are instead caused by
> implementation and procedural blunders. The presentation is enlivened by nu-
> merous case studies drawn from the author's experience in banking security.

[9] Ross Anderson (ed.). *Information Hiding: First International Workshop proceed-
     ings*, vol. 1174 of *Lecture Notes in Computer Science*. Springer-Verlag, 1996. ISBN
     3-540-61996-8. (Ref: p. 210, 221.)

[10] Ross Anderson. "GSM hack—operator flunks the challenge". *The RISKS Digest*,
     19(48), Dec 1997. `http://catless.ncl.ac.uk/Risks/19.48.html#subj5`.
     (Ref: p. 192.)

> A report on the planned Cambridge attack on GSM which exploited a basic
> operational failure, namely the fact that the microwave links between base sta-
> tions are left unencrypted. Possible reasons why the hole is left in place are
> considered and the risks to all the parties involved are highlighted. Interestingly
> and provocatively, Anderson discusses not only cryptographic protocols but also
> wider policy issues.

[11] Ross Anderson. *Security Engineering—A Guide to Building Dependable Distributed
     Systems*. John Wiley & Sons, 2001. ISBN 0-471-38922-6. (Ref: p. 3, 59, 60, 78,
     87, 176, 189.)

★ The computer security textbook that best conveys the feeling for the impact of the discipline on the Real World™. More than on "building", the emphasis is on "breaking"—I can see Ross's evil grin in my mind's eye when he tells time and again of grandiose security systems brought down by incompetence, blunders and opportunistic exploits. Just as one should be suspicious of any cryptosystem whose designer is not experienced in breaking ciphers, similarly one should be suspicious of any security system engineered by a designer unaware of how such systems fail in practice. *Security Engineering* provides the awareness. Dense with anecdotes and war stories, readable and entertaining, up to date and full of pointers to first-hand research, this volume will be extremely useful to any security practitioner. (Yes, this sentence somehow travelled back in time from my bibliography to the back cover of his book. :-)) No other book contains such a wide-ranging, cross-disciplinary, insightful, irreverent and entertaining investigation of the many unexpected ways in which secure systems actually fail.

[12] Ross Anderson. "The Sklyarov case", 26 Jul 2001. http://www.eff.org/IP/DMCA/US_v_Sklyarov/20010726_anderson_mueller_letter.html. Letter to US Atty. Mueller. (Ref: p. 202.)

> Russian security researcher Dmitry Sklyarov broke the (weak and proprietary) security of Adobe's electronic book format and was arrested and criminally prosecuted in the US under the controversial Digital Millennium Copyright Act. This letter "points out the widespread alarm about this incident in international academic circles" (EFF).

[13] Ross Anderson, Francesco Bergadano, Bruno Crispo, Jong-Hyeon Lee, Charalampos Manifavas and Roger Needham. "A New Family of Authentication Protocols". *Operating Systems Review*, 32(4):9–20, Oct 1998. http://www.ftp.cl.cam.ac.uk/ftp/users/rja14/fawkes.ps.gz. (Ref: p. 125.)

> Introduces the Guy Fawkes protocol, a hash chain construction providing inexpensive signing of a stream of messages. The narrative is readable and entertaining, but the short section describing the actual protocol is somewhat elliptical. The learned discussion that follows gives a useful perspective on related constructions and raises interesting questions about the nature of digital signatures.

[14] Ross Anderson and Markus Kuhn. "Tamper Resistance—A Cautionary Note". In "Proc. 2nd USENIX Workshop on Electronic Commerce", 1996. ISBN 1-880446-83-9. http://www.cl.cam.ac.uk/~mgk25/tamper.pdf. (Ref: p. 54, 104, 121, 128.)

> ★ The seminal paper exposing the vulnerabilities of supposedly tamper resistant computing hardware such as smart cards.

[15] Ross Anderson and Markus Kuhn. "Low Cost Attacks on Tamper Resistant Devices". In Mark Lomas (ed.), "Security protocols: 5th international workshop, Paris,

France, April 7–9, 1997: proceedings", vol. 1361 of *Lecture Notes in Computer Science*, pp. 125–136. Springer-Verlag, 1998. ISBN 3-540-64040-1 (paperback). ISSN 0302-9743. `http://www.cl.cam.ac.uk/~mgk25/tamper2.pdf`. (Ref: p. 121, 130.)

[16] Ross Anderson and Jong-Hyeon Lee. "Jikzi: A New Framework for Secure Publishing". In Christianson *et al.* [68], pp. 21–36. `http://www.cl.cam.ac.uk/ftp/users/rja14/jikzi-cpw.ps`. (Ref: p. 84.)

[17] Ross Anderson, Frank Stajano and Jong-Hyeon Lee. "Security Policies". In Marvin V. Zelkowitz (ed.), "(untitled)", vol. 55 of *Advances in Computers*, pp. 185–235. Academic Press, 2001. ISBN 0-12-012155-7. (Ref: p. xix, 84.)

> A comprehensive survey of security policy models, with extensive discussion. The general concept of a policy is distilled from many case studies as being the security specification of a system—a blueprint that is useful as a communication tool as well as a yardstick to verify the adequacy of a design or implementation.

[18] Ross J. Anderson. "The Correctness of Crypto Transaction Sets". In Christianson *et al.* [69], pp. 125–127. `http://www.cl.cam.ac.uk/ftp/users/rja14/protocols00.pdf`. (Ref: p. 130.)

[19] Ross J. Anderson and S. Johann Bezuidenhoudt. "On the Reliability of Electronic Payment Systems". *IEEE Transactions on Software Engineering*, **22**(5):294–301, May 1996. `http://www.cl.cam.ac.uk/ftp/users/rja14/meters.ps.gz`. (Ref: p. 146.)

[20] Ross J. Anderson, Bruno Crispo, Jong-Hyeon Lee, Charalampos Manifavas, Vaclav Matyáš and Fabien A. P. Petitcolas. *The Global Trust Register 1998*. Northgate Consultants Ltd., Cambridge, Feb 1998. ISBN 0-9532397-0-5. `http://www.cl.cam.ac.uk/Research/Security/Trust-Register/gtr1998.pdf`. An updated second edition was published by the MIT Press in 1999, ISBN 0-262-51105-3. (Ref: p. 80.)

> An ad hoc directory of hashes of public keys of individuals and organizations. Apart from its practical usefulness in establishing a hard-to-corrupt base for a chain of trust towards an unknown key, it is significant because it exploits the "freedom of the press" legislation to protect the independence of the Certification Authority it implements.

[21] Anonymous. *Maximum Security: A Hacker's Guide to Protecting Your Internet Site and Network*. Sams.net Publishing, 1997. ISBN 1-57521-268-4. (Ref: p. 175.)

> A grand compilation of tidbits on Internet security. Lists many system- and version-specific vulnerabilities, along with attacks, attack tools and countermeasures. Easy reading (if somewhat verbose) as introductory material, but technically too superficial to be useful as a reference. It nevertheless provides a wealth of bibliographic pointers and covers Windows as well as UNIX (the Macintosh occasionally gets a token mention but is not treated in any detail). Wide rather

than deep ("The children's—or maybe the journalists'—encyclopædia of Internet security"), it does contain some nuggets but on the whole there are more useful books on the subject.

[22] R. Atkinson. "Security Architecture for the Internet Protocol". RFC 1825, IETF, Aug 1995. http://www.ietf.org/rfc/rfc1825.txt. Category: Standards track. (Ref: p. 226.)

The official high level description of IPSEC. A fairly readable overview, since the actual details are delegated to the following two RFCs in the series.

[23] AT&T Laboratories Cambridge. "Sentient Computing Project Home Page". http://www.uk.research.att.com/spirit/. (Ref: p. 38.)

[24] AT&T Laboratories Cambridge. "The Smart Beverage Dispenser". http://www.uk.research.att.com/cgi-bin/coffee/. (Ref: p. 32.)

The home page of AT&T's badge-activated coffee machine, with dynamically updated statistics.

[25] AT&T Laboratories Cambridge. "Virtual Network Computing". http://www.uk.research.att.com/vnc/. (Ref: p. 33.)

The home page of AT&T's Virtual Network Computing project, whence source, binaries and documentation can be freely downloaded.

[26] AT&T Laboratories Cambridge. "Sentient Computing", Aug 2000. ftp://ftp.uk.research.att.com/pub/videos/qsif-200/sentient-qsif-200.mpg. First shown by Andy Hopper during his keynote speech at MobiCom 2000. (Ref: p. 38.)

A video showing the Active Bat and its back-end software in action.

[27] Tuomas Aura, Pekka Nikander and Jussipekka Leiwo. "DOS-resistant authentication with client puzzles". In Christianson et al. [69], pp. 170–177. http://www.tcs.hut.fi/Publications/papers/aura/aura-nikander-leiwo-protocols00.pdf. (Ref: p. 138.)

[28] Autonomous Zone Industries. http://www.mojonation.com/. (Ref: p. 136.)

[29] D. Elliot Bell and Leonard J. LaPadula. "Secure Computer Systems: Mathematical Foundations". Mitre Report ESD-TR-73-278 (Vol. I–III), Mitre Corporation, Bedford, MA, Apr 1974. (Ref: p. 83, 101.)

[30] Steven M. Bellovin and Michael Merritt. "Limitations of the Kerberos Authentication System". In USENIX (ed.), "Proceedings, Winter 1991", pp. 253–267. USENIX, Dallas, TX, Jan 1991. (Ref: p. 181.)

A detailed constructive criticism on Kerberos versions 4 and 5 (written at the time when version 5 was still in draft). Includes proposals for remedies to some of the problems it highlights.

[31] Frazer Bennett, David Clarke, Joseph B. Evans, Andy Hopper, Alan Jones and David Leask. "Piconet: Embedded Mobile Networking". *IEEE Personal Communications*, **4**(5):8–15, Oct 1997. `ftp://ftp.uk.research.att.com/pub/docs/att/tr.97.9.pdf`. (Ref: p. 44.)

First published description of Piconet. Good overview which also goes into reasonably technical detail.

[32] Berkshire Products. "ISA PC Watchdog Board User's Manual". Manual, Berkshire Products, Suwanee, GA, 2000. `http://www.berkprod.com/docs/isa-wdog.pdf`. (Ref: p. 147.)

Detailed and instructive user's manual for an ISA card providing a watchdog timer.

[33] Kenneth J. Biba. "Integrity Considerations for Secure Computer Systems". Tech. Rep. MTR-3153, MITRE Corporation, Apr 1975. (Ref: p. 84, 90, 102.)

[34] Eli Biham and Adi Shamir. *Differential Cryptanalysis of the Data Encryption Standard*. Springer-Verlag, 1993. ISBN 0-387-97930-1. (Ref: p. 64.)

[35] Alex Biryukov, Adi Shamir and David Wagner. "Real Time Cryptanalysis of A5/1 on a PC". In "Proceedings of Fast Software Encryption 2000", New York, NY, Apr 2000. `http://cryptome.org/a51-bsw.htm`. (Ref: p. 191.)

[36] Matt Blaze. "Oblivious Key Escrow". In Anderson [9], pp. 335–343. `http://www.crypto.com/papers/netescrow.ps`. (Ref: p. 159, 162.)

[37] Matt Blaze. "A few thoughts on the September 11th tragedy", 12 Sep 2001. `http://www.crypto.com/wtc.html`. (Ref: p. 167.)

[38] Matt Blaze, Joan Feigenbaum, John Ioannidis and Angelos D. Keromytis. "The KeyNote Trust-Management System". RFC 2704, Network Working Group, Sep 1999. `http://www.ietf.org/rfc/rfc2704.txt`. (Ref: p. 94, 101, 104.)

[39] Matt Blaze, Joan Feigenbaum and Jack Lacy. "Decentralized Trust Management". In "Proceedings of the 17th IEEE Symp. on Security and Privacy", pp. 164–173. IEEE Computer Society, 1996. `ftp://ftp.research.att.com/dist/mab/policymaker.ps`. (Ref: p. 94, 101.)

[40] Bluetooth SIG. `http://www.bluetooth.com/`. (Ref: p. 2, 194.)

[41] Bluetooth SIG. "Specification of the Bluetooth System, Volume 1: Core, v1.0B". Bluetooth Doc 1.C.47/1.0 B, Bluetooth SIG, 1 Dec 1999. `http://www.bluetooth.com/developer/specification/core_10_b.pdf`. (Ref: p. 193, 196, 197, 198, 199, 225.)

This volume is somewhat daunting at over 1000 pages—definitely a reference as opposed to a cover-to-cover read. On the other hand the chapters are pretty much independent, so it's all manageable after the initial shock. The chapter devoted to security is short (less than 30 pages) but could be organized more clearly in places. The main problems, however, are with the contents (design choices) rather than with the presentation.

[42] Bluetooth SIG. "Specification of the Bluetooth System, Volume 2: Profiles, v1.0B". Bluetooth Doc 1.C.47/1.0 B, Bluetooth SIG, 1 Dec 1999. `http://www.bluetooth.com/developer/specification/profile_10_b.pdf`. (Ref: p. 166, 193.)

> Bluetooth profiles are predefined usage scenarios for Bluetooth devices. Examples include file transfer, dial-up networking, synchronization, serial port, headset, fax and so on. The functionality and protocols for each profile are standardized up to the application layer in order to guarantee interoperability between compliant Bluetooth devices from different manufacturers. This volume specifies 13 different profiles.

[43] Bluetooth SIG. "Specification of the Bluetooth System, Volume 1: Core, v1.1". Bluetooth doc, Bluetooth SIG, 22 Feb 2001. `http://www.bluetooth.com/files/Bluetooth_11_Specifications_Book.pdf`. (Ref: p. 193, 194, 225.)

[44] Bluetooth SIG. "Specification of the Bluetooth System, Volume 2: Profiles, v1.1". Bluetooth doc, Bluetooth SIG, 22 Feb 2001. `http://www.bluetooth.com/files/Bluetooth_11_Profiles_Book.pdf`. (Ref: p. 193, 194.)

[45] Mike Bond. "Attacks on Cryptoprocessor Transaction Sets". In Çetin Kaya Koç, David Naccache and Christof Paar (eds.), "CHES", vol. 2162 of *Lecture Notes in Computer Science*, pp. 220–234. Springer, 2001. ISBN 3-540-42521-7. `http://www.cl.cam.ac.uk/users/mkb23/research/Attacks-on-Crypto-TS.pdf`. (Ref: p. 130.)

[46] Mike Bond and Ross J. Anderson. "API-Level Attacks on Embedded Systems". *IEEE Computer*, **34**(10):67–75, 2001. `http://www.cl.cam.ac.uk/users/mkb23/research/API-Attacks.pdf`. (Ref: p. 130.)

[47] Mike Bond and Richard Clayton. "Extracting a 3DES key from an IBM 4758", 2001. `http://www.cl.cam.ac.uk/~rnc1/descrack/index.html`. (Ref: p. 64, 130.)

> ★ In this ingenious and inexpensive attack the authors combine sleight-of-hand and raw processing power to extract all the useful key material out of a tamper-resistant 4758 cryptoprocessor running its standard CCA cash-machine software. This means free access to all the PINs handled by the device!

[48] Nikita Borisov, Ian Goldberg and David Wagner. "Intercepting Mobile Communications: The Insecurity of 802.11", Feb 2001. `http://www.isaac.cs.berkeley.edu/isaac/wep-draft.pdf`. Draft paper. A higher-level presentation of the same material is available at `http://www.isaac.cs.berkeley.edu/isaac/wep-faq.html`. (Ref: p. 70, 201, 202.)

The authors highlight a number of flaws in the Wired Equivalent Privacy (WEP) protocol of the 802.11 wireless LAN standard, most of which stem from misapplication of cryptographic primitives. Practical attacks to exploit these flaws are demonstrated. The lack of peer review for WEP before ratification as a standard is blamed for these failures.

[49] Jennifer Bray and Charles F. Sturman. *Bluetooth: Connect Without Cables*. Prentice Hall PTR, Dec 2000. ISBN 0-13-089840-6. (Ref: p. 194.)

A gentle, readable and substantially more compact alternative to the official Bluetooth documentation. Technical accuracy and completeness are not sacrificed.

[50] David F.C. Brewer and Michael J. Nash. "The Chinese Wall Security Policy". In "Proceedings of the 1989 IEEE Computer Society Symposium on Security and Privacy", pp. 206–214. IEEE Technical Committee on Security and Privacy; and International Association for Cryptologic Research, IEEE Computer Society Press, Oakland, CA, 1–3 May 1989. ISBN 0-8186-1939-2. (Ref: p. 95, 101.)

This security policy regulates cases in which conflicts of interest might occur, e.g. in a consultancy firm whose associates work for competing companies. The policy prevents the flow of "insider knowledge" from a company to a competing one through the consultants.

[51] David L. Brock. "The Electronic Product Code". Tech. Rep. MIT-AUTOID-WH-002, MIT, Jan 2001. http://www.autoidcenter.org/research/MIT-AUTOID-WH-002.pdf. (Ref: p. 25.)

[52] Dan Brown. "Techniques for Privacy and Authentication in Personal Communications Systems". *IEEE Personal Communications*, **2**(4):6–10, Aug 1995. (Ref: p. 191.)

Short and readable high level overview of the authentication and key agreement techniques of the GSM and IS-41 cellular telephone systems, plus discussion of a proposed new system based on public key cryptography.

[53] Jeremy Bruestle and Blake Hegerle. "AirSnort Homepage", Aug 2001. http://airsnort.sourceforge.net/. (Ref: p. 201, 234.)

Yet another implementation of the Fluhrer *et al.* [109] attack on the Wi-Fi WEP protocol. It's open source, works under Linux and, in the description of its direct competitor WEPCrack [214], it has "a much more useable and complete implementation for both collection and cracking".

[54] Barry Brumitt and JJ Cadiz. " 'Let There Be Light!' Comparing Interfaces for Homes of the Future". Tech. Rep. MSR-TR-2000-92, Microsoft Research, 21 Sep 2000. ftp://ftp.research.microsoft.com/pub/tr/tr-2000-92.pdf. (Ref: p. 55.)

[55] E. Loren Buhle, Jr. "NeXT microphone problem?" *The RISKS Digest*, **10**(65), Dec 1990. http://catless.ncl.ac.uk/Risks/10.65.html#subj5. (Ref: p. 56.)

At a time when it was newsworthy for a computer's standard configuration to include a microphone, this article pointed out that the one that came with the NeXT had no visible indicator of whether it was on or off, and that it could therefore be abused as an office bug. (Hey, and what about the microphone on your current computer?)

[56] Michael Burrows, Martín Abadi and Roger Needham. "A Logic of Authentication". Tech. Rep. 39, Digital Equipment Corporation Systems Research Center, Feb 1989. (Ref: p. 179, 205, 213.)

The landmark paper that introduced the BAN logic, a tool for formal verification of authentication protocols.

[57] Michael Burrows, Martín Abadi and Roger Needham. "A Logic of Authentication". *ACM Transactions on Computer Systems*, **8**(1):18–36, Feb 1990. (Ref: p. 179.)

A revised and shortened journal version of [56], which the authors made substantially more readable by simply trading their previous hieroglyphs for boldface English words.

[58] Carnegie Mellon University, Computer Science Department. "CMU SCS Coke Machine", 2001. http://www-2.cs.cmu.edu/~coke/. (Ref: p. 32.)

Home page of the CMU SCS Coke Machine, the classic 1982 hack that allowed potential customers to query via finger the status of the coke cans inside the vending machine so as to delay purchase when the available cans had not been exposed to the refrigerating apparatus for a sufficient time. Provides recent and ancient history and pointers to other similar exploits.

[59] CCITT. "Data Communications Networks Directory". Tech. Rep. 8, CCITT, Melbourne, Nov 1988. Recommendations X.500-X.521, 9th Plenary Assembly. (Ref: p. 181.)

[60] CERT/CC and FedCIRC. "Denial-of-Service Developments". CERT Advisory CA-2000-01, CERT, 3 Jan 2000. http://www.cert.org/advisories/CA-2000-01.html. (Ref: p. 136.)

Reports on the discovery of new DDOS attack tools that were surreptitiously planted on hosts belonging to various organizations. Explains the problem and suggests some detection tools and prevention measures.

[61] David Chaum. "Untraceable Electronic Mail, Return Addresses, and Digital Pseudonyms". *Communications of the ACM*, **24**(2):84–88, Feb 1981. Unofficial copy at http://www.wiwi.uni-frankfurt.de/~kcotoaga/offline/chaum-acm-1981.html. (Ref: p. 153, 162.)

[62] David Chaum. "Security without identification: transaction systems to make big brother obsolete". *Communications of the ACM*, **28**(10):1030–1044, Oct 1985. `http://www.acm.org/pubs/articles/journals/cacm/1985-28-10/p1030-chaum/p1030-chaum.pdf`. (Ref: p. 153.)

[63] David Chaum. "The Dining Cryptographers Problem: Unconditional Sender and Recipient Untraceability". *Journal of Cryptology*, **1**:65–75, 1988. Unofficial copy at `http://www.scu.edu/SCU/Programs/HighTechLaw/courses/ccp/diningcr.html`. (Ref: p. 160, 162.)

[64] David Chaum. "Achieving Electronic Privacy". *Scientific American*, pp. 96–101, Aug 1992. `http://www.eff.org/pub/Privacy/Digital_money/chaum_privacy_id.article`. (Ref: p. 153.)

[65] David Chaum, Amos Fiat and Moni Naor. "Untraceable Electronic Cash". In S. Goldwasser (ed.), "Advances in Cryptology—CRYPTO '88", vol. 403 of *Lecture Notes in Computer Science*, pp. 319–327. Springer-Verlag, 1990, 21–25 Aug 1988. (Ref: p. 153.)

[66] David L. Chaum. "Blind signature systems". US patent 4,759,063, US Patent Office, Jul 1988. `http://www.delphion.com/details?pn=US04759063__`. Filed 1983-08-22, issued 1988-07-19. (Ref: p. 153.)

[67] David Chess, Benjamin Grosof, Colin Harrison, David Levine, Colin Parris and Gene Tsudik. "Itinerant Agents for Mobile Computing". *IEEE Personal Communications*, **2**(5):34–49, Oct 1995. `http://www.research.ibm.com/massdist/rc20010.ps`. (Ref: p. 145.)

[68] Bruce Christianson, Bruno Crispo, James A. Malcolm and Michael Roe (eds.). *Security Protocols, 7th International Workshop, Proceedings*, vol. 1796 of *Lecture Notes in Computer Science*. Springer, 2000. ISBN 3-540-67381-4. ISSN 0302-9743. (Ref: p. 93, 208, 238.)

[69] Bruce Christianson, Bruno Crispo and Michael Roe (eds.). *Security Protocols, 8th International Workshop, Cambridge, UK, April 3-5, 2000, Revised Papers*, vol. 2133 of *Lecture Notes in Computer Science*. Springer, 2001. ISBN 3-540-42566-7. (Ref: p. 208, 209, 238.)

[70] David D. Clark and David R. Wilson. "A Comparison of Commercial and Military Computer Security Policies". In "Proceedings of the 1987 IEEE Symposium on Security and Privacy", pp. 184–194. IEEE Technical Committee on Security and Privacy; and International Association for Cryptologic Research, IEEE Computer Society Press, Oakland, CA, 27–29 Apr 1987. ISBN 0-8186-0771-8. (Ref: p. 95, 101.)

> This influential paper introduced the Clark-Wilson security policy model for integrity, which abstracts the best practice in banking and accounting systems.

[71] Richard Clayton. "Brute force attacks on cryptographic keys", 2001. `http://www.cl.cam.ac.uk/~rnc1/brute.html`. (Ref: p. 64.)

[72] Richard Clayton and Michael Bond. "Experience using a low-cost FPGA design to crack DES keys", 2002. To appear. (Ref: p. 64.)

[73] Clifford Cocks. "Split Knowledge Generation of RSA Parameters". In Mike Darnell (ed.), "Cryptography and coding: 6th IMA conference, Cirencester, UK, December 17–19, 1997: proceedings", vol. 1355 of *Lecture Notes in Computer Science*, pp. 89–95. Springer-Verlag, 1997. ISBN 3-540-63927-6. ISSN 0302-9743. http://www.cesg.gov.uk/downlds/math/rsa.pdf. (Ref: p. 159.)

[74] Computer Emergency Response Team. "/usr/lib/sendmail, /bin/tar, and /dev/audio Vulnerabilities". Advisory CA-1993-15, CERT, 21 Oct 1993. http://www.cert.org/advisories/CA-1993-15.html. (Ref: p. 56.)

> The third part of this advisory explains that, in all the versions of SunOS that existed at the time, the permission bits on the audio device were such that any user with access to the system (even across the net) could eavesdrop on the conversations held near the workstation's microphone.

[75] Jeremy R. Cooperstock, Sidney S. Fels, William Buxton and Kenneth C. Smith. "Reactive Environments". *Communications of the ACM*, **40**(9):65–73, Sep 1997. ISSN 0001-0782. http://www.acm.org/pubs/citations/journals/cacm/1997-40-9/p65-cooperstock/. (Ref: p. 49.)

[76] Joan Daemen and Vincent Rijmen. "AES Proposal: Rijndael", 3 Sep 1999. http://www.esat.kuleuven.ac.be/~rijmen/rijndael/rijndaeldocV2.zip. For further (pointers to) information on Rijndael, see http://www.rijndael.com/. (Ref: p. 62.)

> The official documentation for the block cipher Rijndael (now the AES), as submitted to NIST. Includes design motivation and performance figures.

[77] O.-J. Dahl, E. W. Dijkstra and C. A. R. Hoare. *Structured Programming*. Academic Press, 1972. ISBN 0-12-200550-3. (Ref: p. 113.)

> A cute little classic dispensing pearls of wisdom about how to structure programs and their data in order to produce more understandable and more reliable software.

[78] Dallas Semiconductor. http://www.ibutton.com/. (Ref: p. 97, 128, 130.)

> The iButton is a secure processing node (with CPU, memory and battery) enclosed in a tamper-resistant steel enclosure the size of a thick coin. It has a two-contact I/O interface, like a coin cell. It can be mounted on a ring, a key fob or other fashion accessory and used, among other things, like an electronic key. This web site is continuously updated with new iButton products and applications.

[79] Dallas Semiconductor. "Secure Microcontroller User's Guide". User guide, Dallas Semiconductor, May 1996. http://www.dalsemi.com/datasheets/pdfs/secguide.pdf. (Ref: p. 122.)

[80] Dallas Semiconductor. "Secure Microprocessor Chip". Data Sheet DS5002FP, Dallas Semiconductor, May 1999. `http://www.dalsemi.com/datasheets/pdfs/5002fp.pdf`. (Ref: p. 122.)

[81] Dallas Semiconductor. "Using the High-Speed Micro's Watchdog Timer". Application Note 80, Dallas Semiconductor, Oct 1999. `http://www.dalsemi.com/datasheets/pdfs/app80.pdf`. (Ref: p. 147.)

[82] Dallas Semiconductor. "Using the Secure Microcontroller Watchdog Timer". Application Note 101, Dallas Semiconductor, Nov 1999. `http://www.dalsemi.com/datasheets/pdfs/app101.pdf`. (Ref: p. 147.)

[83] Dallas Semiconductor. "Watchdog Timekeeper". Application Note 66, Dallas Semiconductor, Jul 1999. `http://www.dalsemi.com/datasheets/pdfs/app66.pdf`. (Ref: p. 147.)

[84] Dallas Semiconductor. "DS1921L-F5X Thermochron iButton". Data Sheet DS1921L-F5X, Dallas Semiconductor, 18 Jul 2000. `http://www.dalsemi.com/datasheets/pdfs/1921.pdf`. See also [85]. (Ref: p. 130, 216.)

[85] Dallas Semiconductor. "Thermochron iButton", 26 Oct 2000. `http://www.ibutton.com/ibuttons/thermochron.html`. See also [84]. (Ref: p. 130, 216.)

Web page giving an informal overview of the features of the DS1921 Thermochron, an iButton capable of logging timestamped temperature measurements and meant to be attached to thermally vulnerable products such as fresh foods.

[86] Dorothy E. Denning and Giovanni Maria Sacco. "Timestamps in Key Distribution Protocols". *Communications of the ACM*, **24**(8):533–536, Aug 1981. ISSN 0001-0782. (Ref: p. 177.)

Highlights a vulnerability of the Needham-Schroeder protocol (under the assumption that session keys may be compromised) and suggests a fix based on timestamps. The public key version is also examined. The dubious point of the argument is that, if it is sound to assume that session keys might be stolen by exploiting design flaws, by the same reasoning this might happen with private keys (the keys that users share with the authentication server), in which case the addition of timestamps would not help. The authors acknowledge and discuss this.

[87] Department of Defense. "National Industrial Security Program Operating Manual (NISPOM)". Tech. Rep. DoD 5220.22-M, Department of Defense, Department of Energy, Nuclear Regulatory Commission, Central Intelligence Agency, Jan 1995. `http://cryptome.org/nispom/nispom.htm`. (Ref: p. 120.)

[88] Michael L. Dertouzos. "The Future of Computing". *Scientific American*, Aug 1999. `http://www.sciam.com/1999/0899issue/0899dertouzos.html`. (Ref: p. 25.)

A "promise" article describing the vision and goals of the then newly established Oxygen project at MIT.

[89] T. Dierks and C. Allen. "The TLS Protocol, Version 1.0". RFC 2246, IETF, Jan 1999. http://www.ietf.org/rfc/rfc2246.txt. Category: Standards track. (Ref: p. 188.)

[90] Whitfield Diffie and Martin E. Hellman. "New Directions in Cryptography". *IEEE Transactions on Information Theory*, **IT-22**(6):644–654, Nov 1976. (Ref: p. 66, 72, 80, 91, 136, 225.)

The classic paper that introduced the ideas of public key cryptography and digital signature. A fascinating read which also provides a good historical perspective on cryptography.

[91] Whitfield Diffie and Martin E. Hellman. "Exhaustive Cryptanalysis of the NBS Data Encryption Standard". *Computer*, **10**(6):74–84, Jun 1977. ISSN 0018-9162. (Ref: p. 64.)

[92] Whitfield Diffie and Susan Eva Landau. *Privacy on the Line: The Politics of Wiretapping and Encryption*. MIT Press, Jan 1998. ISBN 0-262-04167-7. (Ref: p. 6, 65.)

★ Serious and authoritative, yet as gripping and fascinating as a good spy novel. The authors explore wiretapping and encryption from many angles; their undiscussed technical competence does not distract them from focusing on law, history and civil liberties. They offer a lucid, impartial and extremely well documented analysis of a controversial and delicate topic. This is an essential book for anyone wishing to understand the impact that technology has on society.

[93] eBay. http://www.ebay.com/. (Ref: p. 154.)

First and most popular auction site on the web.

[94] Electronic Frontier Foundation. *Cracking DES—Secrets of Encryption Research, Wiretap Politics & Chip Design*. O'Reilly & Associates, Jul 1998. ISBN 1-56592-520-3. http://cryptome.org/cracking-des.htm. (Ref: p. 64.)

The complete design blueprint for the dedicated hardware machine that cracked DES in a couple of days for less than $250,000—a detailed scientific report allowing other researchers to reproduce this remarkable result and to improve on it. Publication as a paper book instead of on the Internet was partly chosen as a way to circumvent US export restrictions. The book was later scanned in by volunteers and the source code is now available on servers outside the US.

[95] Electronic Frontier Foundation. "*EFF DES Cracker* Machine Brings Honesty to Crypto Debate". Press release, EFF, 17 Jul 1998. http://www.eff.org/pub/Privacy/Crypto_misc/DESCracker/HTML/19980716_eff_descracker_pressrel.html. (Ref: p. 64.)

The EFF proudly announce their success in cracking RSA's DES II-2 challenge in less than 3 days.

[96] Electronic Privacy Information Center. "United States vs. Scarfo (Key-Logger Case)", 2001. http://www.epic.org/crypto/scarfo.html. (Ref: p. 164.)

In June 2001 the FBI installed a keyboard bug on the computer of a suspect, thereby capturing his PGP passphrase. This has subtle legal implications because it is much more difficult to obtain a court-approved wiretap than a search warrant, yet the latter is sufficient to plant a keyboard bug that might have the practical effect of the former. The defence asked for the technique to be disclosed, hoping thereafter to suppress the evidence yielded by the device. This site holds a collection of documents on the court case, which is still open at the time of writing.

[97] Electronic Privacy Information Center, JunkBusters and Privacy International. http://www.bigbrotherinside.org/. (Ref: p. 88, 95.)

An advocacy site against the Pentium III processor ID and its negative repercussions on personal privacy. Includes an extensive and well-organized bibliography of opinions, papers and news articles from a wide spectrum of sources.

[98] J. H. Ellis. "The history of Non-Secret Encryption". Tech. rep., CESG (Communications-Electronics Security Group), Dec 1997. http://www.cesg.gov.uk/about/nsecret/ellis.pdf. (Ref: p. 66, 243.)

The British comsec agency CESG claims to have invented public key cryptography before Diffie and Hellman, but to have kept it secret in the interest of national security. This is an account of these early developments written by the inventor in 1987 and made public shortly after his death. (More technical papers from the 1970s have since been declassified and made available at http://www.cesg.gov.uk/about/nsecret/home.htm.) The consensus is to believe this version of history but, as for the details, various authoritative parties [268] have expressed doubts about the integrity of the documents, which were only released as electronic transcripts rather than photographs of the originals.

[99] Carl Ellison. "The Trust Shell Game". In Bruce Christianson, Bruno Crispo, William S. Harbison and Michael Roe (eds.), "Security Protocols, 6th International Workshop, Proceedings", vol. 1550 of Lecture Notes in Computer Science, pp. 36–40. Springer, 1998. ISBN 3-540-65663-4. ISSN 0302-9743. (Ref: p. 94.)

[100] Carl M. Ellison. "The nature of a useable PKI". Computer Networks, 31(8):823–830, 23 Apr 1999. ISSN 1389-1286. http://www.elsevier.nl/cas/tree/store/comnet/sub/1999/31/8/2123.pdf. (Special Issue on Computer Network Security.) URL inaccessible without subscription. (Ref: p. 182.)

[101] Carl M. Ellison, Bill Frantz, Butler Lampson, Ron Rivest, Brian M. Thomas and Tatu Ylonen. "SPKI Certificate Theory". RFC 2693, IETF, Sep 1999. http://www.ietf.org/rfc/rfc2693.txt. (Ref: p. 182.)

[102] Deborah Estrin, Ramesh Govindan and John Heidemann. "Embedding the Internet". *Communications of the ACM*, **43**(5):38–41, May 2000. (Ref: p. 2.)

> This brief article is the editors' introduction to five more papers that form the cover feature of this issue. An excellent high level presentation of the many visions of ubiquitous networked computing: hundreds of computers per human on Earth, swarms of sensing micro-robots the size of grains of sand, and the problem of programming smart paint.

[103] European Telecommunications Standards Institute. "European digital cellular telecommunications system (Phase 2); Security related network functions". Tech. Rep. GSM 03.20 version 4.3.1, ETSI, Sep 1994. http://www.etsi.org/. Online copy available at no cost, but registration required, so no direct URL available. (Ref: p. 191.)

> The authoritative definition of the security functionality of GSM, including the procedure for authentication of a subscriber and the mechanisms to prevent traffic analysis.

[104] European Telecommunications Standards Institute. "Digital cellular telecommunications system (Phase 2+); Abbreviations and acronyms". Tech. Rep. GSM 01.04 version 8.0.0 release 1999, ETSI, May 2000. http://www.etsi.org/. Online copy available at no cost, but registration required, so no direct URL available. (Ref: p. 190.)

> The authoritative definition of GSM terminology. An uncommented list of acronyms and their expansions—it tells you what LMSI stands for, but not what it is or does.

[105] William M. Farmer, Joshua D. Guttman and Vipin Swarup. "Security for Mobile Agents: Issues and Requirements". In "Proceedings of the 19th National Information Systems Security Conference", pp. 591–597. Baltimore, MD, Oct 1996. http://csrc.nist.gov/nissc/1996/papers/NISSC96/paper033/SWARUP96.PDF. (Ref: p. 146.)

[106] Niels Ferguson and Bruce Schneier. "A Cryptographic Evaluation of IPsec". Tech. rep., Counterpane Internet Security, Dec 1999. http://www.counterpane.com/ipsec.pdf. (Ref: p. 187.)

> A strong, self-confident and enlightening paper that boldly cuts through the fog of IPSEC RFCs with a sharp laser, exposing the many problems and vulnerabilities introduced by featuritis and lack of clarity about the protocols' goals.

[107] FIPS. "Data Encryption Standard". FIPS pub 46, FIPS, 15 Jan 1977. (Ref: p. 63.)

> The authoritative reference on the inner workings of the DES algorithm.

[108] Scott Fluhrer and Stefan Lucks. "Analysis of the E_0 Encryption System". In "Proceedings of SAC 2001, Eighth Annual Workshop on Selected Areas in Cryptography, Toronto, Ontario, Canada, Aug 2001", Lecture Notes in Computer Science. Springer-Verlag. To appear. (Ref: p. 195.)

[109] Scott Fluhrer, Itsik Mantin and Adi Shamir. "Weaknesses in the Key Scheduling Algorithm of RC4", Jul 2001. http://www.crypto.com/papers/others/rc4_ksaproc.ps. (Ref: p. 201, 202, 212, 234.)

[110] Simson Garfinkel. *Database Nation*. O'Reilly, 2000. ISBN 1-56592-653-6. (Ref: p. 49, 113, 118, 152.)

> ★ A brilliant and disturbing book that documents how the modern information society tracks and records every movement of the individual. Garfinkel shows how our "data shadow" is surreptitiously and meticulously analysed. Seemingly innocent transaction logging activities become tentacles of an unwieldy monster when the logs of various organizations are merged, stored indefinitely, and unethically misused. This is a book written to upset—to wake up those who believe they have nothing to hide and that therefore privacy protection is only for paranoids. Extremely well researched, well written, richly illustrated and with an excellent commented bibliography.

[111] Simson Garfinkel and Gene Spafford. *Practical Unix and Internet Security, 2nd ed.* O'Reilly and Associates, 1996. ISBN 1-56592-148-8. (Ref: p. 175.)

> No Unix sysadmin should be without this book: it is competently written, full of worked examples and code, and exhaustive in its coverage of the topic.

[112] Linda Geppert. "Pentium serial number pains privacy groups". *IEEE Spectrum*, **36**(6):92–92, Jun 1999. ISSN 0018-9235. (Ref: p. 95.)

[113] John Gilmore. "What's Wrong With Copy Protection", 16 Feb 2001. http://www.toad.com/gnu/whatswrong.html. Originally posted to the mailing list cryptography@c2.net on 2001-01-18 in response to an invitation by Ron Rivest. (Ref: p. 59.)

> An informed and well reasoned essay on the dangers of the technical and legal measures being enacted to enforce copy protection on digital media.

[114] Gray Girling, Jennifer Li Kam Wa, Paul Osborn and Radina Stefanova. "The Design and Implementation of a Low Power Ad Hoc Protocol Stack". In "Proceedings of the IEEE Wireless Communications and Networking Conference", Chicago, IL, Sep 2000. ftp://ftp.uk.research.att.com/pub/docs/att/tr.2000.13.pdf. Also available as AT&T Laboratories Cambridge Technical Report 2000.13. (Ref: p. 44, 140.)

[115] Gray Girling, Jennifer Li Kam Wa, Paul Osborn and Radina Stefanova. "The PEN Low Power Protocol Stack". In "Proceedings of the 9th IEEE International Conference on Computer Communications and Networks", Las Vegas, NV, Oct 2000. ftp:

`//ftp.uk.research.att.com/pub/docs/att/tr.2000.12.pdf`. Also available as AT&T Laboratories Cambridge Technical Report 2000.12. (Ref: p. 44.)

[116] Brian Gladman. "The AES Algorithm (Rijndael) in C++". `http://fp.gladman.plus.com/cryptography_technology/rijndael/index.htm`. (Ref: p. 63, 110.)

> Provides source code, comments and timing information for the author's optimized implementation of the AES winner.

[117] Brian Gladman. "Implementation Experience with AES Candidate Algorithms". In "Proceedings of the 2nd AES Conference", Mar 1999. `http://csrc.nist.gov/encryption/aes/round1/conf2/papers/gladman.pdf`. (Ref: p. 63.)

[118] Virgil D. Gligor. "A Note on the Denial-of-Service Problem". In "Proceedings of the 1983 Symposium on Security and Privacy (SSP '83), Oakland, CA", pp. 139–149. IEEE Computer Society Press, Los Alamitos, CA, Apr 1983. ISBN 0-8186-0467-0. (Ref: p. 75, 134, 221.)

> This influential paper presents a clear and general definition of denial of service in operating systems based on "maximum waiting time". The author shows that his definition includes all previously known ones.

[119] Virgil D. Gligor. "A Note on Denial-of-Service in Operating Systems". *IEEE Transactions on Software Engineering*, **SE-10**(3):320–324, May 1984. ISSN 0098-5589. (Ref: p. 75, 134.)

> A more concise and polished journal version of [118].

[120] David Goldberg and Cate Richardson. "Touch-Typing With a Stylus". In "Conference proceedings on Human factors in computing systems", pp. 80–87. ACM Press, New York, Apr 24–29 1993. `http://www.acm.org/pubs/articles/proceedings/chi/169059/p80-goldberg/p80-goldberg.pdf`. (Ref: p. 11, 12.)

> Describes the Unistroke input method for pen-based computers—a specially designed symbol set in which each character is drawn with only one pen stroke and in which characters are widely separated in "sloppiness space" (i.e. they are still easily distinguishable even when written quickly). This concept became popular a few years later with the commercial success of the Palm Pilot's Graffiti, which was much easier to learn because its glyphs were more closely modelled on the corresponding letters.

[121] L. Goldberg. "Recycled Cold-War Electronics Battle Cellular Telephone Thieves". *Electronic Design*, **44**(18):41–42, 3 Sep 1996. (Ref: p. 164.)

[122] David M. Goldschlag, Michael G. Reed and Paul F. Syverson. "Hiding Routing Information". In Anderson [9], pp. 137–150. `http://www.onion-router.net/Publications/IH-1996.ps`. (Ref: p. 162.)

[123] Dieter Gollmann. *Computer Security*. John Wiley & Sons, 1999. ISBN 0-471-97844-2. (Ref: p. 60, 75, 175.)

> ⋆ A solid, readable and comprehensive primer on computer security offering valuable insights. Comparable to Amoroso [7], but more dense and with much better coverage of real-world systems (e.g. Unix, Windows NT, TCP/IP).

[124] Eric Greenberg. *Network Application Frameworks: Design and Architecture*. Addison-Wesley, 1999. ISBN 0-201-30950-5. (Ref: p. 175, 190.)

> An excellent book that gives a high level perspective of modern networking technologies in an enterprise context. Covers a lot of ground, from TCP/IP to CORBA and X.500, from Microsoft (NT and 2000) to Novell and IBM, going in detail through all the buzzwords such as SSL, IPv6, COM+, ActiveX and so on, not just with glossary entries but with full sections if not entire chapters. A well balanced and up to date book that offers a unifying picture of a fragmented and complex universe.

[125] Peter Gutmann. "Secure Deletion of Data from Magnetic and Solid-State Memory". In "6th USENIX Security Symposium", USENIX, San Jose, CA, Jul 1996. http://www.cs.auckland.ac.nz/~pgut001/pubs/secure_del.html. (Ref: p. 119.)

[126] Jaap Haartsen, Mahmoud Naghshineh, Jon Inouye, Olaf J. Joeressen and Warren Allen. "Bluetooth: Visions, Goals, and Architecture". *ACM Mobile Computing and Communications Review*, **2**(4):38–45, Oct 1998. (Ref: p. 2, 194.)

> Good high level overview of Bluetooth, but no useful information on its security.

[127] N. Haller. "The S/Key One-Time Password System". RFC 1760, Network Working Group, Feb 1995. http://www.ietf.org/rfc/rfc1760.txt. Category: Informational. (Ref: p. 77.)

[128] N. Haller and C. Metz. "A One-Time Password System". RFC 1938, Network Working Group, May 1996. http://www.ietf.org/rfc/rfc1938.txt. Category: Standards Track. (Ref: p. 77.)

[129] N. Haller, C. Metz, P. Nesser and M. Straw. "A One-Time Password System". RFC 2289, Network Working Group, Feb 1998. http://www.ietf.org/rfc/rfc2289.txt. Category: Standards Track. Obsoletes: 1938. (Ref: p. 77.)

[130] Neil M. Haller. "The S/Key™ One-Time Password System". In Dan Nesset (General Chair) and Robj Shirey (Program Chair) (eds.), "Proceedings of the ISOC Symposium on Network and Distributed System Security", Internet Society, San Diego, CA, Feb 1994. ftp://thumper.bellcore.com/pub/nmh/docs/ISOC.symp.ps. (Ref: p. 77.)

[131] Richard W. Hamming. *Coding and Information Theory*. Prentice-Hall, 1980. ISBN 0-13-139139-9. (Ref: p. 61, 70.)

A textbook of outstanding clarity, written by a pioneer in the field, that provides useful unifying insights as well as explaining how things work and why.

[132] D. T. Heitkemper, S. F. Platek and K. A. Wolnik. "Elemental and Microscopic Analysis in the 1993 Soft Drink/Syringe Product Tampering Incidents". *Journal of Forensic Sciences*, **40**:664–669, 1995. (Ref: p. 129.)

In 1993, numerous alleged product tamperings were reported to the US Food and Drug Administration. This forensic report investigates the veracity of the claims.

[133] Andy Hopper. "Pandora - An Experimental System for Multimedia Applications". *ACM Operating Systems Review, SIGOPS*, **24**(2):19–34, Apr 1990. `ftp://ftp.uk.research.att.com/pub/docs/att/tr.90.1.pdf`. Also available as ORL Technical Report 90.1. (Ref: p. 31.)

Pandora was one of the first systems to bring network-based video and audio streams to the desktop, at a time when multimedia usually meant little more than CD-ROMs. This paper gives an overview of the hardware and software design decisions for the system and then discusses usage and perspectives based on experience with a network of about 20 deployed nodes.

[134] Andy Hopper. "Sentient Computing", 1999. `ftp://ftp.uk.research.att.com/pub/docs/att/tr.1999.12.pdf`. The Royal Society Clifford Paterson Lecture. (Ref: p. 27.)

An excellent high level overview of many research projects at AT&T Labs Cambridge related to the unifying theme of sentient computing, with a discussion of the applications made possible by these developments.

[135] Andrew C. Huang, Benjamin C. Ling, John J. Barton and Armando Fox. "Running the Web backwards: appliance data services". *Computer Networks (Amsterdam, Netherlands: 1999)*, **33**(1–6):619–631, Jun 2000. ISSN 1389-1286. `http://cooltown.hp.com/dev/wpapers/runningbackwards/index.asp?print=yes`. (Ref: p. 27.)

[136] IBM. "Systems Application Architecture, Common User Access: Advanced Interface Design Guide". Manual SC26-4582-0, IBM, Jun 1989. (Ref: p. 117.)

An interesting relic from the times in which IBM and Microsoft were partners working on OS/2 2.0. This essential little manual was the authoritative reference on the user interface aspects of the graphical ancestor of Windows 3.0. Most of the behaviour of the system described here was carried over to Windows with no change, with only a few cosmetic enhancements such as the addition of a three-dimensional look and feel.

[137] IBM. "IBM Coprocessor First to Earn Highest Security Validation", 2 Dec 1998. `http://www.research.ibm.com/news/detail/fips.html`. (Ref: p. 130.)

IBM press release about their 4758 being the first device to earn FIPS 140-1
Level 4.

[138] ICS Advent. "Model PCI-WDT 500/501 Product Manual". Manual 00650-144-
1A, ICS Advent, San Diego, CA, 1998. http://www.icsadvent.com/techlib/
manuals/00650144.pdf. (Ref: p. 147.)

Detailed and instructive user's manual for a PCI card providing a watchdog
timer.

[139] IEEE. "Information technology—Telecommunications and information exchange
between systems—Local and metropolitan area networks—Specific requirements—
Part 11: Wireless LAN Medium Access Control (MAC) and Physical Layer (PHY)
Specifications". ANSI/IEEE Std 802.11, IEEE, 1999. http://standards.ieee.
org/getieee802/802.11.html. The web page also holds the 802.11a and 802.11b
documents. (Ref: p. 200.)

[140] Infrared Data Association. http://www.irda.org/. (Ref: p. 43.)

[141] Hiroshi Ishii, Craig Wisneski, Scott Brave, Andrew Dahley, Matt Gorbet, Brygg
Ullmer and Paul Yarin. "ambientROOM: Integrating Ambient Media with Architectural Space". In "Proceedings of ACM CHI 98 Conference on Human Factors in Computing Systems (Summary)", vol. 2 of *Videos*, pp. 173–
174. 1998. http://www.acm.org/pubs/articles/proceedings/chi/286498/
p173-ishii/p173-ishii.pdf. (Ref: p. 16.)

[142] ITOX, Inc.   http://www.itox.com/pages/products/LitTig/TCub/
bulletintc1a.htm. (Ref: p. 147.)

Technical bulletin for the Tiger Cub BIOS which supports a watchdog timer.
Gives programming information for controlling the watchdog.

[143] Ian W. Jackson. *Who goes here? Confidentiality of location through anonymity*.
Ph.D. thesis, University of Cambridge, Feb 1998.   http://www.chiark.
greenend.org.uk/~ijackson/thesis/. (Ref: p. 58, 153, 163.)

Jackson studies the privacy aspects of the ORL Active Badge system, seeking a
way to allow users to retain control over the disclosure of their location information. The system he proposes, whose anonymity layer is based on Chaum's
mixes, allows users to define personal security policies that specify what can be
disclosed to whom and under what circumstances. He also develops a BAN-style
logic to aid formal analysis.

[144] Markus Jakobsson and Susanne Wetzel. "Security Weaknesses in Bluetooth". In
David Naccache (ed.), "CT-RSA", vol. 2020 of *Lecture Notes in Computer Science*,
pp. 176–191. Springer, 2001. ISBN 3-540-41898-9. http://link.springer.de/
link/service/series/0558/bibs/2020/20200176.htm. Online access requires
registration. (Ref: p. 195, 199, 200.)

To my knowledge this is the first paper to offer a critical examination of the security of Bluetooth. The authors present various attacks, based on a purely static analysis of the 1.0B specification [41] and propose a variety of countermeasures to protect against them. Unfortunately, none of these suggestions were adopted in the 1.1 spec [43], which is therefore still vulnerable to the same attacks.

[145] Roger G. Johnston and Anthony R.E. Garcia. "Vulnerability Assessment of Security Seals". *Journal of Security Administration*, **20**(1):15–27, Jun 1997. http://lib-www.lanl.gov/la-pubs/00418796.pdf. (Ref: p. 130.)

[146] Alan Jones and Andrew Hopper. "The prototype embedded network (PEN)". *Computer Networks*, **35**(4):377–390, Mar 2001. ISSN 1389-1286. ftp.uk.research.att.com:/pub/docs/att/tr.2000.15.pdf. Also available as AT&T Laboratories Cambridge Technical Report 2000.15. (Ref: p. 44, 45, 46, 148.)

[147] Ari Juels and John Brainard. "Client Puzzles: A Cryptographic Defense Against Connection Depletion Attacks". In S. Kent (ed.), "Proceedings of NDSS '99 (Networks and Distributed Security Systems)", pp. 151–165. 1999. (Ref: p. 137.)

[148] David Kahn. *The Codebreakers: The Story of Secret Writing*. MacMillan Publishing Company, New York, NY, 1967. (Ref: p. 225.)

A monumental historical account of cryptography and cryptanalysis from ancient times to WWII. Orchestrated like a movie with emphasis on the characters rather than a technical textbook with emphasis on the mechanisms. A fascinating read.

[149] David Kahn. *The Codebreakers—The Comprehensive History of Secret Communication from Ancient Times to the Internet—Revised and updated*. Scribner, New York, NY, 1996. ISBN 0-684-83130-9. (Ref: p. 60, 61, 65, 66.)

New edition of the out-of-print 1967 original [148]. Despite the new subtitle, very little has been added about the Internet era, or even about the cryptological renaissance of the past quarter century spawned by Diffie and Hellman's *New Directions* paper [90]. Still, as a reprint that makes the old classic available, this is nonetheless an essential book.

[150] Joe M. Kahn, Randy H. Katz and Kris S. J. Pister. "Next Century Challenges: Mobile Networking for 'Smart Dust'". In "Proceedings of International Conference on Mobile Computing and Networking (MobiCom 99)", Seattle, WA, Aug 1999. http://robotics.eecs.berkeley.edu/~pister/publications/1999/mobicom_99.pdf. (Ref: p. 100, 140.)

A fascinating and innovative research project, combining nanotechnology with ad hoc networking and distributed sensing.

[151] C. K. Kantarjiev, A. Demers, R. Frederick, R. T. Krivacic and M. Weiser. "Experiences with X in a wireless environment". In "Proceedings of the USENIX Mobile and Location-Independent Computing Symposium", pp. 117–128. Aug 1993. (Ref: p. 12.)

[152] S. Kent and R. Atkinson. "IP Authentication Header". RFC 2402, IETF, Nov 1998.
       http://www.ietf.org/rfc/rfc2402.txt. Category: Standards track. Obsoletes:
       1826. (Ref: p. 185.)

[153] S. Kent and R. Atkinson. "IP Encapsulating Security Payload (ESP)". RFC 2406,
       IETF, Nov 1998. http://www.ietf.org/rfc/rfc2406.txt. Category: Standards
       track. Obsoletes: 1827. (Ref: p. 185.)

[154] S. Kent and R. Atkinson. "Security Architecture for the Internet Protocol". RFC
       2401, IETF, Nov 1998. http://www.ietf.org/rfc/rfc2401.txt. Category:
       Standards track. Obsoletes: 1825. (Ref: p. 184.)

       The new official high level description of IPSEC, substantially more compli-
       cated than its 1995 predecessor [22]. Despite the fact that the details are once
       more delegated to related RFCs (of which there are so many that one of them
       has to be a "roadmap" for the others), even the top-level one is now much harder
       to follow.

[155] Auguste Kerckhoffs. "La cryptographie militaire *(Military cryptography)*". *Journal
       des Sciences militaires*, **IX**:5–38, Jan 1883. http://www.cl.cam.ac.uk/~fapp2/
       kerckhoffs/. In French. The second part of the article appears in the Feb 1883
       issue, pp. 161–191. (Ref: p. 61, 191.)

       A timeless classic containing some of the fundamental axioms of modern cryp-
       tology, most importantly the principle that security should reside in the secrecy
       of the key, not of the algorithm.

[156] Tim Kindberg and John Barton. "The Cooltown User Experience". Tech. Rep. HPL-
       2001-22, HP Labs, Feb 2001. http://www.hpl.hp.com/techreports/2001/
       HPL-2001-22.pdf. (Ref: p. 26.)

[157] Neal Koblitz. *A Course in Number Theory and Cryptography, 2nd ed.*, vol. 114 of
       Graduate Texts in Mathematics. Springer-Verlag, 1994. ISBN 0-387-96576-9 (New
       York), 3-540-96576-9 (Berlin). (Ref: p. 60, 230.)

       A concise and very dense textbook on the mathematical aspects of (mostly pub-
       lic key) cryptography. Good if followed from cover to cover, but of little use as a
       random-access reference since every formula depends on everything else, while
       the internal cross-referencing is somewhat lacking. Contrast with Menezes *et al.*
       [187].

[158] Paul Kocher, Joshua Jaffe and Benjamin Jun. "Differential Power Analysis". In
       Michael Wiener (ed.), "Advances in Cryptology—CRYPTO '99: 19th Annual Inter-
       national Cryptology Conference, Santa Barbara, CA, August 15–19, 1999 proceed-
       ings", vol. 1666 of *Lecture Notes in Computer Science*, pp. 388–397. Springer-Ver-
       lag, 1999. ISBN 3-540-66347-9. http://www.cryptography.com/dpa/Dpa.pdf.
       (Ref: p. 130.)

[159] Paul C. Kocher. "Timing Attacks on Implementations of Diffie-Hellman, RSA, DSS, and Other Systems". In Neal Koblitz (ed.), "Advances in Cryptology—CRYPTO '96", vol. 1109 of *Lecture Notes in Computer Science*, pp. 104–113. Springer-Verlag, 1996. (Ref: p. 130.)

[160] J. Kohl and C. Neuman. "The Kerberos Network Authentication Service (V5)". RFC 1510, IETF, Sep 1993. http://www.ietf.org/rfc/rfc1510.txt. (Ref: p. 179, 180, 181.)

> The authoritative specification of Kerberos V5. The introductory chapter is particularly clear, despite the lack of diagrams enforced by the typical RFC ASCII-only format.

[161] Oliver Kömmerling and Markus G. Kuhn. "Design Principles for Tamper-Resistant Smartcard Processors". In "Proceedings of the USENIX Workshop on Smartcard Technology (Smartcard '99)", pp. 9–20. USENIX Association, Chicago, IL, 10–11 May 1999. ISBN 1-880446-34-0. http://www.cl.cam.ac.uk/~mgk25/sc99-tamper.pdf. (Ref: p. 128.)

[162] H. Krawczyk, M. Bellare and R. Canetti. "HMAC: Keyed-Hashing for Message Authentication". RFC 2104, IETF, Feb 1997. http://www.ietf.org/rfc/rfc2104.txt. Category: Informational. (Ref: p. 71, 125.)

> Describes the HMAC construction, which builds a MAC out of a hash function according to the following formula:
>
> $$\mathrm{HMAC}_K(\mathit{text}) \triangleq \mathrm{h}(K \oplus \mathit{opad}, \mathrm{h}(K \oplus \mathit{ipad}, \mathit{text})).$$
>
> The specification is crafted in such a way that code for existing hash functions can be plugged in without modifications.

[163] Harry M. Kriz. "Phreacking reconnu par la DG de France Télécom *(Phreaking recognized by the directorate-general of France Télécom)*". *Chaos Digest*, **1**(3), 18 Jan 1993. http://the.wiretapped.net/security/info/textfiles/chaos-digest/chaos-digest-03.txt. (Ref: p. 87.)

[164] Markus G. Kuhn. "Cipher Instruction Search Attack on the Bus-Encryption Security Microcontroller DS5002FP". *IEEE Transactions on Computers*, **47**(10):1153–1157, Oct 1998. http://dlib.computer.org/tc/books/tc1998/pdf/t1153.pdf. (Ref: p. 122.)

[165] Markus G. Kuhn and Ross J. Anderson. "Soft Tempest: Hidden Data Transmission using Electromagnetic Emanations". In David Aucsmith (ed.), "Information Hiding: Second International Workshop", vol. 1525 of *Lecture Notes in Computer Science*, pp. 124–142. Springer-Verlag, 1998. ISBN 3-540-65386-4. http://www.cl.cam.ac.uk/~mgk25/ih98-tempest.pdf. (Ref: p. 164.)

[166] Mik Lamming and Mike Flynn. " 'Forget-me-not': Intimate Computing in Support of Human Memory". In "Proceedings of FRIEND21, International Symposium on Next Generation Human Interfaces, Tokyo, Japan", 1994. http://www.xrce.xerox.com/publis/cam-trs/pdf/1994/epc-1994-103.pdf. Also available as RXRC TR 94-103. (Ref: p. 11.)

Describes "Forget-me-not", a prototype memory prosthesis that helps users remember events, locate documents and generally keep a self-writing diary of their
activities. The hardware of the system is the ParcTab, taken as a representative
of a potentially much smaller wearable computer.

[167] Leslie Lamport. "Password Authentication with Insecure Communication". *Communications of the ACM*, **24**(11):770–772, Nov 1981. ISSN 0001-0782. (Ref: p.
77, 127.)

This brilliant short article introduces Lamport's one-time password technique
based on a reverse hash chain.

[168] Steve Lawrence. "Online or Invisible?" *Nature*, **411**(6837):521,
2001. http://www.neci.nec.com/~lawrence/papers/online-nature01/
online-nature01.pdf. (Ref: p. 204.)

[169] David Matthew Leask. *Low Power Radio Networking*. Ph.D. thesis, University of
Cambridge, Jun 2000. (Ref: p. 111, 140.)

[170] Torsten Lif. "Bugging ISDN". *The RISKS Digest*, **13**(29), Mar 1992. http://
catless.ncl.ac.uk/Risks/13.29.html#subj10. (Ref: p. 56.)

An Ericsson engineer who worked on designing ISDN phones discovers that
"his" hi-tech phone is so programmable that its microphone can be turned on remotely and unobtrusively even while the handset is on hook. In a public-spirited
civil disobedience act, the design team adds extra hardware that makes this impossible without turning on the "hands free" LED. (This does not *prevent* remote
bugging: it only makes it partially visible, assuming that the victim can see the
LED, recognize it from all the others that grace the phone, and realize that something suspicious is going on.)

[171] Peter H. Lindsay and Donald A. Norman. *Human Information Processing; An Introduction to Psychology*. Academic Press, New York, 1972. ISBN 0-12-450950-9.
(Ref: p. 13.)

[172] Diego López de Ipiña. *Visual Sensing and Middleware Support for Sentient Computing*. Ph.D. thesis, University of Cambridge. To appear. (Ref: p. 40.)

[173] Diego López de Ipiña. "Video-Based Sensing for Wide Deployment of Sentient
Spaces". In "Proceedings of 2nd PACT 2001 Workshop on Ubiquitous Computing
and Communications", Barcelona, Spain, 8–12 Sep 2001. http://www-lce.eng.
cam.ac.uk/~dl231/PACT01/pact01.pdf. (Ref: p. 40.)

[174] Konrad Lorenz. *Er redete mit dem Vieh, den Vögeln und den Fischen* (King
Solomon's ring). Borotha-Schoeler, Wien, 1949. (Ref: p. 88.)

[175] Steve Mann. "SeatSale". http://wearcam.org/seatsale/. (Ref: p. 20.)

[176] Steve Mann. "The Witnessential Computer and Witnessential Networks". http:
//wearcam.org/witnessential.htm. (Ref: p. 20.)

[177] Steve Mann. "Privacy Issues of Wearable Cameras versus Surveillance Cameras", Jul 1995. http://wearcam.org/netcam_privacy_issues.html. (Ref: p. 19, 54.)

> A provocative discussion of the threat from surveillance cameras in public places. The author argues that one way to fight back is for people to point their own personal cameras at the entities (governments and businesses) behind the surveillance cameras, since this would make them accountable for their behaviour.

[178] Steve Mann. "'Smart Clothing': Wearable Multimedia and 'Personal Imaging' to restore the balance between people and their intelligent environments". In "Proceedings, ACM Multimedia 96", pp. 163–174. Boston, MA, 18–22 Nov 1996. http://wearcam.org/acm-mm96.htm. (Ref: p. 18, 20, 58.)

[179] Steve Mann. "An historical account of the 'WearComp' and 'WearCam' inventions developed for applications in 'Personal Imaging'". In "Proceedings of the first ISWC", pp. 66–73. IEEE, 13–14 Oct 1997. http://www.wearcam.org/historical/. (Ref: p. 17.)

[180] Steve Mann. "Wearable Computing: A First Step Toward Personal Imaging". *Computer*, **30**(2):25–32, Feb 1997. ISSN 0018-9162. http://www.wearcam.org/ieeecomputer/r2025.htm. (Ref: p. 18.)

[181] Steve Mann. *Cyborg: Digital Destiny and Human Possibility in the Age of the Wearable Computer*. Randomhouse Doubleday, Nov 2001. ISBN 0-38-565825-7. (Ref: p. 21.)

[182] Steve Mann. *Intelligent Image Processing*. Wiley, Nov 2001. ISBN 0-471-40637-6. (Ref: p. 21.)

[183] Steve Mann. "WearComp.org, WearCam.org, UTWCHI, and Steve Mann's Personal Web Page/research", 2001. http://www.wearcam.org/. (Ref: p. 17.)

[184] L. Masinter. "Hyper Text Coffee Pot Control Protocol (HTCPCP/1.0)". RFC 2324, Network Working Group, 1 Apr 1998. http://www.ietf.org/rfc/rfc2324.txt. (Ref: p. 32.)

> An April's Fool standards document describing a protocol for controlling coffee pots.

[185] Mitsuru Matsui. "Linear Cryptanalysis Method for DES Cipher". In Tor Helleseth (ed.), "Advances in Cryptology—EUROCRYPT 93", vol. 765 of *Lecture Notes in Computer Science*, pp. 386–397. Springer-Verlag, 1994, 23–27 May 1993. (Ref: p. 64.)

[186] Andrew D. McDonald and Markus G. Kuhn. "StegFS: A Steganographic File System for Linux". In Pfitzmann [210], pp. 463–477. http://www.cl.cam.ac.uk/~mgk25/ih99-stegfs.pdf. (Ref: p. 117.)

[187] Alfred J. Menezes, Paul C. van Oorschot and Scott A. Vanstone. *Handbook of Applied Cryptography*. CRC Press, Oct 1996. ISBN 0-8493-8523-7. http://www. cacr.math.uwaterloo.ca/hac/. (Ref: p. 60, 226.)

> A thick encyclopedia of cryptography covering everything from the number theory (with proofs of all the theorems) to the algorithms (with numerical examples) and the protocols (with discussion of the relative security of possible variants). Extremely well cross-referenced: the individual items are self-contained or clearly refer by number to any other items upon which they build. Ideal as a reference work, though its size discourages attempts at cover-to-cover reading. Contrast with Koblitz [157].

[188] Perry Metzger. "A Parable", Apr 1993. http://cypherpunks.venona. com/date/1993/04/msg00559.html. Originally posted to sci.crypt and alt.privacy.clipper. Now archived in many places on the net: if you can't find it at this URL, search for the author's name and "Ruritania". (Ref: p. 114.)

> ★ This carefully crafted one-page story about the land of transparent walls, written while the three-letter agencies were heavily pushing the Clipper chip, is a brilliant dramatization of the mechanics and consequences of giving up one's right to privacy. Clipper was later defeated by public outcry, but other initiatives towards legalized mass eavesdropping, including Echelon, Carnivore and RIP, have since taken its place with renewed vigour. Metzger's witty classic is therefore still as topical as ever.

[189] Linda J. Miller and Jean Marx. "Apoptosis". *Science*, **281**:1301, 28 Aug 1998. (Ref: p. 105.)

> This is a one-page introduction to a special section on apoptosis (pages 1301–1326) containing 5 articles by leaders in the field. The topic of apoptosis, "the highly orchestrated form of cell death in which cells neatly commit suicide by chopping themselves into membrane-packaged bits", is described as "one of the hottest in biology". A related editorial elsewhere in this issue mentions "20,000 publications [on the topic of cell death] within the past 5 years".

[190] Martin Minow. "Call Your OPERATER!" *The RISKS Digest*, **16**(9), May 1994. http://catless.ncl.ac.uk/Risks/16.09.html#subj1. (Ref: p. 123.)

> The hilarious 1-800-OPERATER scam with which MCI "has been scooping up calls intended for its arch-rival" AT&T.

[191] MIT. "MIT Oxygen Project", 2001. http://oxygen.lcs.mit.edu/. (Ref: p. 25.)

[192] MIT Auto-ID Center. "The Networked Physical World — Proposals for engineering the next generation of computing, commerce, and automatic-identification". Tech. Rep. MIT-AUTOID-WH-001, MIT, Dec 2000. http://www.autoidcenter.org/ research/MIT-AUTOID-WH-001.pdf. (Ref: p. 21, 22.)

[193] MIT Auto-ID Center. "How much does this technology cost?", Aug 2001. `http://www.autoidcenter.org/questions2.asp`. (Ref: p. 22.)

> A (probably volatile) pointer into the questions-and-answers page of the Auto-ID web site, containing ambitious predictions of extremely inexpensive ePC chips being available in 2001.

[194] Giancarlo Mola. "Domini, Grauso si lancia alla conquista del web *(Domains: Grauso runs off to conquer the web)*", 16 Feb 2000. `http://www.repubblica.it/online/tecnologie_internet/domi/grauso/grauso.html`. (Ref: p. 136.)

> This article from the online version of daily newspaper *La Repubblica* reports on Nichi Grauso's cybersquatting—he bought 500,000 domain names in two months. The newspaper also makes the full list of his purchases available at `http://www.repubblica.it/online/tecnologie_internet/lista/list/Lista.zip`.

[195] Robert Morris and Ken Thompson. "Password Security: A Case History". *Communications of the ACM*, **22**(11):594–597, Nov 1979. (Ref: p. 76.)

> A brief but significant article describing the evolutionary history of the Unix password system. A clear primer on the fundamental techniques of password security (such as "salting") that have since spread to many other systems.

[196] Roger M. Needham and Michael D. Schroeder. "Using Encryption for Authentication in Large Networks of Computers". *Communications of the ACM*, **21**(12):993–999, Dec 1978. ISSN 0001-0782. (Ref: p. 176, 179.)

> A fundamental paper that introduces, among other things, two of the first authentication protocols, one based on conventional cryptography and one on public key techniques. Very readable, motivates all its design decisions and sets the standard for much of the subsequent literature in this field.

[197] NIST. "NIST Announces Encryption Standard Finalists", 9 Aug 1999. `http://csrc.nist.gov/encryption/aes/round2/AESpressrelease-990809.pdf`. (Ref: p. 62.)

> Press release announcing MARS, RC6, Rijndael, Serpent and Twofish as the 5 finalists for the AES.

[198] NIST. "Commerce Department Announces Winner of Global Information Security Competition", 2 Oct 2000. `http://www.nist.gov/public_affairs/releases/g00-176.htm`. (Ref: p. 62.)

> Press release announcing Rijndael as the winner of the Advanced Encryption Standard competition.

[199] Donald A. Norman. *The Psychology of Everyday Things*. Basic Books, New York,
       1988. ISBN 0-385-26774-6. (Ref: p. 13.)

[200] Donald A. Norman. *The Invisible Computer: Why Good Products Can Fail, the
       Personal Computer Is So Complex, and Information Appliances Are the Solution*.
       MIT Press, 1998. ISBN 0-262-14065-9 (hardcover); 0-262-64041-4 (paperback).
       (Ref: p. 13, 51, 232.)

> ★ A readable and entertaining book by one of the world experts on cognitive
> psychology and computer usability. One of Norman's main points is that the de-
> sign of today's personal computer is driven by technology for technology's sake
> rather than by the actual needs of the users. This, he argues with examples rang-
> ing from Edison's phonograph to the "home motors" of the early 1900s, is what
> happens in the early stages of a product's lifetime. For the computer industry
> to reach maturity and, consequently, the lucrative consumer market, Norman's
> solution is to get rid of the general-purpose and technology-centric computer
> of today in favour of specialized information appliances. The somewhat con-
> troversial argument is developed in a convincing way because the author looks
> at it from several points of view, giving due importance not just to the tension
> between technology and human factors, but also to the needs and constraints of
> marketing, organizational structure and the overall business case for the product.

[201] Andrew Odlyzko. "The visible problems of the invisible computer: A skeptical
       look at information appliances". *First Monday*, **4**(9), Sep 1999. http://www.
       firstmonday.dk/issues/issue4_9/odlyzko/index.html. (Ref: p. 14.)

> A critical response to Norman's *Invisible Computer* [200]. The author's argu-
> ment is that the consolidation and simplification advocated by Norman are only
> possible under the conditions of technological stability that are typical of a ma-
> ture market, whereas the mere introduction of the information appliance will
> produce a new wave of innovation and product development that will completely
> negate such stability. The result, for Odlyzko, is that we will continue to be frus-
> trated by information appliances as much as we were by the personal computer,
> only at a different level.

[202] Joann J. Ordille. "When agents roam, who can you trust?" In "First Conference on
       Emerging Technologies and Applications in Communications (etaCOM)", Portland,
       OR, May 1996. http://cm.bell-labs.com/cm/cs/doc/96/5-09.ps.gz. (Ref:
       p. 146.)

[203] Oxford University Press. *Oxford English Dictionary*. Oxford University Press, 2000.
       http://dictionary.oed.com/. Online version of the 20-volume edition, updated
       monthly. Access by subscription. (Ref: p. 2, 139, 176.)

> A monumental dictionary and an invaluable resource for any writer. I have the
> two-volume "shorter" edition at home and use it frequently, but nothing beats
> the convenience of being able to access the full length edition electronically. An
> extremely professional translation from paper to bits.

[204] Ron Perez and Sean Smith. "Secure Coprocessing", 1999. http://www.research. ibm.com/compsci/security/secsystems/4758.htm. (Ref: p. 130.)

> A web page on the 4758 by members of the IBM team that designed it, with references to selected technical publications about it.

[205] Adrian Perrig, Ran Canetti, Doug Tygar and Dawn Song. "Efficient Authentication and Signature of Multicast Streams over Lossy Channels". In "Proceedings of the IEEE Symposium on Research in Security and Privacy", IEEE Computer Society, Technical Committee on Security and Privacy, IEEE Computer Society Press, Oakland, CA, May 2000. http://paris.cs.berkeley.edu/perrig/projects/ stream/stream.ps.gz. (Ref: p. 126.)

> An excellent paper, dense with original constructions and results, yet readable and well presented. Two separate stream authentication protocols are proposed: TESLA, based on time-delayed release of MAC keys that authenticate previous packets; and EMSS, which provides non-repudiation as well as authentication and works without the need for time synchronization between sender and receivers, at the price of higher computational costs and longer delays before verification. Both schemes cope with lossy channels and scale well to large numbers of recipients.

[206] Andreas Pfitzmann. "Ein dienstintegriertes digitales Vermittlungs-/Verteilnetz zur Erhöhung des Datenschutzes *(An Integrated Digital Services Switching/Distribution Network for Increased Privacy)*". Tech. Rep. 18/83, Institut für Informatik IV, University of Karlsruhe, 1983. (Ref: p. 164.)

[207] Andreas Pfitzmann. "A switched/broadcast ISDN to decrease user observability". 1984 International Zürich Seminar on Digital Communications, Applications of Source Coding, Channel Coding and Secrecy Coding, March 6-8, 1984, Zürich, Switzerland, Swiss Federal Institute of Technology, Proceedings IEEE Catalog no. 84CH1998-4, 6–8 Mar 1984. (Ref: p. 164.)

[208] Andreas Pfitzmann. "How to Implement ISDNs Without User Observability—Some Remarks". Tech. rep., Institut für Informatik, University of Karlsruhe, 1985. (Ref: p. 164.)

[209] Andreas Pfitzmann. *Diensteintegrierende Kommunikationsnetze mit teilnehmerüberprüfbarem Datenschutz* (Integrated services communication networks with end-user verifiable privacy). No. 234 in Informatik-Fachberichte. Springer-Verlag, Heidelberg, 1990. (Ref: p. 161, 164.)

[210] Andreas Pfitzmann (ed.). *Information Hiding. Third International Workshop, IH'99. Dresden, Germany, September/October, 1999. Proceedings*, vol. 1768 of *Lecture Notes in Computer Science*. Springer-Verlag, Berlin Heidelberg New York, 1999. ISBN 3-540-67182-X. ISSN 0302-9743. (Ref: p. 229, 238.)

[211] Andreas Pfitzmann and Michael Waidner. "Networks Without User Observability". *Computers and Security*, **6**(2):158–166, Apr 1987. ISSN 0167-4048. http://www. semper.org/sirene/publ/PfWa_86anonyNetze.html. (Ref: p. 164.)

[212] Phoenix Technologies. http://www.phoenix.com/platform/awardbios.html.
     (Ref: p. 147.)

        Product literature for a BIOS ROM with support for watchdog timer. No techni-
        cal info, just a feature list.

[213] Charles Platt. "Satellite Pirates". *Wired*, **2**(08), Aug 1994. http://www.wired.
     com/wired/archive/2.08/satellite_pr.html. (Ref: p. 62.)

[214] Anton T. Rager. "WEPCrack—An 802.11 key breaker", Aug 2001. http:
     //wepcrack.sourceforge.net/. (Ref: p. 201, 212.)

        An open-source PERL script for cracking the WEP encryption of 802.11 wire-
        less LANs. The first (by a short margin of about a week, see AirSnort [53])
        public implementation of the Fluhrer *et al.* [109] attack.

[215] Kasim Rehman. "101 Ubiquitous Computing Applications". http://www-lce.
     eng.cam.ac.uk/~kr241/html/101_ubicomp.html. (Ref: p. 9.)

        An extensive survey of, and online bibliography about, ubiquitous computing
        applications. Projects are classified into nine categories. For each entry there
        is a short description, a bibliographic entry and, where available, a link to the
        online paper.

[216] Martin Reichenbach, Herbert Damker, Hannes Federrath and Kai Rannenberg. "In-
     dividual Management of Personal Reachability in Mobile Communication". In
     Louise Yngström and Jan Carlsen (eds.), "IFIP TC11 13th International Conference
     on Information Security (SEC '97)", pp. 164–174. Copenhagen, Denmark, May
     1997. ISBN 0-412-81780-2. http://www.iig.uni-freiburg.de/dbskolleg/
     public/ps/ReiDFRa_97.IFIP_SEC.ps. (Ref: p. 137.)

[217] Tristan Richardson, Frazer Bennett, Glenford Mapp and Andy Hopper. "Teleporting
     in an X Window System Environment". *IEEE Personal Communications Magazine*,
     1(3):6–12, Third Quarter 1994. ftp://ftp.uk.research.att.com/pub/docs/
     att/tr.94.4.pdf. Also available as AT&T Laboratories Cambridge Technical Re-
     port 94.4. (Ref: p. 12, 33.)

        Describes the Teleporting system, which gives mobility to the user interface of
        your X session. Because it works at the X server level, applications run unmod-
        ified, and unaware that their I/O is being redirected. Thanks to its integration
        with the Active Badge, the Teleporting system was an important step towards
        global personalization of computing resources.

[218] Tristan Richardson, Quentin Stafford-Fraser, Kenneth R. Wood and Andy Hop-
     per. "Virtual Network Computing". *IEEE Internet Computing*, **2**(1):33–38, Jan/Feb
     1998. ftp://ftp.uk.research.att.com/pub/docs/att/tr.98.1.pdf. Also
     available as AT&T Laboratories Cambridge Technical Report 98.1. (Ref: p. 33.)

VNC is a cross-platform system for mobile computing in which the desktop of a server computer can be displayed on a viewer on another computer—crossing networks, architectures and operating systems. This paper describes the design and implementation of the system (now released as open source) and draws lessons from experience.

[219] R. L. Rivest, A. Shamir and L. Adleman. "A Method for Obtaining Digital Signatures and Public Key Cryptosystems". *Communications of the ACM*, **21**(2):120–126, Feb 1978. ISSN 0001-0782. (Ref: p. 67, 72, 107.)

The classic paper introducing the RSA public key cryptosystem. Describes in a relatively readable way all the mathematical detail of how and why it works, and of how to perform all the ancillary operations efficiently.

[220] Ronald L. Rivest and Butler W. Lampson. *SDSI – A Simple Distributed Security Infrastructure*, Apr 1996. http://theory.lcs.mit.edu/~cis/sdsi.html. V1.0 presented at USENIX 96 and Crypto 96. (Ref: p. 182.)

[221] Michael Roe. *Cryptography and Evidence*. Ph.D. thesis, University of Cambridge, 1997. http://www.research.microsoft.com/users/mroe/THESIS.PDF. (Ref: p. 73.)

The author investigates the non-repudiation properties offered by various cryptographic constructions. Interestingly, this also leads to an examination of the problem from the dual point of view, which he calls "plausible deniability". These are the two sides of the "evidence" coin: what is a disadvantage in one case becomes an advantage in the other, and it would be naïve simply to "feel sympathy for Alice and Bob, while regarding the protagonists with names later in the alphabet with some suspicion".

[222] RSA Data Security. "Team of Universities, Companies and Individual Computer Users Linked Over the Internet Crack RSA's 56-Bit DES Challenge". Press release 970619-1, RSA Data Security, Redwood City, CA, 19 Jun 1997. http://www.rsasecurity.com/news/pr/970619-1.html. (Ref: p. 63.)

Announces Rocke Verser's team as the winner of the first RSA DES challenge.

[223] Aviel D. Rubin. *White-hat Security Arsenal*. Addison-Wesley, Jun 2001. ISBN 0-201-71114-1. (Ref: p. 60, 175, 176.)

★ This excellent and up-to-date resource is a rare combination of authoritativeness and clarity. Rubin's problem-oriented approach, based on a wealth of case studies, will be greatly appreciated by professionals who need to address real-world security issues, from secure backups to firewalls and e-commerce. Recommended.

[224] Tony Sammes and Brian Jenkinson. *Forensic Computing: A Practitioner's Guide*. Springer, 2000. ISBN 1-85233-299-9. (Ref: p. 54, 120.)

★ This disquieting book is best described as a torture manual. It gives accurate descriptions of the anatomy, showing the most sensitive spots and highlighting the treatments that are most likely to extract all the desired secrets from the subject under investigation. Search and seizure advice is included: early morning raids are recommended in order to catch the suspects off-guard, and "the first priority at the search scene is to gain total control both of the premises and of the occupants". The fact that the targets of such torture are computers rather than humans mitigates only slightly the uneasy feeling that one gets by imagining a totalitarian police force being trained on books such as this, to be able to suck out your most private information with or without your consent. (Of course such arguments always cut both ways.) Written by law enforcement practitioners with extensive field experience, this is a technically sound and up to date book, and therefore one to be taken seriously.

[225] Greg Sandoval. "eBay auction goes up in smoke". *CNET News.com*, Sep 1999. http://news.cnet.com/news/0-1007-202-123002.html. (Ref: p. 155.)

News report of an incident in which people attempted to sell marijuana on the online auction site eBay, with bids reaching 10 M$ before the auction was noticed and closed by eBay officials.

[226] D. Curtis Schleher. *Electronic Warfare in the Information Age*. Artech House, 1999. ISBN 0-89006-526-8. (Ref: p. 135, 164.)

[227] Bruce Schneier. *Applied Cryptography, 2nd ed., Protocols, Algorithms, and Source Code in C*. Wiley, 1996. ISBN 0-471-11709-9. (Ref: p. 4, 60, 66, 68, 191, 236.)

★ The bestselling ($> 10^5$ copies) technical book on cryptography is very well organised and a pleasure to read. Its abundant and accurate technical material, carefully cross-referenced to the original research publications, is made more palatable by being thickly sugar-coated in jokes. Schneier is great at giving clear and entertaining explanations of complex technical subjects. Despite being at times tantalisingly frustrating, since the author sometimes omits the details and design motivations of some of the items he presents, this book nevertheless deserves its classic status and it would be hard to recommend a better introduction to the subject.

[228] Bruce Schneier. *Secrets and Lies: Digital Security in a Networked World*. Wiley, 2000. ISBN 0-471-25311-1. (Ref: p. 4.)

★ Schneier has a gift for writing about security in a clear and entertaining way. Unlike his previous *Applied Cryptography* [227], this is a high level book without technical formulæ: after extensive experience as a security consultant, the author's new message is that the cryptographic details are nowhere near as important as the big picture of "security as a process". If you want to learn from the horse's mouth what real-world computer security is about, this easy read will provide awareness through many interesting anecdotes.

[229] Bruce Schneier. "The Futility of Digital Copy Prevention", 15 May 2001. `http://www.counterpane.com/crypto-gram-0105.html#3`. (Ref: p. 59.)

> Discusses the technical (e.g. DVD's CSS) and legal (e.g. DCMA) measures taken by the entertainment industry to prevent copying of digital media, concluding that the only profitable course of action would instead be a change of business model.

[230] Adi Shamir. "How to Share a Secret". *Communications of the ACM*, **22**(11):612–613, Nov 1979. ISSN 0001-0782. (Ref: p. 90.)

> A brilliant and very concise paper which introduces a method for (k, n) threshold secret sharing using polynomial interpolation. Split a secret into n shares of which only k are needed for reconstruction.

[231] G. J. Simmons. "Proof of Soundness (Integrity) of Cryptographic Protocols". *Journal of Cryptology*, **7**(2):69–77, Spring 1994. ISSN 0933-2790. (Ref: p. 108.)

> Introduces an invited paper that takes up the rest of the issue. Discusses the idea of verifying crypto protocols using formal methods. A two-page appendix describes a now famous attack on the TMN protocol.

[232] Slashdot. "Security in wireless networks", 20 Oct 1999. `http://slashdot.org/articles/99/10/20/1017231.shtml`. (Ref: p. 88.)

> On the day the Duckling article [240] was featured on Slashdot, the Duckling's web site was visited about 47,000 times. Unfortunately, though, the comments offered by readers and archived on this page were mostly noise.

[233] Sean W. Smith and Steve Weingart. "Building a high-performance, programmable secure coprocessor". *Computer Networks*, **31**(8):831–860, 23 Apr 1999. ISSN 1389-1286. (Special Issue on Computer Network Security). (Ref: p. 130.)

[234] Sony. "eMarker.com Connects Radio Listeners With Their Favorite Music Through New Internet Service", 5 Sep 2000. `http://www.sel.sony.com/SEL/corpcomm/news/consumer/622.html`. (Ref: p. 115.)

> A commercial press release announcing and describing the eMarker device, which allows one to "make a note" of a song being played on the radio in order later to retrieve information about song title and artist.

[235] Quentin Stafford-Fraser. "On site: The life and times of the first Web Cam". *Communications of the ACM*, **44**(7):25–26, Jul 2001. ISSN 0001-0782. `http://www.cl.cam.ac.uk/coffee/qsf/cacm200107.html`. (Ref: p. 32.)

> The entertaining history of the Trojan Room Coffee Pot, by one of its creators.

[236] Frank Stajano. "The Resurrecting Duckling—What Next?" In Christianson *et al.* [69], pp. 204–214. http://www-lce.eng.cam.ac.uk/~fms27/papers/duckling-what-next.pdf. Also available as AT&T Laboratories Cambridge Technical Report 2000.4. (Ref: p. xix, 102.)

Extends the Resurrecting Duckling policy to non-master-slave relationships.

[237] Frank Stajano and Ross Anderson. "The Cocaine Auction Protocol: On The Power Of Anonymous Broadcast". In Pfitzmann [210], pp. 434–447. http://www-lce.eng.cam.ac.uk/~fms27/cocaine/. Also available as AT&T Laboratories Cambridge Technical Report 1999.4. (Ref: p. xix.)

This paper offers several original contributions. First, it examines the trust relationships in an electronically mediated auction, highlighting the difficulties that arise when participants are not ready to trust an arbitrator unconditionally. Second, it offers a protocol for conducting an auction anonymously without a trusted arbitrator, and examines various scenarios of attacks and countermeasures. Third, it presents an efficient anonymity primitive based on physics rather than on cryptography and shows how, despite its obvious theoretical weakness, it is in practice as strong as the "unbreakable" solutions when faced with a realistic threat model. Fourth, it shows how this primitive may be used in protocol modelling to represent more accurately what actually happens at the lower levels.

[238] Frank Stajano and Ross Anderson. "The Resurrecting Duckling: Security Issues in Ad-Hoc Wireless Networks". In "Proceedings of 3rd AT&T Software Symposium", Middletown, NJ, Oct 1999. http://www-lce.eng.cam.ac.uk/~fms27/duckling/. Abridged and revised version of [240]. Also available as AT&T Laboratories Cambridge Technical Report 1999.2b. (Ref: p. 88, 238.)

For this shorter refereed version of [240], the main innovation is the repudiation of centralized escrowed seppuku in favour of local backup of the keys.

[239] Frank Stajano and Ross Anderson. "The Grenade Timer: Fortifying the Watchdog Timer Against Malicious Mobile Code". In "Proceedings of the 7th International Workshop on Mobile Multimedia Communications", Waseda, Tokyo, Japan, Oct 2000. http://www-lce.eng.cam.ac.uk/~fms27/papers/grenade.pdf. Also available as AT&T Laboratories Cambridge Technical Report 2000.8. (Ref: p. xix.)

Introduces the Grenade Timer construction as an inexpensive safeguard against denial of service from mobile code for microcontrollers without a protected mode.

[240] Frank Stajano and Ross Anderson. "The Resurrecting Duckling: Security Issues in Ad-Hoc Wireless Networks". In Christianson *et al.* [68], pp. 172–182. http://www-lce.eng.cam.ac.uk/~fms27/duckling/. See also [238]. Also available as AT&T Laboratories Cambridge Technical Report 1999.2. (Ref: p. xix, 88, 139, 237, 238.)

First presentation of the Resurrecting Duckling security policy model, the sleep deprivation torture and bearer certificates from tamper-evident devices.

[241] Frank Stajano and Alan Jones. "The Thinnest Of Clients: Controlling It All Via Cellphone". *ACM Mobile Computing and Communications Review*, **2**(4):46–53, Oct 1998. `ftp://ftp.uk.research.att.com/pub/docs/att/tr.98.3.pdf`. Also available as ORL Technical Report TR.98.3. (Ref: p. 42, 141.)

Presents the architecture of the SMS server, which lets mobile users access personalized computing facilities using the Short Message Service of GSM phones. User applications and experience with the deployed system are also described. Security features include logging and various quota systems. Phone bill protection against bugs by legitimate authors is considered alongside protection from malicious attackers.

[242] Radina Stefanova. *Power Efficient Routing in Radio Peer Networks*. Ph.D. thesis, University of Cambridge, Jul 2000. (Ref: p. 44.)

[243] Pete Steggles, Paul Webster and Andy Harter. "The Implementation of a Distributed Framework to support 'Follow Me' Applications". Tech. Rep. TR.98.8, ORL, 1998. `ftp.uk.research.att.com:/pub/docs/att/tr.98.8.pdf`. (Ref: p. 38.)

[244] W. Richard Stevens. *TCP/IP Illustrated, Volume 1: The Protocols*. Addison-Wesley, 1994. ISBN 0-201-63346-9. (Ref: p. 175, 184.)

One of the clearest and most competent explanations of the TCP/IP protocol suite. A sound theoretical foundation is complemented and expanded by a wealth of examples in which useful diagnostic programs are incidentally demonstrated to show what is effectively being transmitted between the hosts of the example setup.

[245] Adam Stubblefield, John Ioannidis and Aviel D. Rubin. "Using the Fluhrer, Mantin, and Shamir Attack to Break WEP". Tech. Rep. TD-4ZCPZZ, AT&T Labs, Aug 2001. `http://www.cs.rice.edu/~astubble/wep/wep_attack.pdf`. (Ref: p. 201.)

[246] Makoto Tatebayashi, Natsume Matsuzaki and David B. Newman Jr. "Key Distribution Protocol for Digital Mobile Communication Systems". In Gilles Brassard (ed.), "Advances in Cryptology—CRYPTO '89, 9th Annual International Cryptology Conference, Santa Barbara, CA, August 20-24, 1989, Proceedings", vol. 435 of *Lecture Notes in Computer Science*, pp. 324–334. Springer, 1990. ISBN 3-540-97317-6. (Ref: p. 107.)

[247] Ubicomp. "Ubicomp Conference". `http://www.ubicomp.org/`. (Ref: p. 9.)

The home page of the Ubicomp conference, with links to the pages of the individual editions from 1999 onwards.

[248] Brygg Ullmer and Hiroshi Ishii. "The metaDESK: Models and Prototypes for Tangible User Interfaces". In "Proceedings of the 10th annual ACM symposium on User interface software and technology", pp. 223–232. 1997. ISBN 0-89791-881-9. http://www.acm.org/pubs/articles/proceedings/uist/263407/p223-ullmer/p223-ullmer.pdf. (Ref: p. 16.)

[249] Uniform Code Council, Inc. "UPC Symbol Specification Manual", Jan 1986. http://www.uc-council.org/reflib/01302/d36-t.htm. (Ref: p. 24.)

[250] Uniform Code Council, Inc. "UCC and EAN International Announce Initiative for RFID Standards Development". Press release, UCC, 17 Mar 2000. http://www.uc-council.org/news/ne_rfid.html. (Ref: p. 25.)

[251] US Department of Commerce, Bureau of Export Administration. "Revisions to Encryption Items". *Federal Register*, **65**(203), 19 Oct 2000. http://www.bxa.doc.gov/Encryption/pdfs/EncryptionRuleOct2K.pdf. (Ref: p. 63.)

> The USA now allows the export of some previously restricted encryption products to the European Union and other trading partners of the USA. Related documents and explanatory charts are available from http://www.bxa.doc.gov/Encryption/.

[252] US Department of Commerce, Bureau of Export Administration. "Revisions to Encryption Items; Interim Final Rule". *Federal Register*, **65**(10), 14 Jan 2000. http://www.bxa.doc.gov/Encryption/pdfs/Crypto.pdf. (Ref: p. 63.)

> Announces a change in the US encryption policy, relaxing export controls for strong encryption software.

[253] US Department of State, Bureau of Politico-Military Affairs. "Amendments to the International Traffic in Arms Regulations". *Federal Register*, **58**(139), 22 Jul 1993. http://www.toad.com/gnu/export/itar.in.full. (Ref: p. 63.)

> Archived copy of the 1993 version of the International Traffic in Arms Regulations of the United States, classifying cryptographic software as "munitions". A very large text-only document.

[254] Roy Want, Andy Hopper, Veronica Falcao and Jonathan Gibbons. "The Active Badge Location System". *ACM Transactions on Information Systems*, **10**(1):91–102, Jan 1992. ftp://ftp.uk.research.att.com/pub/docs/att/tr.92.1.pdf. Also available as AT&T Laboratories Cambridge Technical Report 92.1. (Ref: p. 28, 30.)

> The original paper on the Active Badge gives motivation and architectural overview of the project. Since the pilot system had been deployed for over a year when the paper was written, there is also an insightful section on experience, comparing the expectations with the benefits actually perceived by the users. The privacy issues raised by personnel location systems are also discussed.

[255] Roy Want, Bill N. Schilit, Norman I. Adams, Rich Gold, Karin Petersen, David Goldberg, John R. Ellis and Mark Weiser. "An overview of the PARCTAB ubiquitous computing experiment". *IEEE Personal Communications*, **2**(6):28–33, Dec 1995. (Ref: p. 11.)

[256] Andrew Martin Robert Ward. *Sensor-driven Computing*. Ph.D. thesis, University of Cambridge, Aug 1998. `http://www.uk.research.att.com/~amrw/thesis. pdf`. (Ref: p. 37.)

[257] Andy Ward, Alan Jones and Andy Hopper. "A New Location Technique for the Active Office". *IEEE Personal Communications*, **4**(5):42–47, Oct 1997. `ftp: //ftp.uk.research.att.com/pub/docs/att/tr.97.10.pdf`. Also available as AT&T Laboratories Cambridge Technical Report 97.10. (Ref: p. 37.)

[258] M. Weiser, R. Gold and J. S. Brown. "The origins of ubiquitous computing research at PARC in the late 1980s". *IBM Systems Journal*, **38**(4):693–696, 1999. ISSN 0018-8670. `http://www.research.ibm.com/journal/sj/384/weiser.html`. (Ref: p. 9, 32, 49.)

> A brief and significant article, published shortly after Weiser's sudden death, giving a high level overview of the ubicomp research conducted at PARC.

[259] Mark Weiser. "The Computer for the Twenty-First Century". *Scientific American*, **265**(3):94–104, Sep 1991. `http://www.ubiq.com/hypertext/weiser/ SciAmDraft3.html`. (Ref: p. 2, 9, 10, 48, 50.)

> ★ A historical milestone, this readable and insightful visionary article was the one that introduced the phrase "ubiquitous computing" to the general public. In one of many felicitous metaphors, most of which have been reused (with or without acknowledgement) on several occasions by many other players in this field, Weiser compares computing to writing and argues that computing has yet failed to "disappear" like writing has: people still focus on "using a computer" rather than on the actual task that the computer helps them perform. This paper is required reading for anyone interested in ubicomp.

[260] Mark Weiser. "Some computer science issues in ubiquitous computing". *Communications of the ACM*, **36**(7):75–84, 1993. `http://www.acm.org/pubs/articles/ journals/cacm/1993-36-7/p75-weiser/p75-weiser.pdf`. (Ref: p. 9, 10.)

> After a brief perspective on the vision of ubicomp as shifting the focus of attention from the machine to the task, the author highlights some of the technical challenges faced by his team at Xerox PARC while building prototypes of ubicomp devices such as tabs, pads and boards (described as inch-sized, foot-sized and yard-sized displays). The issues explored in the article include power conservation, wireless communication capabilities with Gb/s aggregate bandwidth, protocols for mobility and real-time multimedia, and privacy of location.

[261] Mark Weiser and John Seely Brown. "The Coming Age of Calm Technology". In Peter J. Denning and Robert M. Metcalfe (eds.), "Beyond Calculation: The Next Fifty Years of Computing", pp. 75–85. Springer-Verlag, 1 Mar 1997. ISBN 0-3-879-4932-1. http://www.ubiq.com/hypertext/weiser/acmfuture2endnote. htm. Previously appeared as "Designing Calm Technology" in *PowerGrid Journal*, v 1.01, July 1996, http://powergrid.electriciti.com/1.01. (Ref: p. 12.)

[262] M.J. Wiener. "Efficient DES key search". Tech. Rep. TR244, School of Computer Science, Carleton University, Ottawa, Canada, May 1994. ftp://ripem.msu.edu/ pub/crypt/docs/des-key-search.ps. (Ref: p. 64.)

[263] Maurice V. Wilkes. *Time-Sharing Computing Systems*. Elsevier, New York, 1969. (Ref: p. 76.)

[264] Wireless Ethernet Compatibility Alliance. "WEP Security Statement", 7 Sep 2001. http://www.wi-fi.com/pdf/20011015_WEP_Security.pdf. (Ref: p. 202.)

> A two-page cross between a press release, a disclaimer and a user-oriented security alert. It admits there is a problem, explains that the relevant IEEE Task Group is working on a fix, and suggests some interim precautions for users of the current system.

[265] Stuart Wray, Tim Glauert and Andy Hopper. "The Medusa Applications environment". *IEEE MultiMedia*, **1**(4):54–63, Winter 1994. ISSN 1070-986X. ftp: //ftp.uk.research.att.com/pub/docs/att/tr.94.3.ps.Z. Also available as ORL Technical Report 94.3. This is an extended version of a paper by the same name that appeared in the Proceedings of the International Conference on Multimedia Computing and Systems, Boston, MA, May 1994. (Ref: p. 31.)

> Describes the software architecture of the Medusa multimedia system, which brought multiple simultaneous streams of multimedia data to the desktop using a high speed ATM network. Data sources, sinks and processors are represented as software objects ("modules"), instantiated on distributed hardware nodes and linked by data channels ("connections"). Access control security is provided by capabilities and proxies.

[266] Peter Wright. *Spycatcher: The Candid Autobiography of a Senior Intelligence Officer*. Viking Penguin, 1987. ISBN 0-670-82055-5. (Ref: p. 152.)

> The author, former assistant director of Britain's MI5, specialized in bugging, interception and counter-intelligence (chasing moles). The book is an entertaining read that shows how actual spies can be as gadget-friendly and as ruthlessly cynical as those featured in spy stories. The British government repeatedly attempted to thwart the publication of this book when it first came out.

[267] Jianxin Yan, Alan Blackwell, Ross Anderson and Alasdair Grant. "The Memorability and Security of Passwords—Some Empirical Results". Tech. Rep. 500, Computer Laboratory, University of Cambridge, Sep 2000. http://www.cl.cam.ac. uk/ftp/users/rja14/tr500.pdf. (Ref: p. 76.)

[268] John Young (ed.). "Diffie on GCHQ/CESG PK Forgery Allegation", 1999. `http://cryptome.org/ukpk-diffie.htm`. (Ref: p. 66, 218.)

> A compilation of messages on the dubious integrity of the CESG documents [98] about the origin of public key encryption.

[269] Gideon Yuval. "How to Swindle Rabin". *Cryptologia*, **3**(3):187–189, Jul 1979. ISSN 0161-1194. (Ref: p. 71.)

> A very concise and readable paper showing how the birthday paradox can be exploited to find collisions and therefore break Rabin's signature scheme.

[270] Philip R. Zimmermann. *PGP Source Code and Internals*. MIT Press, 1995. ISBN 0-262-24039-4. (Ref: p. 80.)

[271] Philip R. Zimmermann. "Testimony of Philip R. Zimmermann to the Subcommittee on Science, Technology, and Space of the US Senate Committee on Commerce, Science, and Transportation", 26 Jun 1996. `http://www.cdt.org/crypto/current_legis/960626_Zimm_test.html`. (Ref: p. 167.)

> ★ A lucid, poignant and concise essay on why the widespread availability of strong cryptography is good for democracy. Zimmermann, who put at stake his finances, his career and his personal freedom in order to write and give away PGP, is a qualified speaker on this topic.

Index

244